THE CHRISTIAN HOPE AND
THE TASK OF THE CHURCH

Second Assembly of the World Council of Churches

THE CHRISTIAN HOPE
AND THE TASK
OF THE CHURCH

Six Ecumenical Surveys
and
the Report of the Assembly prepared by
the Advisory Commission on the Main Theme
1954

HARPER & BROTHERS, Publishers, New York

GENERAL PREFACE

The ecumenical and missionary movements of our time are converging in the conviction that the whole Church is commissioned to bring the whole Gospel to the whole world. In intercession and mutual aid, in concerted endeavors of thought and action, the churches are beginning to grow together as members of the one body. They are realizing the meaning of solidarity—solidarity with sister-churches in need, with men in distress. They are engaging in the difficult art of learning from one another.

Growth in fellowship and in imaginative understanding of common needs and common tasks, however, does not come by itself. It involves knowledge of the facts of the Christian world scene. It involves the ability to see and to appraise the situation of one's own Church in the context of the Church Universal.

The present series of ecumenical Surveys should provide both an instructive and inspiring source of information for every person who is, or ought to be, concerned with Christian world affairs. In these documents a rather unusual attempt has been made to ascertain the general patterns of thought and action that seem to emerge in the manifold battlefronts, forward movements, and also failures and weaknesses, of ecumenical Christendom today. The immediate purpose of their preparation has been to provide background information for the Second Assembly of the World Council of Churches at Evanston, Illinois, U.S.A., August, 1954. But since they present a conspectus of areas of church life which are of continuing and, indeed, growing importance, it is hoped that they will remain useful for years to come as guidebooks that open up wider horizons for the Christian advance.

The program of the Evanston Assembly encompasses an exceptional range of subjects, each of which presents issues of the most immediate urgency and import for man's life today. It is focused on the great affirmation of faith:

CHRIST—THE HOPE OF THE WORLD.

In this overarching perspective it seeks to illumine the problems and responsibilities confronting the contemporary Church in six particular fields:

Faith and Order—Our Oneness in Christ and Our Disunity as Churches.

Evangelism—The Mission of the Church to Those outside Her Life.

Social Questions—The Responsible Society in a World Perspective.

International Affairs—Christians in the Struggle for World Community.

Intergroup Relations—The Church Amid Racial and Ethnic Tensions.

The Laity—The Christian in His Vocation.

The Central Committee of the World Council, when laying the groundwork at its meeting in 1951, asked the Study Department Committee to assume responsibility for the co-ordination and supervision of the study preparations. An Advisory Commission on the Main Theme, appointed by the Central Committee and consisting of some thirty Christian thinkers widely representative of different churches and theological outlooks, has held three annual meetings and produced a report for discussion by the Assembly. In 1952 the Central Committee appointed a Preparatory Commission for each of the six other topics, to consider the questions demanding particular attention by the Assembly and to produce three documents: an Introductory Leaflet for general study within the churches; a descriptive Survey of recent thought and activity of the churches in its field; and a Working Paper to be submitted to the corresponding Assembly Section as a starting point for its deliberations. The Surveys thus take the place of the volumes of essays, published in connection with the First Assembly at Amsterdam in 1948.

In their present form the Surveys are the outcome of an extensive program of fact-finding and of consultation with denominational and interdenominational agencies and individual correspondents in many lands. During well over a year, the officers of the Commissions and the Study Department staff have been engaged in the complicated and often baffling task of collecting and digesting source data. The responses to the questionnaires and queries which were sent out have been uneven, both in quantity and in quality. The process has revealed how inadequately equipped the churches still are when it comes to investigating, and realistically assessing, facts and trends in their own situation. Yet, judging from the wealth of statements and reports received (some of them well deserving separate publication in full), it would appear that the usefulness of such synoptic, ecumenical surveys has been fully recognized.

Drafts of the Surveys were scrutinized and partly revised at meetings of the Commissions held in or near Geneva in August, 1953. On the instruction of the Commissions, final editing was subsequently undertaken by officers and staff, who in several instances faced the painful task of drastically reducing valuable material in order to keep within the allotted limits of space. Time has not permitted resubmission of the present texts to the members of each Commission concerned for approval.

It is appropriate to acknowledge here the great debt of thanks which is due to all those who in various ways have shared in this co-operative venture—the many contributors of source materials; the officers and members of the Preparatory Commissions; the substitutes and consultants who attended the meetings of the Commissions in August, 1953, when the draft Surveys were discussed; and last but not least the members of the Study Department Committee.

This account of the manner in which the Surveys have been produced will make it evident that they may not be taken as expressing the position of the World Council of Churches on the matters under review. Rather, they are intended to present background material for the Assembly. Such value and authority as they possess is intrinsic. It lies in the measure in which they acutely discern the facts and signs of the Christian world scene, lift major issues into prominence, and thus offer signposts for the pilgrim Church.

HENRY P. VAN DUSEN, *New York*
Chairman of the Study
Department Committee
NILS EHRENSTRÖM, *Geneva*
Director of the Study
Department

FAITH AND ORDER—OUR ONENESS IN CHRIST AND OUR DISUNITY AS CHURCHES

An Ecumenical Survey
prepared under the auspices of the
World Council of Churches

(Faith and Order Commission Papers: No. 18)

CONTENTS

xi

I

INTRODUCTION

The Second Assembly of the World Council of Churches in 1954 provides an excellent occasion for the Churches[1] participating in the ecumenical movement to render a provisional account of their stewardship of beliefs, doctrines, ideas and attitudes which refer to the urgent problems of Christian unity. A very great amount of thinking, discussing and writing on the complex subject of unity has been done during recent years, particularly since the World Council of Churches was established in 1948 at the First Assembly in Amsterdam. While many of the old barriers to a living expression of Christian unity are still standing erect and defiant, there are some which have been attacked and partially overcome by the thrusts of new and vigorous appreciation for the will of Jesus Christ, that His Church should be one flock. That we are able to perceive such advance in the struggle against discord and estrangement is a privilege for which all Christians should be grateful to God. At the same time, we must give earnest attention to the formidable obstacles to unity which still persist within the Church at large.

This Survey has been prepared in anticipation of the Second Assembly as a report to the Churches on current thinking regarding the problem "Our Oneness in Christ and Our Disunity as Churches." This is the title which was chosen at Lund, Sweden, in 1952 for the study of questions of Faith and Order by one of the six Sections at the Second Assembly. The title is

[1] Throughout this survey the word "Church" is used, not only in reference to the One, Holy, Catholic and Apostolic Church, but also to those numerous bodies which are associated to form the World Council of *Churches*. No particular doctrine of the Church is implied in this usage.

1

unavoidably paradoxical. It rightly asserts the essential and indestructible unity of the People of God who are united by Jesus Christ as members of His Body. At the same time it indicates how Christians are separated from one another by being divided into many confessions and communions. Responsible Christians need to have a comprehensive understanding of the conflicting ideas held by representative Christian leaders concerning our oneness-and-dividedness in the Church. So far as these ideas have been expressed in literature and periodicals available to the secretary of the Commission on Faith and Order, they are hereby presented in terms of the following aim and scope of the Survey.

A. AIM

(1) To know how representative Christian thinkers of varying confessions, traditions and communions are pondering the fact that we are divided as "Churches" even while always united in Jesus Christ.

(2) To understand the present currents of thought, belief and practice with respect to the relations of Churches to one another, to the World Council of Churches, and to the Church Universal.

(3) To recognize and appreciate the meaning, for the Church's unity and mission, of Jesus Christ as the world's hope.

B. SCOPE

(1) Official statements issued by church councils, synods, conferences, etc.

(2) Statements made for the most part since 1948 by members of Churches in the World Council of Churches.

(3) Significant statements made by recent ecumenical conferences, such as those at Amsterdam, Willingen, Lund, and those of the Central Committee of the World Council of Churches.

II

PRESENT LANDSCAPE OF CHRISTIAN UNITY

Before any specific ideas on the problems of unity are presented, it is worth while to take a brief but broad look at the actual world situation in which the ecumenical movement lives and moves.

Anyone who knows the history of the Church in modern times, since the Reformation of the sixteenth century, cannot avoid being astonished by the most recent trend away from the provincialism and sectarianism of diverse Christian people. From the seventeenth century until the present one, relatively few members of the clergy or laity had any interest at all in the fact that the One, Holy, Catholic and Apostolic Church of Jesus Christ, in which they professed belief, was actually fragmented into exclusive and mutually suspicious bodies called confessions, denominations or sects.

Today these divisions still exist and are plain to see. But the new factor, which has been gaining tremendous strength in our lifetime, is the growing conviction on the part of many Christian people that these "unhappy divisions" are an offense before God and a violation of His purpose for the Church He has created and sustained. This serious concern for the unity of the Church, so far as it affects the thinking of a great number of Christians throughout the world, is surely a matter of immeasurable significance.

Documentation is not needed to support the assertion that the problems of the unity-and-dividedness of the Church are now receiving more serious attention by vaster numbers of Christians than ever before. Despite the fact that huge segments of the Church's membership are still unaffected by the

3

changing climate of belief and attitude toward unity, this encouraging assertion is vindicated by *the growing volume of literature, speeches, sermons, conferences and conversations* which call defenders of disunity before the judgment seat and require answers to the ancient question of St. Paul, "While there is jealousy and strife among you, are you not of the flesh, and behaving like ordinary men?" (I Cor. 3.3, Revised Standard Version)

As the most dramatic evidence of changing thought on Christian unity, facts about *actual unions of Churches* need to be noted. Many Christians believe that church unity demands more than co-operative endeavor or federated organization. Denominational barriers of any kind, at least in a limited geographical area, are intolerable to them, as shamefully evident denials of unity in Christ. One is deeply impressed, therefore, in reading the survey by Stephen C. Neill entitled *Towards Church Union 1937-1952*,[1] in which he records thirteen achievements of complete organic union of denominations; two agreements for unconditional intercommunion and two for limited intercommunion; sixteen progressing negotiations with a view to organic union, seven with the goal of some other kind of closer fellowship, and six which are temporarily suspended or are abandoned. By such ways is the frayed garment of Christ's Church being mended in our time.

Another sign of the degree to which the attitudes of Christians toward members of other confessions are being transformed is *the increasing number of councils of Churches* to be found in many nations. These are so numerous and so diversified in constituency that no generalized description can apply to all. In most instances their expressed purpose is to find opportunities whereby many Churches can work together on projects of mutual concern. In lands where there are large numbers of denominations, as in Great Britain and the United States of America, the co-operative action of Churches in local

[1] Faith and Order Commission papers No. 11, S.C.M. Press, London, 6s.

communities has been deemed a necessity, and hundreds of city councils of Churches now exist.

This generation has likewise beheld the rapid growth of national ecumenical councils or committees. While the older organizations, such as the National Christian Council of India, the National Council of Churches of Christ in the U.S.A., the Swiss Protestant Church Federation and the British Council of Churches continue to thrive, many important new councils have been formed in recent years. Among these may be noted such examples of growing Christian fellowship as the Joint Committee (*Arbeitsgemeinschaft*) of Christian Churches in Germany, the Ecumenical Council in the Netherlands, the National Council of Churches in Indonesia, the Hungarian Ecumenical Committee, etc. The bare fact that such councils are being constituted anew in the present time and are gaining participants is not to be taken lightly. It is a primary evidence of the growing concern for the unity of the Church.

Above the local and national levels, the ecumenical move-ment takes on world-wide organizational forms. Certain de-nominations or confessions—the Lutheran, Methodist, Congre-gational, Anglican, Baptist, Presbyterian, Disciples of Christ—have gathered their Churches into international alliances. Whether these alliances will serve the purposes of church unity or of confessional self-sufficiency depends upon the attitudes of their leaders and constituent churches.

In the sphere of genuine ecumenical fellowship among Christians of 160 different church bodies of many nations and traditions stands the World Council of Churches. Officially constituted in 1948 after preparatory labors lasting more than a decade, this organization is bringing diverse Churches into common studies and projects which serve the cause of unity and strengthen the Churches in their evangelistic mission.

Also rich in its influences is the International Missionary Council. Having membership of missionary societies and Christian councils of more than thirty countries, and carrying the experience of over forty years' activity, the I.M.C. is a

most effective instrument of the Churches for the co-operative
proclamation of the Gospel of Jesus Christ to all people. There
are also various other world-wide Christian organizations
which are considered part of the ecumenical movement in a
broad sense.

It is the accepted practice for participants in the organizations described above to speak of their councils and federa-
tions as aspects of *the* ecumenical movement. However, recognition must be given to the fact that millions of Christians
belong to churches which are technically outside this movement. Certain great Church bodies remain aloof for doctrinal
reasons which prevent collaboration: the Roman Catholic
Church, the Russian Orthodox Church, the Missouri Synod
Lutheran Church, the Southern Baptist Convention (U.S.A.),
as well as dozens of smaller ones. Although there are very
small groups in each of these which maintain cordial and
fruitful relations with Christians outside their Churches (and
this is a hopeful sign not to be underestimated), the majority
of members remain in isolation, either indifferent towards the
tragedy of division or convinced that they possess already the
fullness of the Church's truth.

III

THE CHURCH, THE CHURCHES, AND
THE WORLD COUNCIL OF CHURCHES

The World Council of Churches could not have taken form
if it were not for one fact of profound importance. Separated
Christians had become increasingly conscious of a deep unity
with one another in Christ. This awareness drove them
steadily toward more adequate expression of that fundamental
unity given them by the Lord. Whenever these separated
Christians met as representatives of their churches, they encountered serious problems of differing aspects of faith and
practice; but the fact of unity in Christ made it possible for
them to meet in common despite these problems. When such
meetings eventually led to the formation of the World Council
in 1948, the Churches found themselves obliged to think
afresh about their relations to one another on the basis of their
common belief in the one Church of Christ. They were also
compelled to inquire into the theological significance of the
relationships they had created by forming the Council, and
further, to reflect on the theological meaning of the Council
itself. In respect to these general problems, we shall consider
some of the prevailing attitudes of the churches represented
in the Council.

Concerning the inevitable question of the World Council's
authority relative to member Churches, the Assembly at Amsterdam adopted the following clear resolution:

The World Council of Churches is composed of Churches which
acknowledge Jesus Christ as God and Saviour. They find their
unity in Him. They do not have to create their unity; it is the
gift of God. But they know that it is their duty to make common

7

cause in the search for the expression of that unity in work and in life. The Council desires to serve the Churches which are its constituent members as an instrument whereby they may bear witness together to their common allegiance to Jesus Christ, and cooperate in matters requiring united action. But the Council is far from desiring to usurp any of the functions which already belong to its constituent Churches, or to control them, or to legislate for them, and indeed is prevented by its constitution from doing so. Moreover, while earnestly seeking fellowship in thought and action for all its members, the Council disavows any thought of becoming a single unified church structure independent of the Churches which have joined in constituting the Council, or a structure dominated by a centralised administrative authority.

The purpose of the Council is to express its unity in another way. Unity arises out of the love of God in Jesus Christ, which, binding the constituent Churches to Him, binds them to one another. It is the earnest desire of the Council that the Churches may be bound closer to Christ and therefore closer to one another. In the bond of His love, they will desire continually to pray for one another and to strengthen one another, in worship and in witness, bearing one another's burdens and so fulfilling the law of Christ.[1]

This resolution stated very concisely that the Council could never usurp powers which inhere in member Churches nor mold them by coercion into an artificially unified structure. Moreover, it declared the intention of providing the means whereby the churches might discover and manifest the basic unity already given to them by God in Jesus Christ. It went no further.

There was taking place already, however, a serious discussion on the significance of the Council for the Churches' relations to one another.[2] By 1950 the discussion had led to the formulation of a paper which was received by the Central Committee, meeting in Toronto. This document prompted a debate which laid bare some of the most fundamental cleav-

---

[1] *The First Assembly of the W.C.C.* Official Report, p. 127.
[2] See *The Universal Church in God's Design*, pp. 177-99, by W. A. Visser 't Hooft.

ages which still separate churches from one another, and which, accordingly, amounted to the most vivid "ecumenical encounter" experienced by the committee members. As the General Secretary later wrote:

During the course of that searching discussion, there were moments of anxiety when it seemed that the World Council had come to a real crisis in its history. But it proved to be a crisis unto life, for at the end of the discussion all present had arrived at a deeper understanding both of the very real differences which exist between the member Churches of the Council in their conception of the Church and also of the not less real work of the Holy Spirit by which these Churches are brought into fellowship with each other.[3]

Because this "Toronto Statement" is the keystone of the present survey, we quote it in extensive but abridged form. Note well that this document is just a contribution to an ongoing discussion, and by no means the last word on the nature and function of the World Council and the interrelationships of its member churches. Rather, it is a clarification of how these relations are, in fact, now understood by various Churches; and the statement has been commended to the Churches only for study and comment. It reads as follows:

II. THE NEED FOR FURTHER STATEMENT

The World Council of Churches represents a new and unprecedented approach to the problem of inter-church relationships. Its purpose and nature can be easily misunderstood. So it is salutary that we should state more clearly and definitely what the World Council is and what it is not.

This more precise definition involves certain difficulties. It is not for nothing that the Churches themselves have refrained from giving detailed and precise definitions of the nature of the Church. If this is true of them, it is not to be expected that the World Council can easily achieve a definition which has to take account

[3] *The Ecumenical Review*, III, 1, p. 77.

of all the various ecclesiologies of its member Churches. The World
Council deals in a provisional way with divisions between existing
Churches which ought not to be because they contradict the very
nature of the Church. A situation such as this cannot be met in
terms of well established precedents. The main problem is how one
can formulate the ecclesiological implications of a body in which
so many different conceptions of the Church are represented, without using the categories or language of one particular conception
of the Church. . . .

III. WHAT THE WORLD COUNCIL OF
CHURCHES IS NOT

(1) *The World Council of Churches is not and must never become
a Super-Church*

It is not a Super-Church. It is not the World Church. It is not
the Una Sancta of which the Creeds speak. This misunderstanding
arises again and again although it has been denied as clearly as
possible in official pronouncements of the Council. . . . Each Church
retains the constitutional right to ratify or to reject utterances or
actions of the Council. The "authority" of the Council consists
only "in the weight which it carries with the Churches by its own
wisdom" (William Temple).

(2) *The purpose of the World Council of Churches is not to nego-
tiate unions between Churches, which can only be done by
the Churches themselves acting on their own initiative, but to
bring the Churches into living contact with each other and
to promote the study and discussion of the issues of church
unity. . . .*

(3) *The World Council cannot and should not be based on any
one particular conception of the Church. It does not prejudge
the ecclesiological problem. . . .*

The Council as such cannot possibly become the instrument of
one confession or school without losing its very *raison d'être*. There
is room and space in the World Council for the ecclesiology of
every Church which is ready to participate in the ecumenical conversation and which takes its stand on the Basis of the Council,

which is "a fellowship of Churches which accept our Lord Jesus Christ as God and Saviour." . . .

(4) *Membership in the World Council of Churches does not imply that a Church treats its own conception of the Church as merely relative.*

There are critics, and not infrequently friends, of the ecumenical movement who criticize or praise it for its alleged inherent latitudinarianism. According to them the ecumenical movement stands for the fundamental equality of all Christian doctrines and conceptions of the Church and is, therefore, not concerned with the question of truth. This misunderstanding is due to the fact that ecumenism has in the minds of these persons become identified with certain particular theories about unity which have indeed played a role in ecumenical history but which do not represent the common view of the movement as a whole, and have never been officially endorsed by the World Council.

(5) *Membership in the World Council does not imply the acceptance of a specific doctrine concerning the nature of church unity.*

The Council stands for church unity. But in its midst there are those who conceive unity wholly or largely as a full consensus in the realm of doctrine, others who conceive of it primarily as sacramental communion based on common church order, others who consider both indispensable, others who would only require unity in certain fundamentals of faith and order, again others who conceive the one Church exclusively as a universal spiritual fellowship, or hold that visible unity is inessential or even undesirable. But none of these conceptions can be called the ecumenical theory. The whole point of the ecumenical conversation is precisely that all these conceptions enter into dynamic relations with each other. . . .

IV. THE ASSUMPTIONS UNDERLYING THE WORLD COUNCIL OF CHURCHES

(1) *The member Churches of the Council believe that conversation, co-operation and common witness of the Churches must*

*be based on the common recognition that Christ is the Divine
Head of the Body. . . .*

Therefore, no relationship between the Churches can have any
substance or promise unless it starts with the common submission
of the Churches to the Headship of Jesus Christ in His Church.
From different points of view Churches ask, "How can men with
opposite convictions belong to one and the same federation of the
faithful?" A clear answer to that question was given by the Orthodox delegates in Edinburgh 1937, when they said: "In spite of all
our differences, our common Master and Lord is *one*—Jesus Christ
who will lead us to a more and more close collaboration for the
edifying of the Body of Christ." The fact of Christ's Headship over
His people compels all those who acknowledge Him to enter into
real and close relationships with each other—even though they
differ in many important points.

(2) *The member Churches of the World Council believe on the
    basis of the New Testament that the Church of Christ is one.*

The ecumenical movement owes its existence to the fact that
this article of the faith has again come home to men and women
in many Churches with an inescapable force. As they face the
discrepancy between the truth that there is and can only be one
Church of Christ and the fact that there exist so many Churches
which claim to be Churches of Christ but are not in living unity
with each other, they feel a holy dissatisfaction with the present
situation. The Churches realize that it is a matter of simple Christian duty for each Church to do its utmost for the manifestation of
the Church in its oneness, and to work and pray that Christ's purpose for His Church should be fulfilled.

(3) *The member Churches recognize that the membership of the
    Church of Christ is more inclusive than the membership
    of their own church body. They seek, therefore, to enter into
    living contact with those outside their own ranks who confess
    the Lordship of Christ.*

All the Christian Churches, including the Church of Rome, hold
that there is no complete identity between the membership of the
Church Universal and the membership of their own Church. They
recognize that there are church members "extra muros," that these
belong "aliquo modo" to the Church, or even that there is an

"ecclesia extra ecclesiam." This recognition finds expression in the fact that with very few exceptions the Christian Churches accept the baptism administered by other Churches as valid. . . .

(4) *The member Churches of the World Council consider the relationship of other Churches to the Holy Catholic Church which the Creeds profess as a subject for mutual consideration. Nevertheless, membership does not imply that each Church must regard the other member Churches as Churches in the true and full sense of the word.*

There is a place in the World Council both for those Churches which recognize other Churches as Churches in the full and true sense, and for those which do not. But these divided Churches, even if they cannot yet accept each other as true and pure Churches, believe that they should not remain in isolation from each other, and consequently they have associated themselves in the World Council of Churches.

They know that differences of faith and order exist, but they recognize one another as serving the One Lord, and they wish to explore their differences in mutual respect, trusting that they may thus be led by the Holy Spirit to manifest their unity in Christ.

(5) *The member Churches of the World Council recognize in other Churches elements of the true Church. They consider that this mutual recognition obliges them to enter into a serious conversation with each other in the hope that these elements of truth will lead to the recognition of the full truth and to unity based on the full truth.*

It is generally taught in the different Churches that other Churches have certain elements of the true Church, in some traditions called "vestigia ecclesiæ." Such elements are the preaching of the Word, the teaching of the Holy Scriptures and the administration of the sacraments. These elements are more than pale shadows of the life of the true Church. They are a fact of real promise and provide an opportunity to strive by frank and brotherly intercourse for the realization of a fuller unity. Moreover, Christians of all ecclesiological views have throughout the world, by the preaching of the Gospel, brought men and women to salvation by Christ, to newness of life in Him, and into Christian fellowship with one another.

The ecumenical movement is based upon the conviction that these "traces" are to be followed. The Churches should not despise them as mere elements of truth but rejoice in them as hopeful signs pointing toward real unity. For what are these elements? Not dead remnants of the past but powerful means by which God works. Questions may and must be raised about the validity and purity of teaching and sacramental life, but there can be no question that such dynamic elements of church life justify the hope that the Churches which maintain them will be led into fuller truth. It is through the ecumenical conversation that this recognition of truth is facilitated.

(6) *The member Churches of the Council are willing to consult together in seeking to learn of the Lord Jesus Christ what witness He would have them bear to the world in His Name.*

Since the very *raison d'être* of the Church is to witness to Christ, Churches cannot meet together without seeking from their common Lord a common witness before the world. This will not always be possible. But when it proves possible thus to speak or act together, the Churches can gratefully accept it as God's gracious gift that in spite of their disunity He has enabled them to render one and the same witness and that they may thus manifest something of the unity, the purpose of which is precisely "that the world may believe" and that they may "testify that the Father has sent the Son to be the Saviour of the world."

(7) *A further practical implication of common membership in the World Council is that the member Churches should recognize their solidarity with each other, render assistance to each other in case of need, and refrain from such actions as are incompatible with brotherly relationships . . .*

(8) *The member Churches enter into spiritual relationships through which they seek to learn from each other and to give help to each other in order that the Body of Christ may be built up and that the life of the Churches may be renewed . . .*

V. CONCLUSION

None of these positive assumptions, implied in the existence of the World Council, is in conflict with the teachings of the member

Churches. We believe therefore that no Church need fear that by entering into the World Council it is in danger of denying its heritage.

As the conversation between the Churches develops and as the Churches enter into closer contact with each other, they will no doubt have to face new decisions and problems. For the Council exists to break the deadlock between the Churches. But in no case can or will any Church be pressed to take a decision against its own conviction or desire. The Churches remain wholly free in the action which, on the basis of their convictions and in the light of their ecumenical contacts, they will or will not take.

A very real unity has been discovered in ecumenical meetings which is, to all who collaborate in the World Council, the most precious element of its life. It exists and we receive it again and again as an unmerited gift from the Lord. We praise God for this foretaste of the unity of His People and continue hopefully with the work to which He has called us together. For the Council exists to serve the Churches as they prepare to meet their Lord who knows only one flock.

Far from a majority of the 160 member Churches of the Council have found it practicable or desirable to write official responses to the Toronto statement. Of those which have responded, hardly any showed disfavor toward the statement as a whole.

In 1952, the Canterbury Convocation of the Church of England[3a] welcomed the statement as an adequate reply to certain misinformed critics of the World Council who had unjustified fears about the purpose of the Council. Only the suggestion was made that the term "mystical body" in IV, 3 be deleted, because it is a phrase carrying various connotations and no clarification of its meaning is there offered.

The Swiss Protestant Church Federation gave approval to the statement, pointing out that the word "Church" as applied to member constituents of the Council does not refer to either meaning of the word *ekklesia* in the New Testament, but to

[3a] Which represents the clergy of the Southern of the two English Provinces.

organizational entities of a particular tradition or confession.[4]

General acceptances, without critical comment, were also received in 1951-52 from the Protestant Episcopal Church (U. S. A.), the United Church of Canada, the Moravian Church (*Brüder-Unität*), the Methodist Church (U. S. A.) and the Christian Ecumenical Council in Poland. In Germany there was considerable study of the document by special committees of the various *Landeskirchen* territorial Churches. Their critical comments merit attention later in the survey. In general their attitude is consistent with that of the report from the Evangelical Lutheran Church of Hannover:

> The Lutheran Church possesses in the *Confessio Augustana VII* and *VIII* (cf. also *Apologia VII*) an expression of its conception of the Church. There is nothing in the ecclesiological statements by the World Council of Churches that would contradict these articles.

Only these replies? Have not the other member Churches taken care to answer this important document? They have not; but this need not be considered a lack of interest on their part. Official acceptances are of much less importance than the numerous studies and debates on ecclesiological problems which this document has stimulated. In connection with them we shall also review the important observations and assertions set forth by church groups and individual writers, whose concern for understanding the relationships of the Churches to one another and to the one Church of Jesus Christ may or may not have been aroused by the Council's Toronto statement.

A. Churches and the Church

Two things about each Church need to be known before one can understand its relationship to other Churches. First, on what grounds does it judge other Christian bodies to be entitled to full recognition as belonging to the Church? Sec-

[4] See footnote on p. 4.

ond, by what tokens does it understand its own identity as being a part of the true Church?

(1) *Four Kinds of Recognition among Churches.* The Toronto statement rightly explains that "All the Christian Churches, including the Church of Rome, hold that there is no complete identity between the membership of the Church Universal and the membership of their own Church."[5] This is generally true as applied to *individual* Christians, who in virtue of their Baptism and faith may be reckoned by all Churches as members somehow of the Body of Christ. Granting this degree of latitude respecting individuals, there are Churches which nonetheless hold to the belief that no other *corporate entities* called Churches (denominations or communions) can be considered parts of the true Church in the full sense of the word.

Other Christian bodies, on the contrary, are convinced that no Church has the wisdom or prerogative to pass judgment upon another. This is the business, not of any Church, but of God, they say, and hence remove themselves from the discussion of mutual recognition. Some Lutherans, for example, point out that the very concept of recognition implies the idea that a church *possesses* certain essential attributes of order and doctrine. Recognition is granted only to other bodies possessing the same attributes. They see much danger in this attitude, because they emphasize, instead of possession, the continuing *work of Jesus Christ* in the Sacraments, Word and worship. It is Christ Himself, then, who gives life and substance to a group of believers and makes them the Church.

It is now obvious, nonetheless, that the Central Committee was obliged to pronounce the sentence in the Toronto statement, ". . . membership does not imply that each Church must regard the other member Churches as Churches in the true and full sense of the word."[6] Such is indeed a fact; but it is an intolerable fact for many Christians, a fact which causes

[5] IV, 3.
[6] IV, 4.

them genuine anguish in view of their conviction that the Church of Christ is one [7] and that this oneness needs to be expressed far more clearly and truthfully than it now is. Truthfully—there is the difficulty! A kind of unity of form and appearance, and even of work and witness, could perhaps be effected after some years of common action and negotiation. For this to be a unity in truth, however, which satisfies the conviction of all participating Churches as to what the basic truth is, requires the painful and patient processes of encounter and discussion which have been characteristic of both the Faith and Order movement and the many exhausting endeavors to achieve organic unions of Churches.

In each of these relationships there arise questions of recognition which are based upon matters of faith, ecclesiastical order, worship, or some combination of non-theological factors. And we can describe these kinds of recognition, generally but not in particular, by indicating four major categories of attitude and belief. These do not perfectly coincide with denominational policies so we shall not attempt an exposition of denominational policies *seriatim.*

(a) FULL RECOGNITION OF OTHER CHURCHES, WHETHER THE RECOGNITION IS RECIPROCATED OR NOT. The sole test of such recognition is the confession of faith in Jesus Christ as Divine Lord and Saviour. While variant interpretations of Sacraments, ministry, doctrine and church polity are regarded as being of great importance, they are not thought to be decisive. Open Communion is the mark of this kind of recognition, there being restrictions on neither communicants nor ministers of other Churches.

Churches holding this view believe that their own distinctive practices and those of others are worthy of inclusion in the full life of a Church united. Among these may be numbered believer's Baptism, congregational autonomy, and various doctrinal and ethical emphases. But these are not made binding upon other Churches as necessary for full recognition.

[7] IV, 2.

rolonging the one Apostolic Church and preserving unchanged
without alteration her teaching and tradition. While believing
e things, she does not hesitate to come into contact and com-
ication with the other Christian Churches and to form close
ions with them and even to have negotiations inspired by love
nity, participating in what is termed the Oecumenical Move-
t of the Churches, without meaning thereby that she denies
dogma of the One true Church or that she renounces herself,
nature, and her historical position, by giving up her claim to
he one true and visible Church of Christ on earth. . . . The
odox Catholic Church, as we have said, believes wholeheartedly
she is not one of the many historic Christian Churches and
essions but is herself "the" Church herself, that is, the "one,
catholic and apostolic Church," of the holy symbol of the
, the one and only true and securely saving and infallible and
dox Church [orthodox without marks of quotation], the Church
holds the Christian truth in all fulness and purity and which
, canonically and uninterruptedly, prolongs in a direct line the
itive Church founded according to the will of the Tri-une God
ur Lord Jesus Christ and expanded and organised by the
tles.[12]

cannot be questioned that such rigorous pronounce-
ts of Orthodox belief are offered with a deep measure of
stian charity. But love rejoices in the truth and the right
or. 13:6) and the Orthodox Church is convinced that the
and the right are entrusted to and preserved by her.
is attitude of the Orthodox Church is in full agreement
article IV, 4 of the Toronto statement:

e member Churches of the World Council consider the rela-
ip of other Churches to the Holy Catholic Church which the
s profess as a subject for mutual consideration. Nevertheless,
ership does not imply that each Church must regard the other
er Churches as Churches in the true and full sense of the word.

Karmiris, *The Orthodox Catholic Church and Her Relations with
Churches and with the World Council of Churches*, W.C.C. Study
49E/607A 1949. Cf. G. Florovsky in the *Ecumenical Review*, II, 2,
2 ff.

(b) FULL RECOGNITION BASED UPON COMMON AGREEMENT
ON ESSENTIAL DOCTRINE AND ORDER. Without insisting on uniformity of doctrine, some Churches hold that both agreement
on fundamental doctrines and possession of mutually recognized ministry are indispensable to full recognition. Such a
concept is defined more clearly in the terms of the Lambeth
Quadrilateral, the Anglican Communion's enunciation of those
essentials on which church union may be based: the Holy
Scriptures, the Creeds, the two Sacraments and the universally recognized ministry.

It is on the question of ministry that an important divergence of attitude here obtains. For some who gladly accept
the four marks as necessary to catholicity do not consider it
necessary to insist that a particular doctrinal interpretation
be placed upon the episcopal succession as a condition for
recognition.[8] This reservation was written into the Concordat
of 1931 between the Church of England and the Old Catholic
Church as follows:

Intercommunion does not require from either Communion the
acceptance of all doctrinal opinion, sacramental devotion or liturgical practice characteristic of the other, but implies that each believes the other to hold all the essentials of the Christian faith.

Within this category, but demanding a more precise understanding of the episcopate, are those whose views are represented in the pamphlet *Catholicity*. All four points of the
Lambeth Quadrilateral are indispensable and interrelated as
an expression of the fullness of the Church's life. But they
assert:

The appeal to the *historic Episcopate* will mean the recovery of
the true place of the Bishop in the Church, not as the organiser
of a vast administrative machine, but as a guardian and exponent
of the faith, as the bond of sacramental unity, and as an organ of

[8] Cf. Metropolitan Juhanon Mar Thoma in the *Ecumenical Review*, V, 3,
p. 293. Also the position of the Church of Sweden with regard to its
own episcopate.

the Body of Christ in true constitutional relation to the presbyters and people.[9]

A certain elasticity of thought is therefore to be expected among those whose criteria for recognition include both doctrine and ministerial order.

(c) FULL RECOGNITION OF CHURCHES HOLDING THE SAME DOCTRINES. These Churches believe it necessary for other Churches to be in substantial doctrinal agreement with themselves before recognition may be given and intercommunion practiced. For some a particular confession is considered essential; for others a common understanding of the apostolic *kerygma* and the Sacraments. There is no insistence upon uniformity in the form and meaning of ministry or church order, however. And a partial recognition is granted by these bodies to other Churches whose doctrinal positions approximate but do not coincide with their own.

(d) RECOGNITION AS IDENTIFICATION ONLY. According to the faith and conviction of many Christians—and here we speak distinctly of the Holy Orthodox Churches—there is no possibility of discussing seriously the full recognition of various Christian bodies which do not possess and live by the orthodox faith, Sacraments and hierarchy which these deem indispensable. This position rules out neither the possibility of recognizing individuals' membership in the Church nor the recognition of certain essential elements of the Church in other Christian bodies.

The Orthodox Churches participate in the World Council despite this position, because, as the Oecumenical Patriarch of Constantinople declared, "the task of rapprochement and co-operation between all the Christian confessions and organizations is a sacred obligation and a holy duty, derived from their own function and mission."[10]

[9] A report presented to His Grace the Archbishop of Canterbury, 1947, p. 54.

[10] Encyclical of January, 1952, printed in *The Ecumenical Review*, V, 2, p. 167.

These four conceptions of the ways in whi[ch] can be granted recognition have been he[ld by] various Churches through the centuries. [A] confession or denomination may not find [itself] described accurately by any one of the fou[r but by a combi] nation of elements from two of them, we [ ] the descriptions of these four ways are g[iven] because the four differ from one anothe[r] storms of controversy over church unity h[ave] generations, just as the conflicting pressure[s] cause turbulent weather.

(2) *How Churches Understand Thems[elves].* [The pre] vailing danger in Faith and Order studie[s] movement is that participants are too [ ] "comparative ecclesiology." It is necess[ary for] Churches to explain themselves to one ano[ther] understanding. This is never an easy thin[g] tive work done by the Faith and Order [ ] has been most valuable.[11] In the followin[g] sent in brief form the distinctive teaching[s] with regard to their own understanding [ ] presentation may seem too static and [ ] show what is dynamically evolving am[ong] relation to one another. But such appear[ ] able. It must be noted, moreover, that [ ] attached to the order in which the variou[s] here presented.

(a) Despite membership in the Worl[d] the Church of Greece and other ORTHO[DOX] firm in the conviction expressed by a [ ] follows:

. . . there can be only One Church an[d] Church has the conscientious conviction [ ]

[11] See the very important volume, *The N[ ]* R. N. Flew, S.C.M. Press and Harper, 1952[ ] Churches.

The crucial phrase in this sentence is "the true and full sense" of the word "Church." Here we encounter, in other words, the perennial problem of the meaning of the catholicity or wholeness of the Church. What are the essential characteristics or marks of the One Church Catholic, the lack of any of which prevents a body of Christian believers from being so identified? This question cannot be dodged in ecumenical studies, even though many would prefer to circumvent it.

Only a sampling of the vast amount of writing on this "mutual consideration" is here feasible.

We have noted already the position of the Greek Orthodox Church. It understands its catholicity in terms of the following essentials:[13]

(i) preservation of the revealed and saving faith in Jesus Christ, the God-Man, as Lord and Head of the Church;

(ii) maintenance of the corporate life of worship and charity as proof of faith;

(iii) retention of the unbroken Apostolic succession of the "divinely-constituted Hierarchy";

(iv) right interpretation of Holy Tradition and the canons of the seven Oecumenical Councils;

(v) unfailing and worthy administration of the seven Sacraments.

(b) Very similar dogma concerning the catholicity of the Church is held by the OLD CATHOLIC CHURCH of the Union of Utrecht. In disavowing the "errors" of the Roman Catholic Church, such as the dogmas of immaculate conception and papal infallibility, the Old Catholics believe they have preserved intact the essential faith and order of the Catholic Church as it developed in the West since the apostolic age.[14] As to their identity with the Church in the true and full sense of the word, the Old Catholics therefore have

---

[13] Cf. H. Alivisatos, in *The Nature of the Church*, pp. 48 f., and I Karmiris, *op. cit.*

[14] Archbishop A. Rinkel in *The Nature of the Church*, p. 148.

no doubt. Catholicity is basically defined by the preaching of the whole Gospel of Jesus Christ, the administering of Sacraments and fostering of worship, and the continuing of the Apostolic succession of bishops. So the Archbishop declares:

We believe that the significance of the Old Catholic Church lies only in being truly Catholic and in the faithful maintenance of this catholicity, in faithful witness thereto and in faithfully passing it on. The conviction that she possesses this catholicity is for her no reason to stand haughtily aside and wait until others rally to her, or, stronger still, submit themselves to her dogma. On the contrary, this conviction impels her to take part wholeheartedly in the ecumenical conferences of the Church, to listen to all and to learn from all, and in addition to testify to the faith which she herself possesses.[15]

(c) In the doctrinal thought of churches of the ANGLICAN COMMUNION there is a clear claim to full and valid participation in the Church Universal. Thus the conference of Anglican bishops meeting at Lambeth in 1948 stated this position plainly:

We commence our report by emphasising again the fact that the Churches of the Anglican Communion are Catholic in the sense of the English Reformation. They are Catholic but reformed; they are reformed but Catholic. The embodiment of this character is the Book of Common Prayer. It is not only an important source of Anglican teaching, it is also the means by which the Anglican tradition has been sustained. The English Reformers were not trying to make a new Church. It continued to be the Church of England, the *Ecclesia Anglicana*, as Magna Carta described it in 1215. For this reason the Anglican Communion is not a sect. It is a true part of the Church Catholic.[16]

The Anglican Communion does not regard itself as constituting the whole Church in an exclusive sense, as is well known. However, it has been careful to clarify the minimal terms on which the realization of unity may justly be sought,

[15] *Ibid.*, p. 159.
[16] *Lambeth Conference 1948*, Pt. II, p. 83.

chiefly in the formulation of the "Lambeth Quadrilateral." These terms, first developed in the General Convention of the Episcopal Church in Chicago in 1886, were adopted in a report of the Lambeth Conference in 1888, and were restated and defined in "The Appeal to All Christian People" issued by the Conference in 1920, as follows:

VI. We believe the visible unity of the Church will be found to involve the wholehearted acceptance of:

The Holy Scriptures, as a record of God's revelation of Himself to man, and as being the rule and ultimate standard of faith; and the Creed commonly called the Nicene, as the sufficient statement of the Christian faith, and either it or the Apostles' Creed as the Baptismal confession of belief:

The divinely instituted Sacraments of Baptism and the Holy Communion, as expressing for all the corporate life of the whole fellowship in and with Christ:

A ministry acknowledged by every part of the Church as possessing not only the inward call of the Spirit, but also the commission of Christ and the authority of the whole body.

The Appeal goes on to assert that only the historic episcopate can constitute such a universally acknowledged ministry.

In so delineating the conditions of union the Anglican Communion indicates in outline its understanding of the fundamental basis of catholicity and its own consciousness of possessing that quality. There is, however, tension and disagreement within the Anglican Communion on the question of the interpretation of the Quadrilateral. While these tensions are not such as to affect the claim of Anglicans to be "a true part of the Church Catholic," they do sometimes profoundly influence Anglican attitudes toward non-episcopal Churches.

As the following paragraph of the report of the 1948 Lambeth Conference discloses:

The statement in the Lambeth Appeal of 1920 accords fully with the Preface to the Ordinal, under which all the Churches of the Anglican Communion have retained episcopal ordination as a necessary condition for the exercise within themselves of the ministry of the Church. But this unity in practice has not ruled out a certain diversity of interpretation. Some, holding episcopacy to be of the *esse* of the Church, are bound by their convictions to hold that non-episcopal ministries are not ministries of the Church, and lack that authoritative commission without which there can be no guaranteed priestly ministrations. Others, while holding firmly that episcopacy is the normal method for the transmission of ministerial authority, yet feel themselves bound, in view of the manifest blessing of God on non-episcopal ministries, to recognise those ministries as true ministries and their sacraments as true sacraments. Yet others hold shades of opinion intermediate between these views. It is clear that in any scheme for reunion or intercommunion all these views must be recognised and allowed for. To treat non-episcopal ministries as identical in status and authority with the episcopal ministry rules out the first of the two views mentioned above. To declare the sacraments of non-episcopal bodies to be null and void rules out the second. It follows from the principle set out above as uniting all Anglicans that the acceptance of episcopacy as part of the life of the Church, and of episcopal ordination as the rule of the Church, is a pre-requisite for the formation of a united Church with Anglican participation, or for the establishment of rules of intercommunion. But room must be left for varying interpretations of the fact of episcopacy, provided that the historic succession is maintained, and that the functions of the episcopate are such as have been traditionally assigned to it.[17]

(d) Among the Churches which are generally called LUTH-ERAN there is still to be marked a perennially strong rallying point, which is the Augsburg Confession, Article VII. Few contemporary Lutheran statements on the nature of the Church can be understood apart from the theological implications of this article, which asserts that the One, Holy Church "is the congregation of believers, where the Gospel is purely preached and the Sacraments rightly administered." In relation to the Church Catholic, "it must be observed that the Augsburg Confession does not define the Church as 'a congregation of faithful men in which the Lutheran Confession is

[17] *Ibid.*, Pt. II, p. 50.

taught clean and pure,' but 'in which the Gospel is rightly preached and the sacraments rightly administered'":[18] where this takes place by the grace of God there is, whatever her name, the true Church, because there is, through the Holy Spirit in Word and Sacrament, Christ Himself with all His saving and recreating power. "This means that the Augsburg Confession clearly looks back to Holy Scripture itself and its final authority. The Church is never formally defined as 'Lutheran' as if Luther wanted to found a new Church in his own name."[19]

When Augustana VII thus puts so much stress on the pure proclamation of the Gospel, it does not mean that the possession of doctrinal statements is decisive, but it means that in what is proclaimed Christ Himself comes to us, through the Holy Spirit creating faith in us and so establishing His Kingdom. As Edmund Schlink explains:

Thus the Church is constituted by the event (*Ereignis*) of the preaching of the Gospel and the administering of the Sacraments, and so by Christ Himself acting through and present in Gospel and Sacraments. The Church does not exist where men possess Bible, Confession and Ministry, and yet keep silent, but rather where on the basis of Scripture, and in agreement with our Fathers and brethren, the Gospel is preached and the Sacraments celebrated, where the voice of Christ is heard and Christ offers Himself.

Thus the idea of the Church is separated from a false ontology and also from dissolution into a succession of individual acts without any continuity. The continuity of the Church consists in the identity of the Gospel preached ever anew, and it thereby becomes visible. So long as this Gospel is essentially identical with the apostolic Gospel, preaching occupies its place in apostolic succession. Since public preaching ensues upon ecclesiastical office . . . one can speak of an apostolic succession of office. But this succession rests not on a succession of ordinations . . . but rather on an identity of the Gospel and Sacraments which Jesus Christ instituted and which He commissioned the Apostles to continue. If the chain of ordination in the Lutheran Church from the ancient Church to

[18] K. E. Skydsgaard in *The Nature of the Church*, p. 89.
[19] *Idem.*

the present day remains unbroken, this is to be regarded as an outward sign of the continuity of the Church. The true apostolic succession of office is neither based upon laying on of hands, nor guaranteed by it. The Church through all time and change preaches and believes the Gospel; doing this it is apostolic and will persist "always" until the end of the world. . . . This continuity receives expression in the acceptance by the Lutheran Church of the confessions of the ancient Church, of the Church Fathers, as *testes veritatis*, and of the structure of the liturgy of the ancient Church.[20]

On the basis of such an understanding, the general claims for "the catholicity of Lutheranism"[21] are being set forth today.

(e) When we turn to an examination of current thinking in the REFORMED Churches holding the Presbyterian System, we encounter a somewhat more restricted degree of unanimity concerning the essentials of the Church Catholic and the relationship of denominational Churches thereto.

In general it should be noted that

All the Churches of the Zwinglian and Calvinistic tradition now called Reformed, Churches which declare the Church to exist where the Gospel is purely preached and the Sacraments administered according to the Saviour's institution, believe in and claim to belong to the Holy Catholic Church, acknowledge the sinfulness of schism and a divisive spirit, and desire the unity of the Church which is so plainly urged in Scripture, while at the same time measuring the gifts of the Reformation, including emphasis upon spiritual liberty and individualism, and recognising the need for wide charity as to differences in opinion and practice within the Christian community.[22]

The following statements may be taken as characteristic of the distinctive witness of the Reformed Churches:

(i) ON THE ESSENTIAL RELATION OF THE WORD AND SACRAMENTS: The Gospel is proclaimed and the grace of Jesus

---

[20] In *The Nature of the Church*, p. 61.

[21] Cf. G. Aulén in *World Lutheranism of To-day*, p. 6.

[22] J. Courvoisier, G. D. Henderson, and S. Berkelbach van der Sprenkel in *The Nature of the Church*, p. 108.

Christ is communicated in turn under the two different and complementary modes of the Word and the Sacraments. In other terms, that which is promised in the Gospel is not only *represented* in the Sacraments but is at the same time presented and effectively communicated through the action of the Holy Spirit to him who participates in faith. The grace communicated in the Sacrament is not linked with the material elements of the Sacrament, as though it were enclosed within them; the hearts of those who participate are lifted up by Him toward the glorified Lord.

(ii) ON FACTORS REGARDED BY THE REFORMED CHURCHES AS OF "SUPREME IMPORTANCE" FOR THE CHURCH:

. . . the supreme authority of Holy Scripture in matters of faith and practice; emphasis upon the sovereign grace of God; the Lordship of Jesus Christ over the Church and the World; the reality of the new man in Christ, born of, and empowered by, the Holy Spirit, and relevant to every human situation; a doctrine of the sacrament of the Lord's Supper which admits to the Lord's table communicant members of all Christian Churches; a view of Church organisation which makes full provision both for central authority and for the freedom of the individual conscience; and a vision of a theocratic order in history.[23]

Because the exposition, teaching and proclamation of the Word of God occupy such a primary place in the life and obedience of the Church, a relatively high degree of authority is given to the various Reformed Confessions, always, however, subordinate to Holy Scripture and subject to modification. They are designed not only to guard the Church from error, but to serve as a guide to the interpretation of Holy Scripture. These Confessions testify at the same time to the membership of the Reformed Churches in the Apostolic and Catholic Church, from which Calvin and the other Reformers never admitted separation. Though it was their claim by

[23] *The Presbyterian World*, XXI:3, p. 100.

means of reformation to restore the true face of the Catholic Church, the Reformed Churches lay no claim to perfection in doctrine or polity but insist that they are ever under the judgment and renewal of the Word, and as such a manifestation of the one true Church which is the Body of Christ.

(f) Even as the Reformed Churches are readily able to claim membership in the Church Catholic without denying such privilege to churches of other confessions, so are Churches of the METHODIST movement.

A representative expression of the belief of Methodists concerning their direct continuity with the One, Holy, Catholic and Apostolic Church is found in the *Deed of Union* of Methodist Churches in Great Britain:

> The Methodist Church claims and cherishes its place in the Holy, Catholic Church which is the Body of Christ. It rejoices in the inheritance of the Apostolic Faith, and loyally accepts the fundamental principles of the historic creeds and of the Protestant Reformation. . . . The doctrines of the Evangelical Faith, which Methodism has held from the beginning and still holds, are based upon the divine revelation recorded in the Holy Scriptures. The Methodist Church acknowledges this revelation as the supreme rule of faith and practice. The Methodist Church recognises two sacraments, namely, Baptism and the Lord's Supper, as of divine appointment and of perpetual obligation, of which it is the privilege and duty of members of the Methodist Church to avail themselves.[24]

The belief that any one Church, in the confessional or denominational sense, is fully and exclusively to be identified with the Church Catholic is quite unacceptable to Methodists. As one of their leading spokesmen in the ecumenical movement declared in response to the Toronto statement:

> There are those today holding to exclusive doctrines of the Church who are willing to say that we may be one in Christ though we are not one in the Church. That is a distinction which seems to me to be untenable in the light of the New Testament.[25]

[24] Cf. *The Nature of the Church*, p. 206.
[25] C. T. Craig in *The Ecumenical Review*, III, 3, p. 216.

Thus the Methodists generally share the concept of self-identity which is common to other Churches of Protestantism. Their Church cherishes a true place in the one Church.

But it makes no claim to be *the* Church; and it excludes no Church which confesses Jesus as Lord to the glory of God the Father. It acknowledges that its apprehension of Christian truth is incomplete, that its discipline of the Christian life is imperfect, that its ministry is limited to certain parts only of the world . . . and that its separation from other communions impoverishes its life and witness, and it humbly asserts the same of all other communions.[26]

(g) The churches which bear the name CONGREGATIONALIST continually emphasize their high consciousness of the nature and life of Christ's one Church. As John Marsh asserts:

Congregationalists have claimed, with all other Reformed churchmen, that the marks of the life of Christ in His Body, as these are set out in Scripture for our guidance, are the faithful preaching of the Word, the proper celebration of the Gospel sacraments and the practice of godly discipline. To be in communion with any particular Church is not simply to share in one part, or several parts of that life; it is to share in it all, continually and continuously.[27]

Being true to this concept of the Church's essentials, the Congregationalists also believe that they have a distinctive and indispensable understanding of the meaning of Christ's authority over His Body and of the manner of His exercising it. This is clarified in a statement of the International Congregational Council of 1949 as follows:

(1) While Congregationalists do not require subscription to any man-made creedal statements, they have never differed from other Christian communions in respect of the great doctrines of the Christian faith . . . At the same time they have stood, and still stand, for religious liberty under the Gospel and in obedience to the Gospel.

[26] R. E. Davies in *Intercommunion*, D. Baillie and J. Marsh, eds., pp. 154 f.
[27] *Ibid.*, p. 274.

(2) The distinctive element in the Congregational polity has been the local church, in which each member has his spiritual responsibility. The purpose of church polity is that Christ, and Christ alone, may rule in His Church. We believe that the instrument whereby Christ rules in the local church is the church meeting, at which all the covenant members of the church seek together by prayer and discussion to discover the will of Christ and are guided into a common mind by the Holy Spirit.

(3) . . . It is our fundamental principle that in all the organisation of the Church, at every level, all authority is spiritual, or, as our fathers put it, ministerial, not legalistic, coercive and magisterial. We believe this to be the true principle of government and authority in the whole Church catholic; this we regard as our essential contribution to the universal Church.[28]

It must be added to complete the expression of this principle, that it implies neither individualism nor isolationism of churches, but rather the unity of the whole Church in the community of the Spirit.

It is in the consciousness that it is not the *local* church that Christ designed it to be until it is fully recognised by the congregations of the whole fellowship of Christians on the planet that it finds itself in the midstream of ecumenical zeal. This is the corollary to the Congregational belief in the Universal, Visible Church: ideally *all* congregations must be in fellowship.[29]

(h) The BAPTIST churches also have emphasized the competence of the local congregation under the lordship of Jesus Christ to choose its own ministers and officers and to exercise discipline over its members. Though in the seventeenth century Baptists drew up a number of Confessions, of recent generations they have been shy of regarding such statements as binding or authoritative. A recent declaration, prepared by British Baptists for the Lund Conference, has, however, met with wide approval. It states that:

[28] *The Nature of the Church*, pp. 183 f.
[29] Douglas Horton, *Congregationalism*, p. 84.

Although Baptists have for so long held a position separate from that of other communions, they have always claimed to be part of the one holy catholic Church of our Lord Jesus Christ . . . The origin of the Church is in the Gospel—in the mighty acts of God, the Incarnation, Ministry, Death, Resurrection and Ascension of our Lord and the Descent of the Holy Spirit.[30]

Though in most lands the church order of Baptists has followed a congregationalist pattern, in others a connexional or synodal form has developed. Even where the local churches have been independent and autonomous, it has been recognized that separate congregations have the duty of entering into cordial relations of mutual help with one another, and that fellowships wider than the national or denominational are necessary for the healthy life of the Church. This is not based upon mere convenience or human contrivance but is an expression of the oneness of the Church in Christ.

Baptists recognize the two Sacraments or ordinances of Baptism and the Lord's Supper, holding that both are "means of grace" to those who receive them in faith. Baptism is administered "only to those who have made a responsible and credible profession of 'repentance towards God and faith in the Lord Jesus Christ.' Such persons are then immersed in the name of the Father, the Son and the Holy Spirit."[31] Membership of local churches is normally consequent on such baptism. Most Baptist churches receive into their membership only those who have been baptized as believers. "We see no evidence in the New Testament of any being admitted to Holy Communion who were not church members and baptised as believers."[32] Other churches, though they consist in the main of baptized believers, hold the position that "in view of the situation as it has developed historically through the centuries in Christ's Church on the matter of baptism, and in view of

[30] *The Nature of the Church*, pp. 160-61.
[31] *Ibid.*, p. 166.
[32] Report of the Special Committee on the Question of Union between Baptists, Congregationalists and Presbyterians, February, 1937.

the quality of spiritual life to be found in paedo-baptist churches, we do not believe we should be true to the Mind of Christ in making believer's Baptism a condition of church membership today."[33]

(i) Related to churches which hold a congregational polity, and yet bearing their own distinct witness concerning the Church, are the CHURCHES OF CHRIST (or DISCIPLES OF CHRIST). In all the history of their "movement" they have testified to the unity of the Church, which comprehends the many denominational and confessional bodies. And to expedite the manifestation of this unity they have sought consciously to restore the Church of the New Testament in its essential faith and form. As to the nature of these essentials they have strong conviction. They include, upon the authority of the New Testament: simple affirmation of faith in Jesus Christ and repentance for sins as basis for membership; believer's Baptism by total immersion; preaching of the Gospel; regular weekly observance of the Lord's Supper; and congregational autonomy.[34]

In contrast to the terms of the Lambeth Quadrilateral, for example, the Disciples would reject, on scriptural evidence, the essential need for creeds and a particular order of the ministry, "because the creeds themselves, when taken in any authoritative sense, are inherently divisive and schismatical, and a 'commissioned ministry' can be regarded as essential to the continuity of the Church only in so far as it is necessary to have someone who will make known the Gospel, thus calling men to faith, repentance and obedience."[35]

(j) FRIENDS (Quakers) have sought from their beginnings to witness both to the divine call in the heart of man, and also from within the Church, to faith and worship, ministry and communion in the Spirit of Jesus Christ, independent of formal creeds and liturgies, orders and sacraments.

[33] *Ibid.*
[34] Cf. *The Nature of the Church,* pp. 283-88.
[35] "A Response to Lund" by Disciples of Christ in the U.S.A., 1953.

They did not seek to establish a separate denomination, but regarded themselves, and still regard themselves, as belonging to the Universal Church of Christ.

(k) The CHURCH OF SOUTH INDIA, as a unique union Church, has accepted and intends to maintain the historic episcopate in a constitutional form. But the Church has refrained from giving any particular interpretation of episcopacy and consequently has abstained from making any judgment on the ministries of either the Churches which went into that united church or the Churches with which each uniting church had fellowship before union.

Any communicant member of any Church with which the Church of South India has relations of fellowship shall be at liberty to partake of the Holy Communion in any Church of the Church of S. India, and any minister of such a Church shall be free as a visitor to minister or celebrate the Holy Communion in any Church of the Church of S. India, if he is invited to do so.[36]

The Church of South India has not based itself upon any particular "confession." It accepts the Holy Scriptures of the Old and New Testaments as containing all things necessary to salvation and as the supreme and decisive standard of faith. It also accepts the Apostles' Creed and the Nicene Creed as witnessing to and safeguarding that faith. But the Church also claims in its constitution the right to produce doctrinal statements when the need arises of protecting the truth of the Gospel against some error. The basis of the Church of South India is, however, "the faith that the word 'Church' *ought* to mean the whole company of Christ's people in any place gathered in one visible fellowship."[37]

In summary, the foregoing characterizations of various churches' belief about themselves show that several members of the World Council say: "Here we have all the essential marks of the Church. Dropping for the moment considerations of the status of other Churches, we must confess that we are

[36] Constitution of the Church of South India, II, 14.
[37] A. M. Hollis in *The Nature of the Church*, p. 222.

the true Church." Such an assertion does not imply that this *true* Church is the *perfect* Church. "The Church of Christ has to grow and be built up in history," writes Georges Florovsky of the Orthodox Church, "yet the whole and full truth has been already given and entrusted to the Church."[38] Neither does this assertion imply the necessity to "unchurch" other Christians as individuals, for such a judgment is not in the province of the Church, but of God.

The opposing belief—that various Churches are really parts of the true Church, though none is *the* Church—is held with equal firmness by many member bodies of the World Council. A fundamental disagreement thus lies at the heart of the ecumenical movement.

(3) *Four Signs of Promise.* The purpose of this survey is not so much to report on what have long been regarded as intractable ecclesiastical positions of the various Churches. Our task is rather to keep raising the question of the immutability of these positions. Is there not evidence in the ecumenical movement that the rigorous position of some Churches can be modified in order that the essential oneness of Christ's people may be made more evident, and also that the indifference to doctrine which prevails in other Churches can be corrected in favor of a deeper concern for the wholeness of the Church's truth and life?

(a) LEARNING TO GROW TOGETHER IN UNITY. One of the most important lessons learned in recent years by the advocates of church union is that the achievement of a kind of "legalistic" agreement on matters of faith and order is not only highly improbable but also incapable of effecting actual union of Churches. Since the divisions within the Church Catholic are so numerous and complex, it is felt by some people that negotiators of church unions ought not to look toward a "united Church," which is a static society, but to a "uniting Church," which is dynamic. This insight has been granted especially to church leaders who have had actual

[38] In *Intercommunion,* p. 204.

experience in the planning and fulfilling of church union. Speaking for members of the Church of South India, Bishop Michael Hollis explains:

. . . There is the type of approach in which an attempt is made by conference to produce agreement on all major theological issues before the United Church comes into existence. . . . Yet it surely remains true that centuries of learned discussion in writing and in conference give little reason for belief that this method is likely to have any effective result. . . . What we have done is first to express our conviction that we are all genuinely Christian in faith and that we all desire to learn and to obey the Will of God. We have agreed on certain practical steps, set up an organisation in and through which we can plan and work together. It was our faith that, if we took the decisive step of coming together into one Church, we could count upon the Holy Spirit to make plain to us how we were to proceed from that starting-point of obedience. We believe that we had gone as far in mutual understanding as it was possible for us to go so long as we remained in separation.[39]

The importance of such mutual discovery of unity is expressed in the Report of the Lund Conference:

A faith in the one Church of Christ which is not implemented by *acts* of obedience is dead. There are truths about the nature of God and His Church which will remain forever closed to us unless we act together in obedience to the unity which is already ours.[40]

It must be stressed that this practice of growing together into unity does not constitute an easy solution to problems of disunity. But many Christians are coming to see in it a way of overcoming great obstacles, provided the best of Christian charity and devotion are combined with theological knowledge and practical wisdom.

(b) UNITY IN WITNESS: WITNESS IN UNITY. If Christianity were not inherently and inescapably a missionary faith, it is quite likely that the Churches would never have become

[39] Speech at a conference held in Madras, December, 1948, between Lutherans, Baptists and members of the Church of South India.
[40] P. 6.

aroused in concern over their disunity. The scandal of division is not especially evident so long as congregations are considered as well-settled flocks in need only of worship and pastoral care. It is when efforts are made with intensity and vigor to propagate the Gospel and extend the ministry of Jesus Christ, either locally or in foreign lands, that the failure of the Church to be truly united is a cause for alarm. It is just this sense of alarm which is another sign of hope that some Churches may modify their attitudes toward one another in the direction of full recognition.

While we are continually reminded of the truth that the mission of the Church is important in "Christian" lands as in "pagan" ones, it is clear that for reasons of their being a religious minority the members of so-called Younger Churches are the ones who have been most insistent and instructive in the call for "mission and unity." In reference to these Christians, the Lund Report says:

Their strong awareness of our fundamental oneness in Christ is due not merely to their relative immunity to the influences which produced and still maintain divisions among the older Churches, but also to their response to the demand for full obedience to the requirements of faithful witness and service. In their experience we can surely see the leading of the Holy Spirit. The miracle of this unity has disclosed to the older Churches the tragic extent to which their own witness has been impaired by their separation.[41]

In this regard Christians are thinking, to an encouraging extent, that the *being* of the Church cannot be divorced from what the Church is *doing*. It *is* one; it *does* spread the Gospel. This conviction is the foundation of the challenge directed to the Churches by the Lund Conference: "Should not our Churches ask themselves *whether they should not act together in all matters except those in which deep differences of conviction compel them to act separately?*"[42]

The penetrating power of this prophetic suggestion has yet

[41] P. 49.

[42] *Report*, p. 6. Italics added.

to be felt in most Churches, but the changing climate of thought respecting church unity and mission is preparing the way for such power to be effective in the relationships of Churches to one another.

(c) PARTIAL RECOGNITION. There is no novelty in the fact that some Christian Churches discern "elements of truth" in other Christian bodies, although still considering them to be defective, and being unable to accord them full recognition. Nevertheless this discernment of elements of truth in other Christian bodies involving partial recognition was noted in the Toronto statement as "a fact of real promise" which provides "an opportunity to strive by frank and brotherly intercourse for the realization of a fuller unity."[43] These "elements of truth" were regarded as "more than pale shadows of the life of the true Church . . . not dead remnants of the past but powerful means by which God works." The calling of these by the name *vestigia ecclesiae* ("traces of the Church"), however, has aroused apprehension and misunderstanding:

> Despite its worthy aim, the most unfortunate section of the [Toronto] statement is that found in IV, 5. I do not feel gratified when some other church grudgingly admits that *vestigia ecclesiae* are to be found in the church through which God's forgiving grace was mediated to me. The very phrase indicates that insufferable arrogance which is a major barrier to fellowship as well as to unity.[44]

This is not altogether unjustified because of the apparent identification of the *vestigia ecclesiae* with essential marks of the true Church (*notae ecclesiae*). It is felt now that it would be better not to use the expression *vestigia ecclesiae* any longer in this connection. The conception of *partial recognition,* however, does help considerably to open up the whole problem of ecclesiastical recognition in a way that merits very much fuller investigation.

(d) RECOGNIZED EXCEPTIONS TO CHURCH RULES. When they bear the connotation of a temporary relaxation of ecclesiastical

---

[43] IV, 5.
[44] Clarence T. Craig in *The Ecumenical Review*, III, 3, p. 216.

laws for special cases, the words "economy" and "dispensation" are quite strange to many Christians. Yet this practice, which has a precedent of many centuries in the history of the Church, is another promising opportunity for the breaching of barriers between Churches.

According to an Orthodox theologian, Hamilcar Alivisatos, economy means "suspension of the strict enforcement of Canon Law in cases of urgent need and in a spirit of prudent stewardship, condescension and leniency, practised by the Church's leaders, without overstepping the limits of dogma, in order to regularise abnormal conditions, for the salvation of those concerned,"[45] or, as another authority put it, when "such deviation promotes the higher good of the Church or prevents a greater evil."[46] This by no means alters the doctrine of the Church according to Orthodoxy, but it does allow a slight bending in an otherwise rigid attitude toward other Christians.

Similarly there is a practice known as "dispensation" in certain Churches which permits the temporary suspension of even such important rules as those governing admission to the Eucharist. The Anglican Communion generally allows a diocesan bishop to permit a service of Holy Communion "in the interest of reunion, as a mark of Christian fellowship" at which baptized Christians other than those normally admitted may communicate.[47] Such dispensation is not uncommonly applied at ecumenical conferences of various kinds. This practice was approved by the Upper Houses of the Convocations of Canterbury and York, 1931, and it is believed by many to serve the cause of Christian unity and to extend the hope for more approximate recognition among Churches not in communion with one another.

[45] In *Dispensation in Practice and Theory*, E. J. Palmer, ed., p. 30.

[46] *Ibid.*, p. 92, quoting Archbishop Germanos, Metropolitan of Thyateira.

[47] Cf. A. E. J. Rawlinson, *Problems of Reunion*, p. 83, and *Dispensation in Practice and Theory*, p. 123.

Because the doctrine of the apostolic succession continues to be a major barrier to Christian fellowship and reunion, it is significant that some leading exponents of this doctrine are urging a more lenient attitude toward it, at least temporarily, in the interests of Christian unity. Two principles seem to constitute a dilemma for many Anglicans, writes Leonard Hodgson. The first is the principle that episcopal ordination is willed by God for the ministers of His Sacraments; the second is the recognition of equality of episcopalian and non-episcopalian Sacraments. He continues:

I would suggest that we can be faithful to both principles if we distinguished between God's will for His Church in its unity and His will for it in its present divided condition. There is no inconsistency in maintaining both that we hold the apostolic succession in trust to be our contribution to the fulfilment of God's will in the united Church of the future, and also that in this interim period of disorganisation between the disruption of the past and the re-union of the future, He wills us to recognise the equality of His sacramental activity in episcopal and non-episcopal bodies alike.[48]

On the basis of this judgment, Dr. Hodgson proceeds to argue for the rightness of reciprocal open Communion services when-ever situations favorable to the promotion of Christian unity present themselves.

This insight into the problem of the ecumenical impasse is also not to be considered a cure-all for disunity, as Hodgson carefully points out. But it does express an idea which can lead to a breaking through of an otherwise frozen barrier.

(4) *The Effect of Social and Cultural Factors.* We have been trying to describe and understand the mutual relationships of confessions, denominations and Churches chiefly in doctrinal concepts. But it is obvious to all that matters of doctrine, church order and worship are not the only factors which prevent various Churches from recognizing or being in close fellowship with one another. Conversely, the influences

---

[48] In *Intercommunion*, pp. 265 f. Cf. S. L. Greenslade, *ibid.*, pp. 222-35.

which give impetus to the breaking down of barriers to unity are not only those which have to do with articles of faith and conceptions of church polity. Working both for and against the cause of unity are factors which are primarily social, cultural, political and psychological. To make a list of these factors and provide illustrations of how they have been effective in problems of denominationalism during the past four centuries is not difficult for any person with a modicum of information on church relations. Just to name them is enough to suggest examples of their influence: nationality, race, family traditions, political events, language, economic and social status, morality, temperament and social psychology, externals of worship, aesthetics, leading personalities and so on.[49]

Commonplace as these social and cultural factors may seem to be, it must be admitted that they have been given insufficient attention and study in the recent history of the ecumenical movement. Their undeniable but unrecognized role in all church union negotiations has yet to be adequately described. Neither have we properly perceived how the same categories of non-doctrinal matters which have caused and preserved divisions in the past are now, in diverse ways, impelling Christians to rediscover their true visible unity.

In this survey we can merely point to the exciting opportunity for new and rewarding study in this wide dimension of the ecumenical problem.

B. THE CHURCHES, THE WORLD COUNCIL AND THE CHURCH

(1) *Decision Demanded at Amsterdam.* The many acute difficulties of interchurch relations, which have thus far been surveyed, have a history which recedes many decades before 1948. It is not as though they had first been brought to light by the formation of the World Council of Churches in that year. And yet we may justly say that a wholly new dimension

---

[49] Cf. *Social and Cultural Factors in Church Divisions,* Faith and Order paper No. 10; and *The Ecumenical Review,* III, 4, pp. 339-56.

was added to the existing problems of Christian disunity by the formal constituting of the Council.

Prior to 1948 the Churches which participated in the ecumenical movement were not formally committed to one another. There had been a flourishing zeal for organic unions of Churches before the conference at Lausanne, 1927. This was followed by two decades in which the Churches, chastened by theological encounters, were trying to become better acquainted with one another in the interests of mutual understanding, more charitable attitudes, and united action in certain fields. At Amsterdam this informal relationship became a mutual covenant: "We intend to stay together" was the firm affirmation of the delegates assembled there; ". . . we have been drawn together to discover that, notwithstanding our divisions, we are one in Jesus Christ." That such an affirmation of unity is not merely a pious wish or a theological theory is evident in the fact that the participating Churches have risked their sense of sufficiency by joining this ecumenical organization.

We have already seen (pp. 8, 9) how the Toronto statement of 1950 constitutes a major attempt to deal realistically with the problems of church relationships within the structure of the World Council. It behooves us now to consider the ways in which the Churches are regarding the significance of the Council in respect to the other member Churches and to the unity which they have been given by Jesus Christ.

(2) *Christ Is the Basis.* The only explicit norm of any Church's membership in the World Council is that expressed in the Basis. "The World Council of Churches is a fellowship of Churches which accept our Lord Jesus Christ as God and Saviour."[50] Considerable discussion has centered on both the meaning and the adequacy of this formulation. Therefore it is necessary for the Council to keep the door open for continuing study and debate of the Basis.

[50] Constitution, Article 1.

The words of the Basis were not hastily formulated, but had a long history in the ecumenical movement. They were used in 1910 in the initial discussions about the need for a World Conference on Faith and Order, and later became the basis on which Churches were invited to participate. In the same, or slightly varying, form the basis has been adopted by some national councils of Churches.

What is the purpose of this Basis for the World Council? It is intended essentially to make clear what the Council is, who its members are, and what it does. According to a report made to the Central Committee in 1953,[51] the Basis performs three functions:

(a) It implies an understanding of the nature of Christian fellowship based upon unity in Christ;

(b) It provides a standard or point of reference for faith, so that all activities of the Council find their common reference in Christ;

(c) It defines the range of this fellowship, both inclusively and exclusively.

Granted these functions of the Basis, there are yet some who are not content with its meaning, formulation or adequacy. The theological aspects of their criticisms cannot be examined here, but it is important to know why such criticisms are being made.

The Basis has been criticized because in speaking of the deity of Jesus Christ it does not mention His humanity. But the reply is given that the humanity is unavoidably implied in the fact that *Jesus* Christ is Jesus of Nazareth.

Furthermore, some charge that omission of specific reference to the Holy Spirit throws the Basis out of balance as a statement of Trinitarian faith. This also may be countered by the claim that historically the very doctrine of the Trinity derived from meditation upon the divinity of Jesus Christ.

Some have found it significant that the Basis makes no refer-

[51] Minutes of Fifth Meeting, Lucknow: appendix to report on pp. 95-96.

ence to the authority of the Holy Scriptures, while others say that the Church's concern for the needs and problems of all mankind should be expressed here.

Finally, a conscientious protest has been made against any form of creedal test for membership in the Council, since some Christians cannot accept membership on such terms.

(3) *The Council and Authority.* No authority can be exercised by the Council over its member Churches. On this principle all agree. "Each Church retains the constitutional right to ratify or to reject utterances or actions of the Council."[52]

Acknowledging this constitutional limitation, however, it is a matter for criticism and debate whether the Council has already displayed the intention and ability to maintain a neutral position in its published statements and reports. Certainly it has been accused, whether justly or unjustly, of taking one or another side of a theological question to the dissatisfaction of some member Churches. To such criticisms the answer must be offered, that whatever bias the Council may seem to hold toward certain issues (and what body of representatives of Churches can fully avoid bias?) its pronouncements may be disavowed by any member Church and by its individual members. The Council's purpose is not to embrace the principle that all doctrines and theological concepts are equally true, nor to make *ex cathedra* statements, but rather to seek the truth by bringing the Churches together to face their differences honestly and seriously.[53]

In the area of tension between the Council's quest for truth and its inherent respect for the good faith and integrity of its constituents, whatever their differences among one another, lie two questions which perplex some people:

(a) Is it really true that "no Church need fear that by entering into the World Council it is in danger of denying its heritage"?[54] Although some Churches require such an as-

[52] Toronto, III, 1.
[53] Cf. Toronto III, 3, 4, 5.
[54] Toronto V.

surance, others see in it a barrier to fruitful ecumenical developments. For example, a theological study circle in Lower Saxony declares:

We cannot see any danger in a critical examination of the heritage of the past and even its denial under the Word of God, i.e. in considering it an obstacle rather than a safe possession.

(b) Does membership in the World Council, which implies that member churches "refrain from such actions as are incompatible with brotherly relationships,"[55] include or exclude the right of both evangelizing and proselytizing in one another's provinces? Here again we encounter the problem of mutual recognition of Churches with respect not only to doctrine, ministry and Sacraments but also to the character of individual and corporate Christian life. While many will agree that membership in the Council clearly means not to reject another member Church by anathema or by the making of proselytes, the question remains an open one for others, subject to careful scrutiny in particular areas and with respect to particular circumstances of religious life. The question is further complicated by the lack of a clear distinction between evangelism and proselytism. This is a matter which obviously challenges the member Churches to such a frank inquiry as has not yet been undertaken.

(4) *Unity and Renewal.* One aspect of membership of the Churches in the World Council which is frequently overlooked, or obscured by a preoccupation with divisions, is the fact that the unity of the Church is inseparable from the renewal of the Church. The member Churches learn from one another, support one another in need, and modify the existing thoughts and practices of one another.[56] These mutual influences are not easily detected, but they are an inevitable concomitant of ecumenical relationships.

[55] Toronto IV, 7.
[56] Toronto IV, 8.

We are split apart because we have failed to preserve the "wholeness," the catholicity, the comprehensive experience of Christian faith and life. Only through the restoration of this wholeness can we approach one another again. The ecumenical movement is a symptom, the expression of the call for the restoration of the Church.[57]

(5) *What May the Council Become?* Time and again it has been asserted that the World Council is not now, nor ever is intended to be, the non-Roman rival of the Vatican, an all-embracing World-Church, or the Holy Catholic Church of which the creeds speak.[58] It is a constitutional organization of 160 Churches in which the integrity of each member is respected. But this denial does not satisfactorily answer the question of what the Council may become, in the providence of God.

There are members of participating Churches who look for no other expression of Christian unity than that which they think is already manifest in the Council. They are satisfied if the Council is never more than an association in which autonomous Churches work together so much as they are able and seek mutual edification for the community life and mission of one another. Acceptance of this view would to a large extent reduce the effectiveness of the Council as a servant of Christian unity, and would be an avoidance of the challenge raised by the Churches' "holy dissatisfaction with the present situation."[59]

Many others have asserted the belief that Christian unity can never be adequately expressed within the World Council so long as it remains an association in which co-operative action suffices. The question of what form this more substantial unity may take is one which must remain open. If all had the same concept of Christian unity there would be no ecumenical problem, for the chief difficulty in this prob-

[57] H. van der Linde in *The Ecumenical Review*, III, 3, p. 241.
[58] Toronto III, 1.
[59] Cf. Toronto IV, 2.

lem is that Christians have divergent convictions about the
way to overcome disunity. To say that the Council must
challenge the Churches to show their unity in the mutual
recognition of one another's doctrine, ministry and Sacraments is not enough. That is just to beg the whole question,
observes Oliver S. Tomkins.

If all the Churches now in the Council were in communion with
each other, it could only be because they were not thinking in terms
of the federation of diversely-ordered, independent Churches, but
because they had come to accept a conception of unity as the un-
disputed common acceptance of Sacraments, doctrine and ministry
however defined; no longer a Council but a Church in the sense
that no part of it considered any other part of it to be lacking in
all which is essential for the common life in the Body of Christ.[60]

On account of such a conception of a purpose of the Council, the Lund delegates could urge: "Should not our Churches
ask themselves whether they are showing sufficient eagerness
to enter into conversation with other Churches . . . ?"[61]

Since the purpose of the Council is not to be a federation,
nor to become a World-Church by synthetically appropriat-
ing the diverse doctrines and polities of member Churches,
it must always look forward to its own decrease so that the
manifestation of the oneness of the Church may increase.

[60] *The Ecumenical Review*, IV, 3, p. 265.
[61] Lund Report, p. 6.

IV

THE CHURCH'S HOPE IN CHRIST

A. UNITY IN HOPE

We have reviewed some of the current facts concerning the Churches' attitudes toward one another and the possibilities of their finding exits from those situations of relationship which now appear to be blind alleys. But from the testimony of scriptural faith we are reminded that any discussion of these facts is not only inadequate, but false, if it is not carried on in the framework of the biblical teaching on our hope: that is, hope in the perfect redemptive work of God through Jesus Christ and the Holy Spirit.

The content of this hope is far different from that of the utopianism which has characterized the thinking and hoping of many Christians in this century. Impelled by a strong enthusiasm to see the divine love and righteousness become fully effective in the affairs of men, with the undivided, harmonious Church as the perfect social expression of that divine reign, many Christians yield to two temptations: they underestimate the tenacity of man's sin, which persistently confounds efforts to achieve both church unity and a "Christian" world; and they ignore the New Testament's distinction between the Reign of God as partially experienced within history and as fully consummated beyond history.

A renewed concern about the meaning of history, the Kingdom of God and eternal life is now being expressed increasingly by theological leaders of various confessions. Prompted by recently recovered biblical insights, as well as by the social and political exigencies of the present time, many Christian thinkers are rejecting the concept of God's Kingdom as a social order evolving progressively toward perfection. They realize that the consummation of the Kingdom necessarily involves judgment upon mankind generally and the Church in particular. They are less disposed therefore to expect the full and perfect unity of the Church as an easily achieved historical possibility. The separations within the Church are kindred in cause and kind to the separations within mankind as a whole. The same Judge and Saviour of mankind will judge and save the People of God. This aspect of Christian faith gives to the Church the dual attitude of both fear and joy; fear for its infidelity, and joy in realization that its labors are not in vain. While theologians dispute whether the consummation of God's purpose for mankind and the Church shall take place within or beyond the end of history, there is much agreement that the perfect unity of the Church cannot be expected apart from this final coming of Jesus Christ as Judge and Saviour.

What bearing does this hope have on present relationships of Churches? On the one hand, this kind of faith delivers us from frustration and despair when we consider the seemingly irreparable damage which has been done to the Church by schism and separations. At the same time, it may lead those who *misapprehend* its meaning into an attitude of total irresponsibility, if they think that nothing can now be done about our divisions and that God will ultimately take care of them anyhow.

Two things still confront the divided Churches: the Lord's urgent demand that the unity He has granted them now be expressed in church life; and the hope that He will gather His divided People into one at His final coming. In the face of this demand and this hope, Christians of all traditions are addressed by the Lund Conference:

When we place ourselves in our Churches under His judgment and in obedience to His calling and His sending, we shall know that we cannot manifest our unity and share in His fullness without being changed. Some of us who have been assured that we possess the true order and the true sacraments will find ourselves called to give its rightful place to the preaching of the Living Word. Some who have neglected the sacraments will be confronted by Him who humbled Himself in Baptism and broke bread and shared the cup to make us partakers of His passion and death. Those who have sought to show forth the glory of the Church as the Body and Bride of Christ must stand under the judgment of His simplicity and servanthood. Churches which have valued little His prayer that the oneness of His people be made manifest to men will be summoned to make His prayer their own. Churches complacent in the face of racial divisions in the Body will be brought to repentance by Him in whom bond and free, Jew and Gentile, Greek and barbarian, are one. Churches which have stressed one-sidedly that God in His Church gives Himself to men will be reminded that Christ in His humanity offered Himself to the Father. Those who are ever looking backward and have accumulated much precious ecclesiastical baggage will perhaps be shown that pilgrims must travel light and that, if we are to share at last in the great Supper, we must let go much that we treasure. Churches settled and self-assured will have to hear again the Lord's heart-broken concern for the sheep without a shepherd and know that to be His Church is to share in His world-embracing mission. Churches too much at home in the world will hear themselves called out of the world. Churches too wrapped up in their own piety or their own survival will see again Him who identified Himself with the deprived and the oppressed.

We cannot know all that shall be disclosed to us when together we look to Him who is the Head of the Body. It is easy for us in our several Churches to think of what our separated brethren need to learn. Christ's love will make us more ready to learn what He can teach us through them. The truth we would hold fast is that because Christ is the Head and the Lord of the Church, His way is the Church's way. He calls, He sends, He judges. The shape of His life is the shape of the Church's life. The mystery of His life is the mystery of the Church's life.[1]

B. The Way to Christ Is the Way of Unity

Time and again Christians affirm that there is one Church because there is but one Head of the Church, and that it is

[1] *Report* of the Third World Conference on Faith and Order, pp. 10-11.

Jesus Christ who has given unity to His People. This affirmation, which is fully in accord with the teaching of the New Testament and is supported by theological reflection, is yet in danger of being used as a mere cliché in ecumenical discussions. It is spoken so frequently and casually that its really profound meaning is ignored to a lamentable degree.

Three great conferences of the ecumenical movement at Lausanne, Edinburgh and Amsterdam were seriously occupied with the problem of the nature of the Church's unity. But quite understandably at those stages of modern ecumenical discussion, they chose to seek answers, not in respect to the center of unity, Jesus Christ, but on such important but derivative matters as the ministry, church polity, authority, Sacraments and the Church's function in the world. We must not minimize these matters. But there is a growing conviction which was articulated at the Lund Conference that we must get behind these familiar problems to the source and center of the Church—to the person and redemptive work of Jesus Christ our Lord.

What does it mean to be "in Christ," as St. Paul used the phrase so frequently? In what ways can we understand the Body of Christ, as the Church is designated? What do the other biblical figures for Christ tell of His meaning? How does Christ still live in the Church while the Church lives in Him? What do the Cross and the Resurrection mean for the unity of the Church as a whole? How is the presence of the Holy Spirit manifest in the Church? If the unity of the Church derives from the one Christ in unity with God the Father and with His People, what explanations can be given for existing divisions in the Church? How does Jesus Christ show us the means by which divisions shall be healed?

It is undoubtedly a sign of promise that theological leaders of the World Council have agreed to study such questions as these. The maturity of the ecumenical movement is indicated by the fact that such fundamental theological problems will be explored. Moreover, it is agreed that such study

must not proceed in the isolation of confessional or denominational groups, but rather in the structure of the Commission
on Faith and Order. The second chapter of the Lund Report
has pointed the way to Christ as the way of unity. It is even
possible that formal theological inquiry will not find this
way, since God who is no respecter of persons does not make
His ways known only to theologians. Perhaps it will remain
for the Church as a whole to manifest a new obedience to
its Lord in mission, ministry and worship before Jesus Christ
will be sufficiently recognized as the true vine, giving life
and unity to His branches.

V

CONCLUDING QUESTIONS

So long as no fully adequate solutions for the various problems of church unity are in sight, Christians must continue to seek answers to the questions raised in the Survey. The most important ones, with page references in the Survey, are:

(1) What does the absence of denominations or confessions in the New Testament mean for the existence and interrelationships of such bodies in our present time?

(2) If individual Christians can be accounted by all as members of the Church, why cannot the corporate bodies be recognized in which these Christians received God's grace? (P. 16.)

(3) On what theological grounds do some Churches refuse to be concerned with the problem of recognizing other Churches? (P. 16.)

(4) How does the readiness to give full recognition to other Churches, even without reciprocation, differ from mere indifference to doctrine? (P. 17.)

(5) What attitude should Churches of the World Council take toward the churchly character of the multiverse sects which own Christ as Lord?

(6) Is Professor Peter Brunner right when he asserts:

A Church of one particular confession which has not the perfect right to proclaim to all Christian people, "*Here* is the banner of the Lord! *These* are the insignia round which the Una Sancta rallies in visible form!" thereby admits that it is conscious . . . of elements within itself which do not measure up to the true nature of the Church.[1]

[1] *The Ecumenical Review*, III, 3, p. 228.

(7) On the basis of known examples of "growing into unity," why, or why not, is this a valid principle for overcoming the deepest differences between Churches? (P. 36.) What other factors must be considered?

(8) How can it be demonstrated that evangelism is impeded by disunity? Is it not impelled by confessional loyalty? (P. 37.)

(9) What are the full and specific implications of the dictum, that Churches should do all things together except those which deep difference of conviction compels them to do separately? (P. 38.)

(10) Why, or why not, is Canon Hodgson theologically justified in distinguishing God's abiding will for the Church from His will for the present divided conditions? (Pp. 40-41.)

(11) In what sense do the doctrines of creation and redemption show that social and cultural factors affecting church unity are *not* "non-theological"? (Pp. 41-42.)

(12) How does the Basis of the World Council succeed or fail to fulfill the three functions named on p. 43.

(13) In the light of discussion on p. 47 what view of the future form of the World Council would you defend?

(14) In view of the nature of Christian hope, what degrees and forms of visible unity can we legitimately expect before the fulfillment of all things by Christ? (Pp. 49-50.)

(15) Why does the Christian hope in Christ as the one who will fulfill the unity of the Church not strip Christians of responsibility to work for its clearer manifestation? (P. 50)

(16) Note the profoundly significant questions on p. 52 concerning Christ and the Church.

PREPARATORY COMMISSION I

on

FAITH AND ORDER—OUR ONENESS IN CHRIST AND OUR DISUNITY AS CHURCHES

Members

The Rev. Dr. Oliver S. TOMKINS, United Kingdom, Chairman
The Rev. Dr. J. Robert NELSON, (W.C.C.), Secretary

Mr. Percy W. BARTLETT, United Kingdom
The Rev. Professor J. Russell CHANDRAN, India
*Dean Clarence T. CRAIG, U.S.A., (deceased)
*The Rt. Rev. Bishop Angus DUN, U.S.A.
The Rev. Professor H. d'ESPINE, Switzerland
The Rev. Principal R. Newton FLEW, United Kingdom
The Very Rev. Professor Georges FLOROVSKY, U.S.A.
*The Rev. President H. GEZORK, U.S.A.
*The Rev. President Perry E. GRESHAM, U.S.A.
The Rev. Professor R. R. HARTFORD, Eire
The Rev. Dr. G. JACOB, Germany
*The Most Rev. Metropolitan JUHANON MAR THOMA, India
*The Rev. Professor T. A. KANTONEN, U.S.A.
The Rev. Professor C. KONSTANTINIDIS, Turkey
The Rev. Principal John MARSH, United Kingdom
The Rev. Dr. Ernest A. PAYNE, United Kingdom
*The Rev. Professor Edmund SCHLINK, Germany
The Rev. Professor K. E. SKYDSGAARD, Denmark
The Rev. Professor T. F. TORRANCE, United Kingdom
The Rev. Professor L. J. TRINTERUD, U.S.A.
The Rev. Professor Gustaf WINGREN, Sweden

Central Committee Consultants

*The Rt. Rev. Bishop Angus DUN, U.S.A. (Member of the Commission)
The Very Rev. Professor Georges FLOROVSKY, U.S.A. (Member of the Commission)
*The Most Rev. Metropolitan JUHANON MAR THOMA, India (Member of the Commission)

* Not present at August, 1953, meeting.

Substitutes and ad hoc Consultants attending the August 1953 meeting

The Rt. Rev. Bishop S. F. BAYNE, U.S.A.
The Rev. Professor Carl MICHALSON, U.S.A.
The Rev. Dr. Heinrich MEYER, Germany
Miss Marie NASSIV, Lebanon
The Rev. Dr. J. E. SKOGLUND, U.S.A.
The Rev. Dr. V. VAJTA, Geneva (Lutheran World Federation)

EVANGELISM—THE MISSION OF THE CHURCH TO THOSE OUTSIDE HER LIFE

*An Ecumenical Survey
prepared under the auspices of the
World Council of Churches*

CONTENTS

I

INTRODUCTION

This is an Interpretative Survey on Evangelism in the years 1948-53. Designed, under general directives, to focus attention on the mission of the Church to "intellectuals" and "workers," it has enlarged its scope so as to look at wider horizons, though not unduly neglecting its originally assigned task. The International Missionary Conference held at Willingen, Germany, in the summer of 1952, underscored the conviction increasingly accepted in ecumenical thought, that the day of separation between "missions" and "evangelism" is, or should be, over. Hence, a beginning is made in this Survey to deal with the missionary task of the Church on an equality with evangelism as a specialized activity. The union, or reunion, of the concepts "mission" and "evangelism" should mark a step forward in ecumenical discourse.

Even within enlarged boundaries, the Survey is, because of limited space and incomplete information, guilty of many omissions. The fascinating story of how the great Bible societies have spread the Gospel through the printing press and colportage has received little mention. Certain world areas or countries are given more attention than others—in certain instances for the reason that competent separate pamphlets on evangelism in these regions have recently been published by the World Council's Secretariat for Evangelism, for example, on France, and on India, with others in preparation.

Section I consists of an attempt to locate the topic of evangelism on the ecumenical map and to underscore its relevance to our times. Section II in turn invites the reader to see evangelism round the world. Both success and failure

1

march across the scene. Further sections then invite the churches to hopeful appraisal and to wrestling with unsolved problems. Questions are addressed to the churches in sections I and IV. Much of the value of this study will rest upon an honest attempt by all of us to face and answer them.

II

WALKING TOGETHER

Evangelism is the Ecumenical Theme Par Excellence. One of the characteristic features of the period under survey has been the fact that evangelism has increasingly been in the ecumenical news. The solemn pledge at Amsterdam, 1948, *"We intend to stay together,"* is tested when the churches try *to walk together* in the discharge of the task they are set to do: to confront the whole world—the oikoumene—with the Gospel of the Kingdom. (Matt. 24:14.)

Obviously, evidence of this "walking together" can be found in the proceedings of ecumenical conferences in recent years.

For instance, the Latin-America Conference, Buenos Aires, 1949, put its main emphasis on evangelism and stated that

to evangelize ought to become in the believer a holy obsession, the essential atmosphere of his daily living, the passion of his soul, an unceasing exercise for the sake of his own health.

Again, the Eastern Asia Christian Conference, Bangkok, 1949, was focused on a relevant proclamation of the Gospel in this continent full of change and upheaval. The churches in this area were commended to make

a deliberate effort to enlist their entire membership for evangelism, to train congregations, small groups, youth groups and selected individuals for their task, and to secure the whole-hearted service of every minister in the Church in this part of his duty.

And, to quote only one more example, the Latin Countries Conference, Torre Pellice, 1950, gave special attention to the study of the specific issues of evangelism by minority churches in an often hostile Roman Catholic milieu.

3

The evidence could easily be multiplied: Evangelism is put on the ecumenical map, there to stay. In the programs of Lay (such as Bad Boll, 1951), and Youth (such as Kottayam, 1952) Conferences a resurgence of concern for evangelism is manifest.

But on a much deeper level yet, evangelism has in the past years proved to be the ecumenical theme par excellence. Reports from various parts of the world indicate an ever-increasing awareness of the fact that the churches will achieve unity only in their common mission to the world. The proper context for the consideration of "Faith and Order" issues will consequently be the context of the Missionary Obligation of the Church.

The essential unity between the Church's obligation to be one and its mission to the world has been elucidated in a document *The Calling of the Church to Mission and Unity* which the Central Committee of the World Council of Churches commended to the churches for study (Rolle, 1951). An identical trend of thought is manifest throughout the reports of the International Missionary Council Conference at Willingen, 1952, on *The Missionary Obligation of the Church.*

Both documents identify evangelism as an essential mark of Christian life:

To be a Christian is necessarily to be involved in a Mission to the world. [Rolle]

There is no participation in Christ without participation in His Mission to the world. That by which the Church receives its existence is that by which it is also given its world mission. "As the Father hath sent Me, even so send I you." [Willingen]

With equal emphasis both documents suggest that the ministry for unity can and must be performed within the broader context of the mission to the world: on the one hand by insisting that the word "ecumenical" be only properly used "to describe everything that relates to the whole task of the *whole* Church to bring the Gospel to the whole world," so that it covers equally the missionary movement and the movement toward unity (Rolle), and, on the other hand, by forcibly stating that without unity the mission of the Church will necessarily be frustrated:

> Division in the Church distorts its witness, frustrates its mission, and contradicts its own nature. If the Church is to demonstrate the Gospel in its life as well as in its preaching it must manifest to the world the power of God to break down all barriers and to establish the Church's unity in Christ. [Willingen]

This recovery in thought of the true relationship between the Church's calling to mission and its calling to unity will inevitably have organizational consequences. It is seriously questioned whether the "association" between the missionary movement, as organized in the International Missionary Council, and the movement toward unity, as organized in the World Council of Churches, is a convincing enough demonstration of the essential interrelatedness of these two callings of the Church. Especially in the lands of the "younger" churches, Christians stress the necessity of a speedy integration of the two organizations. Convinced that they are living at the "end of a missionary era," and desirous to correct antiquated relationships as between "sending" and "receiving" churches, they impatiently anticipate a fully integrated ecumenical movement, which will be a convincing symbol of the partnership in the whole Church in its mission to the whole world.

In many different places a beginning has been made to do something about ecumenical evangelism in practice. These joint activities have often been initiated by local or regional councils of churches. It is increasingly felt that this is the area in which the reality of "ecumenicity-at-the-grassroots" is most seriously tested by the unselfish willingness to co-operate in interdenominational evangelistic efforts. Until the present only very little attention has been given to the manifold delicate problems of the underlying theory of such united action.[1]

The conviction is growing, however, that these problems cannot be solved a priori and that common action should not be postponed until all the questions are answered. The problems should rather be dealt with within the context of joint action.

Question

What are the problems of united evangelism in which your church participates? Can they be solved a priori?— How?

It has been suggested that the underlying issues be clarified by reference to the New Testament concepts of proclamation (*kerygma*), i.e. the essentially uniform Christian message to the non-Christian world; and the several teaching traditions (*didachai*) as the diverse definitions of this same message in various groups (denominations), the argument being that a kerygmatic unity in evangelism may be possible concurrent with a didactic diversity in the various churches. Can this distinction be of any help in thinking through the underlying issues of united evangelism? If so, how would you define the content of the common message in evangelism?

Immediately related to the previous questions is the issue which has unfortunately become known as that of "proselytism." In its original meaning of a challenge and invitation to join the Church or any particular church, the attempt at proselytizing should be considered as a legitimate part of the missionary task. Increasingly, however, the word is defined in deprecatory terms and in current language it almost equals "sheep-stealing."

[1] The British Council of Churches has issued a useful document: *United Evangelism*, 1949.

It is commonly agreed that the member churches which have pledged to stay *together* "should recognize their solidarity and refrain from such actions as are incompatible with brotherly relationships."[2] Consequently, they will not regard and treat one another as possible "mission fields," but rather strive to be *"partners"* in the furtherance of the Gospel (Phil. 1.5). In some instances, however, historical developments have produced serious tensions and endangered ecumenical relations, notably so in the Middle East.

Initially, Protestant missions in this area were intended as a Mission of Help "to reform, to revive and to re-equip the ancient churches in this area for a more effective common witness in a Muslim environment." In the end this work has resulted in the formation of independent Evangelical churches. In many parts of the Middle East the development of missionary work has been along the same pattern: attempts to reform the churches from within, growing antagonism, eventual excommunication, and the formation of independent churches which are for the greater part offshoots from the ancient churches and in some instances number not more than one per cent of their members as Muslim converts.

Following the Toronto Declaration (1950) the traditional missionary policy of the Protestant churches has again been scrutinized. It is an almost common conviction now, that the membership of the ancient churches in the Middle East should not be treated as the "objects" of Protestant missionary work, while at the same time the essential freedom to propagate the Faith according to one's own understanding and the freedom to change one's church allegiance should be safeguarded. There are no easy and clear-cut solutions for this problem; the more so, because "the distinction between 'proselytism' and witness is very subtle; it refers not to the content of our preaching, but to the direction and

---

[2] Toronto Declaration of the World Council of Churches, IV, 7.

intention of our will."[3] Every motive of denominational aggrandizement should therefore be eliminated to keep evangelism genuine.

Question

Usually we term our own efforts "evangelistic," and those of the others "proselytizing" in a derogatory sense. By what criteria? Are motives of denominational aggrandizement entirely absent in the evangelistic efforts of your church? If not, by what rationalizations are they justified?

Of extreme importance in the contemporary world scene are the problems posed by the rapidly increasing missionary activities of "non-cooperative groups" of a (more or less) sectarian spirit. The words "spreading like wildfire" occur in many reports to depict their growing activity. It is estimated that some 40 per cent of contemporary Christian missionary efforts lie outside the ecumenical fellowship. Japan reports that "hardly a month goes by without the arrival of representatives of some new non-cooperative church groups. These groups, though the number of their membership is still negligible, are served by about half (834 out of a total of approximately 2,000) of the entire missionary body in the land." Similar reports from various other areas are agreed that these groups drive forward in a way which usually takes no cognizance of existing Christian communities and concentrate their work very often on members of established churches, rather than preaching the Gospel to non-Christians. Wherever these groups are consolidated in a non- (or even anti-) ecumenical council of their own, as in India or Japan, the problems of relationship are greatly intensified.

Alongside the confusion and embarrassment produced by these groups' activities in the minds of many Christians one can detect a mood of curious surprise. Intrigued by the mani-

[3] L. Zander, "Ecumenism and Proselytism," in *The Ecumenical Review*, II, 3, 1951, p. 258.

fest enthusiastic zeal for the winning of souls, they begin
to search for the hidden sources of this powerful stream of
missionary vigor, so often lacking in the churches. Why do
these groups very often find an entrance among the socially
dispossessed, who are usually absent from our respectable
congregations? A whole range of painful questions are
posed by this "ultra-Protestant" evangelism, even though the
churches may be deterred by its unscrupulous methodology.

In most instances there is only one link left with these
non-cooperative groups. In their desire to be strictly "Bible-
centered," and actually engaged in Bible colportage to a degree hardly known in most churches, these groups wholeheartedly participate in the work of the Bible societies. It
may be in the field of Bible colportage that these groups
and the established churches will find and cross-fertilize each
other in a common evangelistic enterprise.

Question
> What are the reasons for the evangelistic "success" (if
> any) of the "sectarian" groups in your country? Is it true
> that these groups have become "the church of the dis-
> possessed"? What is true of their alleged "Bible-centered-
> ness"? What is done to overcome an unwholesome and
> rather negative competition in the field of evangelism?

"To support the churches in their task of evangelization,"
the Amsterdam Assembly set up a *Secretariat for Evangelism*
in the World Council of Churches. Since 1949 this Secretariat
has been in operation, serving the churches primarily as a
center of documentation and information about "the effective
new approaches toward the problem of communicating with
the unchurched." In conjunction with this Secretariat the Research Secretary of the United Bible Societies has been
working since 1951 with the main concern of studying "The
Place of the Bible in Evangelism."[4]

[4] See the book of Dr. A. M. Chirgwin, *The Cutting Edge*.

The inquiry "The Evangelization of Man in Modern Mass Society," initiated in 1949, has not yielded any spectacular results up to the present time. The slow progress seems to be due mainly to an almost chaotic confusion as to the meaning and scope of evangelism. Evangelism has indeed become the ecumenical theme par excellence, but we have hardly begun to make it a concern of serious ecumenical study.

III

EVANGELISM AROUND THE WORLD

A. Asia, the Near East and Africa

A brief analysis of the evangelistic situation in *Asia* is embodied in one of the reports of the Asian Ecumenical Study Conference held at Lucknow, 1952. In the following pages some of the relevant sections of this report are quoted and commented on.[1]

One of the most serious weaknesses in the present evangelistic situation is, reportedly, the Church's isolation *vis à vis* the great classical religions in Asia.

The Christian forces in Asia have not yet come effectively to grips with the greater religious traditions. There have been great accessions to the Church, but invariably, where men and women have been won in large numbers to the Christian allegiance they have been won from a background which is primarily animistic and tribal. It is still true that it is among those simpler, more unsophisticated, more oppressed people that the Word of the Lord runs freely.[2]

In the years under survey this has been particularly manifest in the great "awakenings" among the aborigines in Taiwan (Formosa), in North Laos and North Sumatra. A notable exception is the Church in Japan, whose membership is almost exclusively made up of the urban intelligentsia.

Various reports agree that over the last few decades the

[1] All quotations which follow, unless otherwise noted, are from this report. See *Christ—The Hope of Asia.* Papers and minutes of the Ecumenical Study Conference for East Asia, Lucknow, Dec. 1952, ed. N. Ehrenström, pp. 21 ff.

[2] C. W. Ranson in Bangkok Report, *The Christian Prospect in Eastern Asia*, p. 65.

11

serious concern in the Church for an adequate understanding of these great religions is actually on the decrease:

The Christian Church everywhere has lost the distinction it once possessed that the authoritative scholars in practically every Asian country of the established religions of that country were Christians. The consequent fact is that the Christian Church in these countries is rapidly becoming out of date in its knowledge of the established religions of these countries. Thus, for example, the Hinduism or Buddhism which the Christian evangelist has in mind in forging his apologetic or polemic is a Hinduism or Buddhism which Hindus and Buddhists do not now live by.[3]

A "study group in Asia" stated in unequivocal terms that

Asian Christians seem at present to be not very much interested in the questions of the relations between the Gospel and the ancient cultures (=religious heritage).

Some of them hold that the background is changing rapidly, that the ancient traditions and thought-forms are losing their power, and that to be too much interested in them is archeological rather than practical.[4]

This decrease of interest is the more surprising in view of the fact that from the various areas a *"renascence of the old religions"* is reported.

India: "A revived consciousness of renewed loyalty to Hinduism as a way of life; resurgent and militant Hinduism."
Burma and Ceylon: "A Buddhist revival."
Japan: "The spiritual vacuum after the defeat is showing signs of being filled by revived old religions."
Indonesia: "A recrudescence of militant Islam."

Among the reasons for this decline of concern to communicate effectively with adherents of the traditional religions, most often mentioned are:

"The concealment of the religious renascence." The religious traditions go through a process of reconception in

[3] D. T. Niles in *Christ—The Hope of Asia,* p. 52.
[4] Report, *Christianity in Asia,* prepared for the Kottayam Youth Conference, 1952, p. 11.

modern terms which makes them difficult to identify. Most often they are presented as a social or political program.

A deliberate effort to rationalise the old in terms of the new experience is apparent in all Asian countries. Whenever this is done, it is always termed "a return to the pristine religion." It is not really a return to the original at all but a rethinking and restating of the religion based on carefully selected scripture texts which can be made to seem to apply to the new situations.[5]

Thus the religious traditions are often presented in the disguise of a *national* ideology. For the sake of solidarity with the new nation, Christians are tempted to conform to these ideologies and to ignore the religious roots of these ideas.

A second related factor is reportedly an ubiquitous tendency on the part of the churches to be actively present in the shaping of the new nationhood. The strong conviction that "the ancestral faiths of these lands cannot provide the needed inspiration to support and safeguard the new social ideals"[6] has turned away all vital interest for these religions ("archeological") and concentrated on attention on the new social and ideological movements. The Bangkok conference, for instance, found a vital and relevant message in view of communism, but it failed to be sufficiently articulate in its message with regard to the "cultural heritage of Asia."

Here and there a strong plea is voiced now, to come to grips with the deep-rooted fundamentals of the ancestral religions, and not merely to deal with the transient phenomena on the surface of the Asian scene—but, as yet, the churches in Asia agree in their reports that they live by and large without significant contact with the great religious traditions of this continent.

One of the things that needs urgently to be done is to break the isolation of the Church in its environment. This isolation is first of all the result of an attitude of introversion in the Church. The

[5] K. P. Landon, S. E. *Asia, Crossroad of Religions,* Chicago, 1949, p. 186.

[6] Bangkok Report, p. 118.

churches should be helped to understand their life in terms of their mission. Secondly, this isolation is the result of a lack of real concern for those who are not Christians. Where Christian and non-Christian meet in the normal business of life, the evangelistic encounter is not taking place. And thirdly, there is class isolation on the part of Christian congregations. Congregational life is not possible where those composing the congregation do not share common cultural and social values.

It is reported, for instance, from Japan that:

The Christians in [*Japan*] are a small group influential only in intellectual circles and tending to shut themselves up in their own community, without seeking to break out and penetrate into the life of the common people, to challenge them as to the purpose and meaning of life and history.[7]

The Church in Japan does not reach to the mass of the people, either in the countryside or among industrial workers.[8]

The Protestant Church is on the whole a middle-class phenomenon. Its members are mostly among the social groups which are not too deeply rooted but are movable. It is most at home in cities of secondary size or in the suburbs of large cities. If it is on the side of change at all it would have to be gradual change.[9]

In the post-war period converts have come mainly out of student circles (32%) and generally the white-collar section (26%); with regard to age-groups it is reported that the majority of converts are young people—10-19 years, 34%; 20-25 years, 25%; and that the most significant group in the nation: 30-35 years is almost untouched.[10]

Though the Japanese situation is exceptional in the Asian scene, it is agreed that:

there is a stalemate with regard to evangelistic progress in all the churches in Asia where the Church is almost completely middle

[7] K. Takeda in *The Ecumenical Review*, III, 4, 1951, p. 400.

[8] Report from Japan, 1952.

[9] C. Iglehart, "The Christian Church in Japan," in *International Review of Missions*, p. 276.

[10] Bishop Yashiro in *International Review of Missions*, 1952, pp. 360 ff.

class (Ceylon, Malaya, Japan), and that practically everywhere there is a stalemate where the Church faces the educated non-Christian.[11]

A recent analysis of the evangelistic situation in India[12]

includes a wide range of variations on the theme of the isolation of the Church. The isolated situation of the Church in urban society means that urban Christianity is generally out of touch with the labouring classes. . . . The Communist allegation that the Church is a bourgeois child seems true to the student because of what he sees in his Church life.

In rural areas:

The churches in many places are giving a negative witness of isolation and dependence, rather than a positive witness of community with constantly extending social and economic frontiers, as well as of spiritual and moral reality.

Though any generalization may be unsound, the tenor of reports from other countries is very often the same.

There is need to explore ways and means of developing Christian group life which will meet the needs of social groups as groups, without such a development militating against the oneness of parish life. The problem must be faced that in greater and greater measure the normal unit of social life is not geographically defined, and that therefore the parish cannot easily be the evangelising unit, or become the home of the evangelised. (By "parish" is meant the Christian community living in an area geographically defined.)

The major problem of the Church in fulfilling its mission is the problem of Christians getting alongside their fellowmen in order to communicate the Gospel to them. We must somehow gossip the Gospel. That is, we must learn to talk naturally and spontaneously about the Gospel to our fellows. The evangelist must belong to those whom he is seeking to evangelise. In achieving this the following methods merit serious consideration:
(a) that laymen should be so trained that they can be effective evangelists in their normal life;

[11] D. T. Niles.
[12] R. W. Scott, *Evangelism in India*, Geneva, 1952, *passim*.

(b) that some ordained ministers should earn their living in some lay vocation, thereby becoming more easily members of the community whom they are seeking to serve;

(c) that good Christian men, even though without theological training and academic qualification, be ordained as ministers of the groups to which they naturally belong.

Noteworthy developments in the training of laymen for their evangelistic task are reported from parts of India,[13] Japan (training for visitation evangelism) and in North Sumatra, where among the Simelungun Bataks teams of "Christ's Witnesses" are systematically trained for the evangelization of this region. A great religious awakening has reportedly seized the Simelungun people.[14]

The problem of communication also involves overcoming the foreignness of the form in which the Gospel is presented and the life of the Church is lived. The important thing is not to attempt piecemeal adaptation but to ensure (a) that the leaders of the Church are really indigenous and that the Church is free to order its own life, (b) that the Christian community shares in the culture of the nation so that its expression of Christian thought and life will be inevitably indigenous, (c) and that mission grants are not made available for developing forms of Christian expression which are not congruent with the cultural and social forms of the environment, but that where mission grants are used, they should be used to strengthen the essential life and work of the Church and its evangelistic extension. The danger of syncretism in the way of indigenisation must always be closely watched. The Gospel cannot be indigenised, it is only our response to the Gospel which must be indigenous.

It was reported that new Christian "sects" have been founded and have grown within the last few years in many Asian lands, and that the "sect" type of Christian life was making a successful appeal to many people. Religious emotion is present in them and helps to make their joy contagious. It was felt that among the reasons for the success of the sects were: (a) their insistence on the con-

[13] R. W. Scott, *Evangelism in India*, pp. 43 f.
[14] K. R. Ahn, in *World Dominion*, 1950, pp. 33 ff.

version experience, (b) their ability to meet the people where they were, (c) and the freedom of their ways of worship. The churches are often too procrustean in their methods.

In a factual survey it seems proper not to hazard any guesses on the evangelistic situation in *China*. Such reports as are available suggest an increasing domestication of the churches by the regime, particularly in rural areas; the end of institutional evangelism and possibly of the corporate witness of worship, but—as far as it is known—a continued evangelism by various little Christian fellowship groups and "communistic" sects such as the Jesus Family movement and the Little Flock. Some observers venture to suggest that these "fundamentalist" indigenous sects point in the direction that the Chinese church life may take; others agree with the testimony of one priest that the Church in China will be left with "nothing but the grace of God and personal example as its means of evangelism."

The *Muslim world*,[15] long regarded as one of the most impregnable areas for the Christian Gospel, is showing signs of a serious crisis, if not of disintegration.

With the important shift eastward of the center of gravity of the Muslim world (60 per cent of the Muslims now live east of Karachi) and the spiritual testing Islam has to face in Asia ("new in its history, the issue of which is unpredictable"), Islam now finds itself in a fluid state. "Though well-defined and authoritarian, Islam is yet in a process of redefinition."

In the Middle East nationality seems to be the only allegiance worthy of devotion. A mood critical of all faiths prevails, especially in intellectual circles.

Some reports[16] suggest that the Muslim world, aware of

[15] In this paragraph, statements are quoted from the general survey, "Islam at Mid-Century," in *Muslim World*, 1952, pp. 313 ff.

[16] K. A. Cragg, "The Christian Church and Islam," *ibid.*, and "The Arab World and the Christian Debt," in *International Review of Missions*, 1953, pp. 157 ff.

its new and almost overwhelming problem of modernity, is looking for friendship from Christians, provided this friendship can be offered in a spirit of humility and genuine fraternization, which eventually may live down the historic enmity between Islam and Christendom. In an attitude of "alongsidedness, talking *with* the Muslims rather than *to* them," the Church may discharge its mission to Islam in a promising way.

Though opportunities in some areas of the Muslim world may have ceased to be opportunities (as, for instance, the recent difficulties for missionaries in Iran indicate) and though (Islam-based) "nationalism" may prove to be no less formidable an opponent than traditional Islam has been in the Middle East and North Africa, reports from different areas indicate a greater openness for the Gospel on the part of Muslims.

There may be serious doubts that the Church in Pakistan, mainly consisting of people of low-caste Hindu origin, can represent the Christian faith in the largest Muslim state of the world. Reports indicate, however, that there has never been a time in which there were so many inquirers or converts (since 1947 approximately 5,000) from Islam than in the years after the Partition (1947). "We find the doors open; new areas are showing more interest in the Christian Gospel than ever before."[17]

After the Partition, individual Muslims in India, "sensing their dangerous isolation, have sought security and friendship outside the crumbling walls of Islam. In some areas Muslims come freely and are still coming for baptism. For Muslim evangelism in India the present opportunity has had no parallel in the past, and will probably have none in the near future."[18]

[17] Report from Pakistan; cf. H. Kraemer in *International Review of Missions*, 1953, pp. 149 ff.
[18] K. Anand in *Evangelism in India*, p. 50.

And recent reports from Indonesia, the second largest Muslim country in the world, indicate that there are at present great evangelistic opportunities among Muslims (especially educated young people) in that area.

Africa has in the past few years come into the headlines, there to stay. These years have also witnessed what has been termed "the Christian rediscovery of the Church in Africa," with all its breath-taking opportunities and dangers.

Over the debris of the ancient religions, now crumbling away, Church and Islam confront each other in many parts of tropical Africa. In a continent where the color of a man's skin will increasingly affect everything, it may become of great importance that Islam presents itself as a black man's religion. The rapid advance of Islam in Nigeria and elsewhere has alarmed Christian observers. "There is room for searching inquiry about aims and methods, unless Islam is to possess West Africa within a few decades."[19]

Yet the rapid progress of the Christian cause has been such (approximately 21 million professed African Christians at present) that it seems justified to expect that "in 50 years' time tropical Africa might well be in the main a Christian country."

At the same time there is a growing realization of the fact that "it has been impossible for depth to keep pace with extension."

The Gospel can so readily present itself as no more than a lesson to be learned. Christian discipleship is no more than the substitution of a number of Christian taboos for the traditional taboos of African paganism. . . . the danger becomes serious, when a superficial half-Christianity comes to be accepted as the normal thing. . . . In some areas the young African Churches are already tending to settle down in this wholly unsatisfactory half-pagan, half-Christian state.[20]

[19] E. J. Bingle in *Missions under the Cross*, 1953, p. 172.
[20] S. C. Neill in *The Ecumenical Review*, III, 1, 1950, p. 19.

Reports agree that precisely the rapid extension of the Christian faith is one of the most serious causes of weakness in the life of the African churches.

It would be surprising if the indigenous Church in East Africa failed to double its present membership during the coming generation. The danger is rather that, under the stress of political and social change, it may start to disintegrate at the centre, while it is still expanding on the circumference.[21]

This disintegration at the center is already manifest in the widespread misunderstanding of what the Church is and what it proclaims.

The Church is too often a comfortable little club which gives its members a certain amount of respectability without requiring anything much of them. [Congo][22]

Many detribalized Africans tend to regard the Church as a substitute for the old tribes as a center of loyalty. The "tribal Church" idea is consequently widespread. This implies that Church and former tribe are thought to be coextensive and that there is often little concern for the mission beyond the frontiers of the tribal Church.

This leads to static introversion and may partly explain the strong tendency to rationalize the Christian Gospel in terms of the old tribal religions. Inspired and buttressed by the rise of nationalistic sentiments, nativistic-syncretistic movements have arisen in many African churches throughout the continent, notably in areas of racial tensions (S. Africa), but also in other areas where these tensions are less acute (West Africa). Wherever these movements lead to schism, the separatist churches become very easily syncretistic sects and as such "the bridge over which the Africans are brought back to heathenism."[23]

[21] R. Oliver, *The Missionary Factor in E. Africa*, London, 1952, p. 291.
[22] H. D. Brown, "The Church and Its Missionary Task in Congo," in *International Review of Missions*, 1952, p. 304.
[23] B. G. N. Sundkler, *Bantu Prophets in S. Africa*, London, 1948, p. 297

Against this background the revival movements in East Africa are of great importance. Starting in Ruanda these revival movements have spread since to Kenya, Uganda and Tanganyika and in all these countries there are now strong revival groups, one of them already in existence over a period of more than fifteen years. These groups are a persisting force now in the life of the churches, with a solid background of Bible-teaching, high ethical standards and a strong emphasis on evangelism as the primary function of the Church. Though all reports agree that these movements have had a reviving effect throughout the Church in East Africa as a whole and in Kenya, where the missionary zeal of the rewon Christians is praised as the most marked feature of the movement there, an over-all appraisal of these movements has come to the conclusion that they have had so far only little impact on the untouched African pagans.[24]

As long as "the expansion at the circumference" continues and "Christianity remains fashionable, so that [in Nyasaland] intellectuals and also the working classes like to be classed as Christians," it is reasonable that evangelism be conceived in terms of Christian nurture and training of the laity. Evangelism should be directed to those within the Church.[25]

There is, however, increasing evidence of serious anxiety lest the Church should gradually develop into "an expanding but essentially introverted community" and that the mission to those outside her life will be "suffocated" by the concern for pastoral care of those within the Church. Absorbed by this care for its own life, the Church may easily lack the imagination and the resources to communicate effectively with those outside.[26]

Reports speak more particularly about two groups: the first are the educated young Africans, who tend to break

[24] R. G. N. Colderwood, "Revival in East Africa," in *World Dominion,* 1951, pp. 261 ff.

[25] Based on reports from Nyasaland.

[26] P. Tellkamp, *Gefahr der Erstickung für die christliche Welt-Mission,* Münster, 1950.

away from church life. Though largely still nominal Christians, they increasingly spurn and ignore the Church, because they feel "that it lays far behind the present evolution of their countries and no longer seems capable of giving them anything they want or of meeting their problems and expectations." [Camerouns]

The narrow ecclesiastical outlook, so largely manifest, the low intellectual standards of the ministry, a lack of imagination on the part of church leaders are among the most often heard reproaches. It is felt that mission and Church have tried to "mould the individual only to the Church's purpose, that they have fostered the schools as a recruiting-ground for church membership but have failed to train a younger generation for intelligent and responsible citizenship in the new states." [Gold Coast] There is a great need for new frontier service among the rapidly increasing African intelligentsia.

The second group, mentioned in reports, are the urban population, especially the permanently settled workers in towns and mining centers, who are becoming completely detribalized. The traditional pattern of evangelism in Africa has been that of "rural mass evangelism." These methods cannot be effective for the urban population: "Laymen should be trained for individual work among urban people."[27]

B. Western Europe and Britain

An apt description of the evangelistic situation in Britain and Europe is that provided by an English writer as he attempts to describe the situation faced in that country. His comment comes to this:

The great mass of people are alienated from the churches. This has been a trend which was completed at the time of the great depression in the early thirties when workers particularly affected felt deeply that the churches had let them down. The second World War finally revealed what had taken place. Profound ignorance of

[27] R. Forshaw, "Evangelism among Africans in Urban Areas," in *World Dominion*, 1952, pp. 333 ff.

the first principles of Christianity among large sections of the community was disclosed to chaplains and hostesses of evacuees when the Church took the responsibility of organising their lives. These war years gave a true picture of the attitude of the English people to Christianity. We now know for certain where we are, though we have been where we are for more than twenty years.

Allowing for differences caused by special conditions operating in various countries, this would be a fair description of the situation faced by the Church in Western Europe and Britain. In such a situation, the traditional forms of evangelistic work seem ineffective and yet the special methods by which they are replaced or supplemented have not yet passed the stage of experimentation.

It is better to face unpleasant facts squarely than to segregate certain encouraging tendencies. The over-all impression received when studying the reports coming from many countries is that even where church membership remains high, it is quite impossible to take this fact as an indication of actual participation in the life of the Christian community. For example, though in one diocese of Stockholm reports indicate that 83 per cent of the population are confirmed church members, in the same report the statement is made that indifference to the message of the Church is "frightfully great." Though in Scotland a higher percentage of the population has church membership than in any other country, save the United States, an analysis of a single housing area indicated that only 19.5 per cent had membership in the local parish church.

The isolation of the Church from large segments of society is indicated by the great difficulty found in interesting the families in new housing areas in the life and work of the Church. Uprooted from the old environment and traditional associations, people in overwhelming numbers tend to cut the last surviving ties with the faith to which their parents traditionally conformed. It is not only among workers that the indifference to the Church is noted, but also among those in the middle class. One comment from Scotland is pertinent:

The great achievement of the Church in Scotland in the 19th century was its education of the rising middle class of the cities and towns in Christian service and responsibility. It may well be that its greatest problem in this coming half century will be the evangelisation of their descendents.

From Germany comes the significant comment that in the context of a "national" church, while as many as 95 per cent of the population may belong to a church, very few reveal in their actions a decisive influence exercised by this membership.

The special problems represented by the isolation of the masses of industrial workers from the Church has been carefully explored in the pamphlet, *Evangelism in France.* A particular form of this isolation is noted in the reports from many countries regarding the failure of the Church to contact workers in the new housing districts in industrial areas. Sweden reports that many of these districts have no churches at all. From England comes the comment that "those who live on new housing estates form the section of the community most widely separated from the life of the churches."

It is pointed out that the social and spiritual atmosphere is distinctly worse under the better physical conditions than in the older slums of industrial towns where some tradition of the poor helping the poor survives. It is of some interest to analyze the causes of the Church's failure to a great extent in reaching industrial workers. One comment from Scotland seems of special importance:

It was unemployment (80% of the male population in some areas) that really showed the skilled and unskilled workers that they belong together and finally convinced many that the Church belonged to the other side. It was not so much that the Church did nothing. It was rather that the Church did not care. When the unemployed sent a deputation to the General Assembly they were

9572

not received. Probably the Assembly could have done nothing, but its effect on the men was disastrous. The Church was not concerned with them; that was the impression they received.

It is not clear that a similar indifference to the Church or actual hostility based on deep resentment exists among the intellectuals. There are in many countries indications of the establishment of lines of communication between the Church and the intellectuals. Among students an increased interest in Christianity, increasing Bible study and a desire for a more direct evangelical approach by Christian groups is noted. In Great Britain passing of the Butler Act providing religious instruction for schools creates new opportunities for the development of a high standard of religious instruction and fruitful contact with the teaching profession.

It is frequently pointed out that the new signs of interest in Christian thought among intellectuals seem not to be induced to any great extent by theological writing. Rather this interest finds its sustenance in plays, music, pictures, novels and poetry. It is often in the theater that a sense of responsibility for religious issues is highly developed.

It is at this point that the relative impotence of old forms of evangelism appears most obviously. Mass methods of evangelism have in the past depended on the presumed existence of a Christian community as a reality to which the lapsed may be recalled or into which the converted may be brought. It is necessary to face the fact that such a community does not exist at all among the people with whom the Church is concerned. Therefore, the employment of methods which assume its existence seem to result most often in, at best, a warming of the hearts of those already within the Church, and, at worst, a further alienation of those groups outside the Church's life. A comment by the Swedish Ecumenical Council is pertinent:

Industrial workers who are united in a close fellowship of strong group-consciousness have little appreciation of a religion which means isolation in different groups. If the fact that you want to be a Christian in earnest would mean that you leave your old environment and enter a new organized form of fellowship, the industrial worker must interpret this as treachery against his own class.

The World's Evangelical Alliance comments:

What are generally regarded as the old methods of evangelism, evangelistic campaigns and big mass meetings, very largely leave untouched the great mass of workers and intellectuals.

This does not mean that the Church is to be dispensed with as the agency of evangelism. Quite the contrary, for it is one of the major criticisms of the older types of mass evangelism that the whole Church was in no sense involved. The renewal of the life of the Church by the discovery of the obligation of members of the body of Christ is the indispensable basis for evangelizing activity. One Scottish minister comments:

The main line of opposition to missions in Scotland does not come from the pagan masses outside the Church. By far the most crushing and bewildering conflict arises within the Church when the demands of Christ upon His people are heard by those for whom religion is a matter of comfortable and respectable conformity. The devastating thing about this sort of conflict within the Church is that it cannot be concealed from those who are finding their way back after years outside.

The same commentator goes on to say positively: "The community must discover its own existence."

The most promising developments in evangelism in Western Europe and Britain are those which grow out of a frank facing of the disturbing facts we have previously treated, plus a determination to recover for the Church the distinctive meaning of its own life. These developments can be noted only too briefly and without sufficient reference to national patterns.

First, there are the developments varied in form and application, which are essentially the creation of fellowship groups in which a number of Christian people become a nucleus around which others slowly gather and rediscover the reality of the life with Christ. This kind of fellowship may be found in a parish, among a group of intellectuals united by a common interest, in a profession or in a factory. There are examples of all these types in reports that have been submitted. The one central characteristic that unites them all is the determination to share in terms of human personal interaction the understanding of the Gospel which is found only in deeper personal relationships.

Second, we find an increasing awareness on the part of churches that if the gulf between Church and workers is to be bridged, the existing parochial outlook of the Church must change. Experiments involving the taking of the Church into the factory or into the professional groups are not based on any belief that the traditional pattern of worship and church life can be dispensed with. Rather, they stem from a profound conviction that those who see the Church as quite unrelated to their actual life must be given an opportunity to discover the relationship which does exist between Christianity and their own existence.

A number of experiments in industrial chaplaincies illustrates the absolute necessity of gaining the confidence of industrial workers by exhibiting a concern for them rather than primarily a desire to gain their support for the organized church.

(1) Getting to know the leaders in industrialized society—industrialists, trade union and labor people, union officials, organizers in the plants, plant counselors. (2) Visiting the steel works—the industrial chaplains' daily job is not to hold services or large meetings, but rather to have informal discussions with the men in the hope of becoming accepted by them and being integrated into their natural work groups. (3) Establishing relations with specific groups in industry—chaplains are asked to meet particular groups, especially in the apprentice training schemes, with professional bodies and trade union meetings. (4) Training men to make Christian contributions—helping them to understand the Christian faith and the relation of that faith to the life of industry through

conferences, training courses and development of their innate
capacities for leadership. (5) Providing opportunities for theological students in industry—making it possible for students
to come, in periods of six months or more, into actual work in
the steel mills as part of their training.

A third type of evangelistic pioneering is represented by the
use of developments in the field of communication in direct
relationship to a carefully planned program of parish evangelism. The use of broadcasting, films, drama and other types of
audio-visual aids in relationship to a program which envisages
the full employment of the resources of the parish church is
especially promising, for in this way the intelligent use of
available methods of mass evangelism rests back upon the
careful preparation of the Christian community itself for the
task which only it can do.

The knowledge that great numbers of people and whole
groups in society are outside the life of the Church cannot
help very much unless those already in the churches are
determined to act with this knowledge in full consciousness
of their own responsibility and the means that are available
to them for effective evangelization. Local evangelism carried
out by the parish churches will not be a complete solution to
problems that arise in many cases from the absence of the
Church in certain housing areas. These programs are, however, the most natural and the most promising, where, as in
Britain and Western Europe, the churches still retain a sense
of their responsibility for the whole life of the nation.

The difficulty as well as the challenge is to be seen in the
almost universal comment that the Church itself must be the
true means of evangelism and to that end the Church must be
born again. In actual practice this appears to mean the creation of a new sense of fellowship and concern within the
Church, a fellowship which is more vital and permanent than
that based upon economic or social groupings, a concern
which is manifested in reaching out to the places where
people live and work rather than in bidding them come into

the relatively closed society which the Church has so often become.

C. THE UNITED STATES

The United States is too vast, its population too large and varied, and its numerous Christian denominations too complex in their life for any sweeping statements about the evangelistic situation to be generally valid. Statistics indicate the continuation of a long-established trend toward church membership on the part of Americans. In 1880, 20 per cent of the population was affiliated with the churches; by 1951, 58 per cent had church membership. There are, it is true, large numbers of those recorded on church membership rolls who have little or no active relationship to the churches' life. Many of them must be numbered among those who are actually proper subjects for evangelistic enterprise.

A second general characteristic of the American scene, which renders necessary a definite reservation in regard to generalizations about "workers and intellectuals," is the fact that these groups are not as sharply defined as elsewhere. All careful studies indicate that what may be called "the middle class" is made up increasingly of salaried workers. There is no clearly defined intellectual group in America, with a sense of its distinct position in society, as in other parts of the Western world. With these qualifications, certain important observations may be made concerning the churches' relationship to the groups with whom this Survey is particularly concerned.

A survey of two hundred of the top leaders of the American Federation of Labor and of the Congress of Industrial Organizations, in 1945, revealed that 89 per cent had some connection with the churches and synagogues. There is evidence that among labor leaders there are as many devoted Christians as are to be found in any similar group in America.

Though it is frequently asserted that American Protestantism is middleclass in character, it must be noted that this middle class now includes a very large proportion of skilled industrial workers. In a population group, of which 27 per cent fall into the "skilled and semi-skilled" classification, 29 per cent of the church membership of the Baptists, 27 per cent of the Lutherans and 23 per cent of the Methodists were from this group. This will indicate that, in at least the larger Protestant groups, the proportion of skilled workers in the Church is not very much if any smaller than is their proportion in relation to the whole population. It is also true that among the great mass of semi-skilled and unskilled workers there is much paganism and a minimum of church attendance.

The attempt to procure anything like definite statistics regarding the relationship of intellectuals to the Church is naturally very difficult. The editors of *The Partisan Review*, a leading literary voice of intellectuals, stated in 1950 an opinion which is widely held today:

One of the most significant tendencies of our time, especially in this decade, has been the new turn toward religion among intellectuals and the growing disfavour with which secular attitudes and perspectives are now regarded in not a few circles that lay claim to the leadership of culture. There is no doubt that the number of intellectuals professing religious sympathies, beliefs or doctrines is greater now than it was ten or twenty years ago and that this number is continually increasing or becoming more articulate. If we seek to relate our period to the recent past, the first decades of this century begin to look like decades of triumphant naturalism; and if the present tendency continues, the mid-century years may go down in history as the years of conversion and return.[28]

Many things may be said about this movement of intellectuals toward religion. In part, it is nothing more than a change in fashion; in part, the movement represents a growing willingness to speak out publicly, on the part of those who have always been believers. In part, it is a highly personal movement toward the discovery of adequate foundations for living. Even then, it may not result in contact with the churches.

The adequacy of old forms of evangelism, though doubted

[28] Vol. XVII, p. 103, Feb., 1950.

by many, receives considerable public support through widespread publicity given to the work of professional evangelists. In one campaign in Greensboro, North Carolina, Billy Graham preached to audiences numbering a total of 391,050 persons. Of this number there were 6,443 converts. In contrast with this highly publicized work, the Methodists, in 1950, using the technique of visitation-evangelism, visited 711,207 persons, of whom 138,836 responded by joining the Church. Billy Graham's percentage of 1.6 per cent converts contrasts rather sharply with the Methodist figure of nearly 20 per cent response to their campaign.

There are in the United States interesting experiments in evangelism whose effectiveness should not be too confidently stated, since in most cases they are limited in scope.

(1) *Reclaiming Churches in Slums.* Two experiments are most notable: The East Harlem Protestant Parish in New York City, and the renewal of Grace Church (Episcopal) in Jersey City, New Jersey. These are bold efforts to preach and manifest the Gospel in the worst kinds of city slums, not by establishing charitable or philanthropic "mission homes," but by making the Church live as a community.

The aim of the East Harlem Parish, consisting mostly of Negroes and immigrants from Puerto Rico, is "to establish a church where there has been no church, to proclaim that Jesus Christ is Lord in every area of life, to relate this proclamation to the various areas of life in this community (family, vocation, housing, health, recreation, education, etc.) and to create a group of people, a community, which is witnessing to this Lordship at every point, but especially at points of tension and crucial decision in the area." The Church's life and program are carried on in homes, vacant lots, sidewalks and streets. Emphasis falls upon visiting homes, religious education, social action, developing indigenous forms of worship and leadership, and making Christian community (koinonia) a reality in the coldly impersonal city.

Grace Church, Jersey City, is typical of those many urban churches which have been deserted by their members who move to the suburbs while the poverty-stricken slum dwellers occupy the neighborhood but ignore the church. It was renewed by a group of young priests living in a communal "open rectory"—open, that is, to the entire neighborhood, white and colored, Christian and non-Christian. Those engaged in this effort voice the conviction that the only effective evangelizing agency, in an era of social disintegration, is the Christian community itself—this by way of contrast with trust in older forms of evangelism such as the mass meeting or mere verbal proclamation.

(2) *Evangelism in Mining Areas.* The Mountaineer Mining Mission in the coal area of West Virginia has established a "beachhead" in squalid towns which the churches heretofore have passed by. "It seeks to bring the full-orbed Gospel of Jesus Christ to a culturally neglected and religiously unevangelized segment of our industrial population. It seeks the conversion of miners, their continued spiritual growth and their banding together in organized Christian churches with a specific community outreach." Five congregations have been established by the Presbyterian minister. Worship and preaching are but a part of the mission: also involved are the religious education of children, forming of women's groups, maintaining recreational programs and libraries, sponsoring a preschool medical clinic for children, and struggling constantly to improve the total life of the community. The minister is also a link between the workers and managers of the mines, being neither "Labor's tool" nor the "company preacher" but the human catalyst who heals the wounds of class warfare.

(3) *An Intellectual Approach to Evangelism.* The heart and the mind are both involved in faith, but for some people more attention must be given to the mind. So in Washington, D. C., a series of classes is held on "Christianity and Modern Man" at the National Cathedral (Episcopal). In five years more than one thousand persons have paid tuition fees to attend

evening courses on Christian doctrine. The project is aimed at "the philosophically restless men and women produced by American secular education." Courses run from October to June, two hours a week. The best theologians are secured as speakers and discussion leaders, and mimeographed transcripts of their addresses are sold. The meaning of the Gospel is interpreted through studies of its relation to international affairs, art, psychoanalysis, communism, economic theory, etc. Attendance averages about seventy per meeting, one quarter of these persons having no other contact with the Church and some claiming to be atheists.

Speakers seek to dispel popular misconceptions about the superstitious and moralistic content of Christianity, and they are unafraid of speaking apologetically to all attacks upon the faith. Church members often criticize this program for being too intellectual. It is significant that the outsiders do not consider it so, but find it an effective means of discovering the truth of God in Jesus Christ.

(4) *Christian Evangelism in the Universities.* There are more than two million university students in America. Perhaps three fourths of these have little to do with any church although many call themselves Christians rather than followers of any other religion.

In most universities and colleges there are units of student Christian movements: either denominational organizations, YM-YWCA groups, or united and nondenominational Christian associations. These consider themselves to be related to the Church, as "servants" or "arms" of the Church in academic communities. They have an evangelistic task to be growing Christian communities, to make known the Gospel in every effective way, and to lead students and faculty into faith in Jesus Christ and participation in the life of the Church. This they seek to accomplish, with varying degrees of zeal and success, by conducting study and discussion groups, retreats and conferences, special meetings with speakers, recreational programs, and visitations in students' lodgings.

A distinctive method followed in hundreds of colleges is the "religious emphasis week," or whatever title may be given. Teams of six to twenty clergy and laymen, chosen for their competence, visit the campus for several days, speaking at convocations in regular classrooms, in dormitories and fraternity houses, etc. A local planning committee prepares for the speakers' coming and tries to capitalize on the opportunities for evangelism which the speakers have stimulated. Faculty as well as students, secular groups as well as church groups, are involved. Administrative officers of the university usually co-operate extensively.

The most striking impression to be gained from reading reports on the evangelistic situation in the United States is that while the churches are making regular gains in membership, while regular attendance at church services has increased, while great sums are being expended in church building with special emphasis on the fast-growing communities, there is still too little indication of imaginative and fresh approaches to the task of evangelism. Churches of almost every denomination, both local and national, have attempted evangelistic projects since 1945, with earnestness and zeal unprecedented in this century. Special missions, crusades, campaigns, visitations, etc. by the hundreds have been carried on. While these large-scale, highly organized programs continue to be directed toward small villages, big cities, universities, industrial areas and military camps, there are two fears which are felt about them:

(a) Too often they are directed toward reclaiming nominal or inactive Christians, rather than to converting the unbaptized.

(b) They tend to be conducted in such a mechanically efficient way that they are ineffective for personal evangelism with lasting fruits, and statistical quantity is valued more than spiritual quality.

To brighten the picture, there is evidence of an unmistakable growth in the recognition of the essential role of the laymen in evangelism. There are also many more co-operative interdenominational programs than ever before. Such co-operation finds institutional expression in the Department of Evangelism of the National Council of the Churches of Christ in America.

Finally, a number of resources are worth being more adequately developed. Among these are: the training and sending forth of laymen in visitation-evangelism; the use of data provided by psychological and sociological studies; conferences and retreats; pastors' schools of evangelism; radio and television broadcasting; motion pictures and filmstrips; newspaper advertising and religious books and periodicals.

The conclusions reached by an acute observer of the American religious scene are worthy of quotation:[29]

1. Whether or not the proposition was true in the past, it is not true now that the organized churches are as a whole middle class or "bourgeois" institutions and that the industrial workers on the one hand, the intellectuals on the other, are alienated from them. Churched and unchurched are to be found—and probably in about the same general proportions—in all economic and cultural levels of the population. Individual denominations vary widely from each other, however, in their ability to serve or to appeal to special groups.

2. The number of people at every economic or cultural level who are outspokenly atheistic, anti-Christian or naturalistic is small. However great the number of the unchristian and irreligious may be, anti-Christian and anti-religious movements as such do not constitute an important problem at the present time for the Churches in America.

3. While in the world at large rival faiths, especially in the forms of communism and nationalism have arisen to challenge the Church, such faiths are not represented in America in explicit rivalry with Christianity. Communism is not now an important movement here and since 1939 has lost almost all the religious appeal it once had for certain intellectual and industrial workers.

[29] H. Richard Niebuhr, *Who are the Unbelievers and What Do They Believe?* Report submitted to Secretariat for Evangelism, WCC.

Nationalism is indeed a movement to be reckoned with but more as a corrupter than as a rival of Christian faith.

4. Despite the large proportion of Americans who count themselves members of the Churches there is wide-spread dissatisfaction with these Churches among them. This dissatisfaction is present not only among nominal Christians but also among relatively faithful church attendants and church workers. It is present not only in the laity but among the clergy. The phenomenon is more apparent among Protestants than among Roman Catholics.

5. The rate of religious and particularly Christian illiteracy in a population that by and large regards itself as Christian is very high. Little biblical knowledge can be counted upon among church members and non-members alike. That Christian faith is intimately connected with a theology, that the Church teaches something relatively specific about God, man, the future; that Christianity is not only belief but understanding in the light of belief; not only a code of ethics but an orientation in nature and history—all this is scarcely understood by great numbers of Protestants, perhaps also of Catholics, though there is some evidence that the latter are in general less illiterate than the former.

6. Distinct from and not necessarily connected with this biblical and doctrinal illiteracy is the low intensity of subjective faith upon the part of many of those who count themselves members of the Church and even participate actively in its work. The tepid climate of Laodicea lies heavily upon a large mass of unalert, unawakened Christians who do not know that they are living in despair. The attitude is not peculiar to church members; unbelief is on the whole even more luke-warm than professed belief.

7. In and outside of the Churches, among the religiously literate and illiterate, there is manifest a widespread hunger and thirst for a faith, for a sense of life's meaning, for genuinely good news about man in his history, for a glory that has passed away from life and left it brassy and maculate. The sense of starvation, connected with industrialism on the one hand, with one-sided conceptualism and intellectualism on the other, seeks satisfaction in music and art as well as in cruder pleasures. One cannot say simply that the Gospel is the answer to this quest, unless the Gospel is understood in more than kerygmatic terms. One might say that what is sought is the word becoming flesh.

8. Finally, it appears that much of the most effective work which is being done in the present situation in reaching the unbelievers and half-believers is being accomplished not by the organized Churches through their institutional channels but by confessions of faith and communications of the Christian understanding of life on the part of lay Christians, whether or not they are members of the Churches. This is doubtless most evident in the field of literature where the effectiveness of such writers as T. S. Eliot and W. H. Auden is widely acknowledged. It is, however, more than a literary phenomenon. It is to be encountered in the labour movement also, and in political life. No criticism of the organized Church is implied in this observation. What is implied is that the Church is a much wider (if also narrower) reality than the churches can represent, and that the latter as members of the body of Christ serve and are served by other members not so easily identified as organs of that body.

D. LATIN AMERICA

In few parts of the world is there more continuous and more fruitful day-to-day evangelism than in Latin America. Visitors are impressed by the immense vigor of the work and the determination to grasp to the full the almost fantastic opportunity which confronts the Church. Reports clearly reflect a sense of the part which the evangelistic outreach contributes to the vitality of the Christian community. "Evangelistic zeal" has been identified as one of the outstanding contributions Latin American churches can make to the ecumenical movement, for "in these younger churches the profession of Christ and the missionary obligation are inseparable."[30]

The growth in the Protestant community throughout this continent (though distributed very irregularly) has arrested the attention of the rest of the world.

The Protestant Church in Brazil is reportedly "the fastest growing church in the world." On the whole

---

[30] Dr. Baez-Camargo, "The Place of Latin America in the Ecumenical Movement," in *The Ecumenical Review*, April 1, 1949, p. 318.

Protestant churches have increased their membership five times over during the second quarter of the present century in Latin America. In Argentina a recent report shows that, whereas the population has quadrupled since the beginning of the century, the number of Protestants has multiplied by 12.[31]

Characteristic features of this evangelistic outreach are:

A strong emphasis on *personal-lay-evangelism*. The Latin American Conferences insisted that *personal* work should take first place among evangelistic methods.

The growth of the Church is the function of the laity. Protestantism in Latin America is essentially a movement founded by the laity of the church.[32]

Though evangelistic campaigns are conducted on a wide scale—the Latin American Mission opened the year 1952 with a series of "continental evangelistic campaigns," beginning in Trinidad and subsequently carried out in five Latin American countries—there has arisen some serious misgiving about the evangelistic value of these campaigns and what is usually known as the *direct* mass approach.

The form of direct appeal has been abandoned over a large part of Latin America. But as a means of "breaking the ice," getting rid of prejudices and arousing interest in a town or village where there is no church (or of contacting people who would never enter a church), open-air meetings still play an important part in the programme of evangelism—when a number of meetings have been held in a certain place, we have more than once had the experience of small regular "congregations" springing up spontaneously.[33]

A second characteristic feature of evangelism in Latin America is without any doubt the use of the *Bible* as a means of evangelism. Sometimes reports go as far as to suggest that "evangelism should be regarded as a postscript to Bible colportage." Bible crusades and Gospel "Commando raids" by

[31] J. M. Bonino, *Report on* Evangelism in Latin America, 1953.
[32] *Ibid.*
[33] *Ibid.*

"small bands of specially trained evangelistic shock-troops" have been carried on in several Latin American countries. "Nearly every new church which opens is the outcome of an intense work of colportage."

A third feature is the widespread activity of "ultra-evangelical groups." These groups usually combine a rather emotionalized faith with a deep sense of fellowship and a strong missionary zeal. "The Church is an evangelistic agency first and last and all the way through and does not deviate from its course."[34] This was written about the Pentecostals, who outnumber all other denominations in Chile and are the second largest denomination in Brazil. Reports indicate, however, that in the second or third generation these evangelistic "sects" tend to turn into respectable "churches" with a more or less mild interest in evangelism.

With all its evangelistic fervor, the evangelical churches in Latin America are still practically out of touch with various important groups of the society. The tendency for evangelical work to concentrate on cities and large towns has left the rural population and the "peon" classes largely untouched by the evangelical cause. Among the city population the intellectuals and the working classes are identified as the two groups least touched.

The *intelligentsia*, traditionally indifferent or even hostile to religion, is showing many signs of spiritual restlessness: "wandering, like a thirsty man through a barren desert, seeking the fountain which would satiate the spiritual thirst" (Rojas). Some reports indicate a willingness to listen to the Gospel, if it be presented "in an intellectual framework and the young educated be shown that as a Christian one can be intellectually respectable." As "religion" is often almost instinctively repudiated, this presentation of the Gospel should be performed in "neutral" places, such as theaters and rented halls, and without any "cultic" setting. "Crowds will throng to

[34] D. C. Brackenridge, "Pentecostal Progress in Chile," in *World Dominion*, 1950, p. 298.

listen to a *conferencia* who would never attend a *culto*." The *conferencia sin culto* has consequently become the commonest form of evangelism.

There is also clear evidence of a stronger emphasis on school evangelism in Latin America.[35]

Though there is, on the whole, only very little social distance between the members of evangelical churches and the workers,[36] the traditional pattern of evangelism seems to be inadequate to reach this group. Personal evangelism, most often of the classical revival type, fails to make any significant impact in the workers' world. And "as yet, the churches have often failed to make use of that larger evangelism, which uses social service as a means of Christian witness."[37]

In the last few years, a clearer recognition of the need for a new approach to the workers has arisen in various churches. Conferences to discuss plans and prospects have been held in different countries and these discussions have stimulated further action. "Labor leaders, and to a large degree all labor in these countries, are definitely anti-clerical, though not anti-religious, without any sense of direction." Basic to this field of industrialism, the need is recognized to study the workers' outlook. A beginning has been made with experiments in community approaches; the creation of Christian fellowship in factories, the holding of "shop" discussions; the setting up of Christian industrial schools for boys, etc.; whereas the need for personal evangelism among labor union leaders and direct evangelism in factories and labor union halls has received strong emphasis. Most of these efforts are still in an experimental stage, but already reports indicate that "there are clear evidences of a willingness to listen," though those who are most deeply involved in this Christian approach to labor

[35] E. M. Lee, School Evangelism Grows in Latin America, in *International Review of Missions*, 1952, pp. 185 ff.

[36] The majority of the Evangelicals belong to the "lower-classes within some countries (Argentine, Uruguay), but show a marked tendency to change into lower middle class churches." (*Report,* Bonino.)

[37] G. Baez-Camargo in *International Review of Missions*, 1947, p. 171.

in Latin America give the warning: "The basic answer to
the question 'How do we reach workers with Christ's message?' is that we do not know."[38]

[38] Based on H. D. Jones, *Christian Approaches to Labour in Latin
America, International Review of Missions,* 1951, pp. 435 ff. and in *ibid.*

IV

SOME PROBLEMS AND
OPPORTUNITIES

A survey of the evangelistic situation on a world scale reveals clearly some special areas of opportunity. It is not surprising that these should also be spheres of activity where unsolved problems impair the effectiveness of the Christian witness.

A. The Training of Christian Workers for Evangelism

There are two great areas of concern in relation to the training of Christian workers which our reports stress. First, ministers and laymen in the churches of the West agree that training for evangelism is entirely adequate in the theological curriculum. Second, reports from the Younger Churches in Asia and Africa, and from other areas such as Latin America where the Protestant churches confront an enormous evangelistic opportunity, emphasize the need for extended programs for the training not only of pastors but of full-time lay workers, women workers and voluntary lay workers.

Positive proposals for the strengthening of the theological curriculum to train ministers to be effective evangelists may be summarized briefly in two statements. First, the minister must be taught how to stimulate and maintain group life. Second, he must be trained to give guidance to lay Christians who are concerned to communicate the Christian faith to their friends and fellow workers. These appear to be rather simple matters which, one would suppose, are already dealt with sufficiently in the theological curriculum. However, a knowledge of the meaning of fellowship and its importance in Christian history does not guarantee an understanding of the ways in which Christian fellowship may be achieved in modern life. Nor does the ability to preach imply of necessity an ability to assist laymen in bringing the Christian message to their fellows. Yet these are two essential arts which the minister must possess if he is to lead his people in effective evangelistic work.

The scarcity of trained workers in relation to the needs of the existing Christian community and the opportunities for evangelism poses the special problem of the Younger Churches. The survey, in this regard, confirms the impressions conveyed by studies made in recent years in India and Africa [1] and supports the conclusion of the International Missionary Council at Tamburam in 1938: "For many of the problems of theological education the corporate unity of the Church is the only solution."

Recommended strategy emphasizes the necessity and feasibility of co-operation in theological training that the strength of unity may be achieved while distinctive denominational traditions are preserved. This uniting of effort in the realm of the training of the ordained minister should also open the way for greater accomplishment in the second area cited above. Bishop Neill comments in his report, "The village catechist, with his slender qualifications and very modest pay, is the real hero of the Christian situation in Africa." This statement could be duplicated many times, in reports from many countries contributed to this survey. Yet it appears that facilities for the training of these unordained workers are quite inadequate. The provision of schools for their training, the planning of conferences, summer sessions of study and opportunities for continued training while engaged in their work: these are quite clearly first calls upon the churches if evangelistic opportunities are to be met.

[1] Charles W. Ranson, *The Christian Minister in India*, 1946, and Stephen Neill, *Survey of the Training of the Ministry in Africa*, 1950.

B. Problems Set by Impersonal Methods of Evangelism

Comparatively recent technical developments in the field of communication enable the Christian churches to reach with their message many more people than ever before. Countries in Western Europe, especially Britain, and the United States, have seen in recent years not only very rapid general development of radio and television but their extensive use as vehicles for evangelism. Impressive statistics are cited to demonstrate the large audiences for certain religious programs of the British Broadcasting Corporation or the various major networks in the United States. But it is probably true that radio has been used more definitely as a means of evangelism in parts of the world, such as Latin America and Asia, where the possession of a radio set is an exception rather than the rule in the average family. In notable instances such as Radio Andes, very powerful transmitters are devoted entirely to the broadcasting of the Christian message.

It is apparent that whatever may be the way in which these media of mass communication are employed, a great opportunity involving a major problem is presented to the churches. The opportunity is clearly that of reaching many people who are quite outside the churches' life and influence and who may not be reached in any other way. The problem may be stated bluntly: to what extent does this contact represent true evangelism? If evangelism is the impact of the whole Christian community upon those who are outside its life, can the hearing of a religious message or the witnessing via television of a religious drama be said to constitute evangelism? May it not be possible that the extensive use of radio and television by the churches will lead to a further dilution of the Christian message and encourage great numbers to suppose that they are to be numbered among the Christian believers because they occasionally or even regularly listen to a religious broadcast?

Very promising developments, particularly in Scotland, are

based upon a clear recognition of these limiting factors and a determination to use radio and television as part of a plan of parish evangelism whose total effect is to bring individuals and families into full relationship to the living Christian community. Similar experiments in the United States point clearly to the truth that there must be very careful organization of the churches' efforts in the field of radio, television and films if the work is to be effective. Above all, it must be observed that this is an area demanding a considerable measure of unity among the participating churches both in definition of the aim of evangelism and in planning the total program of which the utilization of these media is but a part.

C. RELIGIOUS AND CULTURAL NATIONALISM

The survey of the evangelistic situation in the Far East reveals a renascence of the old religions in the form of an identification with nationalism. Several dangers here present themselves to the Christian community in its evangelistic enterprise. The religious traditions are often presented in the disguise of a national ideology and for the sake of solidarity with the new nation Christians are tempted to conform to these ideologies, ignoring their religious roots. An aggressive nationalism allied with religious interests may so limit the activities of the Christian community that evangelism is actually impossible. In defense of its freedom, the Christian community may be tempted to seek political recognition thus actually denying its own nature and ultimately negating its possibilities of evangelizing.

Another form of this problem is familiar to Christians in Western nations. Where there is no significant confrontation with other world religions, it is rather easy to assume that the maintenance of a Christian culture or Christian civilization is the main task of the Christian Church and therefore of evangelism. The recognition of religion and the orderly provision of its continued observances is incumbent upon society, not so much that God's will may be done and His rule accepted as that there may be a religious sanction for the prevailing order. Men are called to recognize membership in the Christian Church as an obligation similar to others they assume as responsible members of the community, and the most searching ethical commands are interpreted as admonitions whose fulfillment is well within the powers of the naturally decent citizen. The Christian Gospel is confused with cultural nationalism in such a way that defense of a particular way of life, social, economic and political in its content, is identified with Christian witness.

The Christian Church will surmount these dangers of perversion of its message and misunderstanding of its mission only by an evangelism which refuses to be identified with either religious or cultural nationalism. The Gospel must be preached so freely that its judgment is felt both in relation to individual sin and the sin of national pride itself. Churches that have made significant contributions to the evangelizing achievement of modern missions must recognize the danger of claiming as their own achievement that which the grace of God has made possible, and the folly of holding back from full Christian maturity those whom that grace has set free.

D. The Problem of United Evangelism

To stop short of united evangelism is to countenance the conclusion that Christians do not experience a unity in Christ strong enough to enable them to join in bringing Christ to men and women and men and women to Christ. To effect an entry through the countless doors at present barred to Christianity is a task of too great magnitude for anything less than a united approach.

These sentences, from a report of the British Council of Churches' Committee on Evangelism, state well the argument for united evangelism which appears, both directly and by implication, in many of the reports received for this Survey. There is ample evidence that united evangelism is a fact, and there are persuasive indications that it may be the answer to some of the difficulties faced by the churches as they seek to reach great segments of society now untouched by their influence. . . .

No service is rendered to the cause of evangelism, however, by attempts to evade the serious questions raised in the realm of "faith and order" by proposals for united evangelism. Such proposals imply agreement by the participating churches concerning the content of the Christian message and the nature of the Church. That such agreement is not a reality among all the churches having membership in the World Council of Churches is clearly indicated by the statement in the Toronto Declaration, holding that "membership does not imply that each Church must regard the other member Churches as Churches in the true and full sense of the word."[2] It is therefore true that there will be those who, on doctrinal grounds, are unable to participate in such endeavors. But it is also true that the discipline of preparation in study, prayer and shared experience, so essential for the work of united evangelism, may become a major factor in drawing closer together those churches which venture in the common proclamation of the Gospel.

Uniting for evangelism may thus hasten the coming of the day of full Christian unity, but until that day comes united evangelism will face the further difficulty created by its achievements. It is separate churches that unite their evangelistic effort. Their message may be one, but those who hear it and respond must choose a particular church with which to unite. In practice, the difficulties are lessened by the fact that many new converts will have a hereditary loyalty to or association with some church. It is usually true, also, that acceptance of the message establishes an intimacy with a particular messenger whose counsel is sought and trusted. Most important is the fact that, when churches and their members have united their wills and prayers in preparation and have this together in common action, they are prepared to evange-

problem with wisdom and mutual understanding. . . .

[2] IV, 4

V

THE EMERGING PATTERN

There is virtually universal agreement on the point that recent years show *an increase in concern for evangelism.* This trend is thus described in a recent world survey of evangelism:

Any appraisal of evangelism in the world-Church must first of all take notice of the resurgence of concern for evangelism everywhere. . . .

[This is] not only due to the precarious state of the world and the resulting uncertainties in the spirits of men, but it issues also from a rediscovery of biblical thought and a theological renewal. . . . While the evangelistic spirit and concern has not brought universal revival nor converted the Churches into forces of evangelism, it has nevertheless permeated a number of Churches with a concern for the effective proclamation of the Gospel. . . .

Churches increasingly sense that evangelism is not an extra task which they may undertake as they please; evangelism is of the very essence of the Church. . . .

The subject of evangelism is no longer regarded as a "sect... concern, but as one that is of the utmost concern for the ... such ... for the Churches today are confronted ... situation, wherever they are located and ... evangelism and missions can no longer be ...

Though the term "evangelism" has ... various groups because of its too dubious ... words like "confrontation," "engagement" ... as more adequate substitutes, all reports are ... matter itself has become again a serious ... churches throughout the world. Some schools ... much more mission-conscious now. Sometimes ...

[1] E. G. Homrighausen, "Trends in World Evangelism," ...tian Handbook, 1952, pp. 32 ff.

Evangelism

lism is Christian that does not issue in corporate membership of the Church. United evangelism has demonstrated its potency in enlarging not only the actual dimensions of that corporate membership but also the ways in which it is understood by those who give and those who answer the invitation to come into the Church of Jesus Christ.

Evangelism

the "Apostolate" even tends to become the all-pervading center of thinking.

Question

If there is any increase of concern for evangelism in your Church, analyze its motives. Do you overhear in the call to evangelism any undertones of anxiety, lest the Church be outrun by its powerful rivals?

What is the place of evangelism in current theological thinking in your country? How is it dealt with in the textbooks used for the training of the ministry?

It has often been said that *biblical* scholarship has rediscovered in recent years the "missionary pattern of all Christian theology," that *systematic* theology hesitates to follow the biblical scholars in this view, and that *practical* (pastoral) theology is most stubborn in its refusal to become missionary-minded: is this statement correct? If so, why is it?

A second point, immediately related to the first, is an ubiquitous increase of *the sense of urgency.* The words of the Amsterdam Report, "Now, not tomorrow is the time to act," are echoed to an ever-growing extent. We begin again to take stock of all the resources which should enable the Church to evangelize the world "before the present generation has passed away." A note of "Pauline haste" has come into many discussions on evangelism.

This may be due partly to a rediscovery of the eschatological character of evangelism. More clearly, however, this sense of urgency has been awakened and intensified by the rapid changes in the world picture. We now know that our opportunities of today may cease to be opportunities tomorrow. The missionary retreat from China overshadows all deliberations; recent developments in Africa color the planning. The summons is increasingly for rapidity and mobility.

This sense of urgency is, of course, not equally manifest in all quarters, but there may be only few places where it is entirely lacking. "Haste," together with a sober realization that there will be no easy road ahead, are striking aspects of the temper of contemporary evangelism.

Question

How is this sense of urgency impressed upon the minds of Christians in your Church? Is there any evidence of an "apocalyptic" note?

Reports from various parts of the world indicate that the *Bible* is more systematically used in evangelism. On an unprecedented scale Holy Scripture has been distributed and studied in postwar Japan; the No-Church Movement in this country is centered on Bible study and issues regularly study guides. The Gospel Crusades in Latin American countries, and the Bible Teams in some of the Asian lands are an attempt to bring the Bible into every home of the community as a "paper-missionary" which might stimulate the community to interpret Holy Scripture. In many places Bible colportage has become again an integral part of the total work of the Christian community. Bible discussion groups are an increasingly common feature in the approach to those outside the life of the Church. In Western lands biblical themes are more evident in contemporary literature and drama.

Question

Have any new techniques of Bible colportage been developed during the past few years? How loped in your country during the past few years? How much are means of mass communication used? Is the distribution of Holy Scriptures an integral part of the life of the Christian community or is it still delegated to the special care of the Bible Societies?

A mood of *sober self-criticism* is beginning to become manifest in various ways. First, there is a willingness to *examine the life of the Church itself*, to find out how and where the lines of communication with those outside are blocked. Most reports start off with an extensive section entitled "What is wrong with the Church?" Unsuccessful communication is explained more readily in terms of the scandal of the Church than in terms of the hardening of hearts of those outside.

Question

In a previous ecumenical document on evangelism it was said that the isolated situation of the Church in the modern world is so serious, that nothing short of a revolution in the life of the Church is required to make it again a more useful instrument for evangelism. What has happened in recent years to bring this revolution about? Again it was said that someone engaged in industrial evangelism stated that "the spiritual poverty and unpreparedness of the Church is such that no one can desire that a large number of those now outside should enter the Churches as they are." Do you agree?

Second, a whole process of *re-examination of the traditional methods of evangelism* and especially of their underlying assumptions, is going on. Perhaps there is not (yet?) sufficient radicalism in this re-examination of the techniques, but at least searching questions are posed and partly answered, such as: (in Europe) "How much are the ordinary methods determined by an 'Inner Mission psychology,' i. e., an orientation toward 'reviving the lapsed rather than saving the lost?'" To what extent is our whole evangelistic effort built upon the assumption of a Christendom ideology? etc.

Question

Define the underlying assumptions of the method of work you are engaged in. Do they meet the present situation?

Concurrent with the re-examination of methods is a far greater soberness in the *evaluation of the results*. Perhaps we are less impressed by simple and unqualified statistics. After recent mass meetings the main question was not concerning the numbers of people who attended the meetings, but rather what kind of people they were (church members?) and what happened to them when the meetings were over. There is growing agreement that for the greater part our present evangelism is still "border-mission"—we do not really reach out beyond the "fringe."

Question

What do recent statistics of evangelistic efforts in your country reveal? What do they conceal? Define the untouched groups.

Of the need for constant adjustment of methods we are now deeply convinced. This implies that *new* evangelistic ventures should be regarded as being experimental or even explanatory, rather than definitive. One report speaks of "Dieppe raids," exploratory attacks to enable an effective preparation of the definitive assault. Many of the new experiments in evangelism are not yet beyond the stage of such "Dieppe raids."

In this experimental stage there is, however, one point of almost universal agreement: *evangelism should be conceived in terms of the impact of the Christian Community on its total environment.* Very definitely the general trend is away from considering evangelism as a specialized activity performed by a few specialists. "Our need is not so much for more evangelists, but for an evangelizing Church." There is a new recognition of the fact that the *totality* of the Church's life should be directed toward the evangelization of the entire community. The summons for "total evangelism" is repeated in various ways and with different emphasis.

Question

How would you describe the pattern of a truly evangelizing Church? What is the evangelistic significance of the worship of the Christian community, of its preaching and teaching ministry?

Though this need for total evangelism is recognized to an ever-growing extent, there is still a great deal of confused thinking about the nature of this corporate witness. Avowedly, *laymen* are the spearhead of the Church in the world; "the true XXth-century evangelist is the instructed and witnessing layman." The confusion begins, however, as soon as an attempt is made to define the difference of function between ministry and laity. On the one hand, the function of the laity is simply conceived as an extension of the ministry's function: they simply broaden the scope of what ministers are doing and repeat the same activities on a wider scale. On the other hand, there is increasingly strong evidence of a contrary view: the ministry-centered conception of evangelism is rejected, because the ministry is held to be too much a group apart, enclosed in an ecclesiastical world of their own and therefore unable to communicate the Gospel to those outside in any relevant way. It is their task "to equip the laymen for their service," but they should not (vainly) try to move in the frontlines of evangelism.

This differentiation of function within the evangelizing unit of the Christian community has not yet been worked out with all its practical inferences. The need for a *nonprofessional ministry* is stressed in various parts of the world. Attempts have been made to correct the traditional view of the parish as an exclusively territorial unit and to conceive it also as a social unit (e.g., a factory). Experiments with a more flexible and more "indigenous" ministry are under way, all trying to bring the ministry nearer to the community whom they are seeking to serve. However these things may develop, total evangelism can be nothing short of a convincing, corporate demonstration by the whole Laos ("the people of the Mission") of Christ's solidarity with mankind. The members of the Laos—laymen—are the agents of evangelism in the world.

Question

What is done in your congregation to equip the laymen for their evangelistic task? How effective is this preparation?

It has often been said that laymen who engage in evangelism become "church-domesticated." Is this true? Why?

Is there any evidence in your country that the exclusively territorial concept of the parish ("neighborhood") is corrected? Is it necessary? What are the special groups which should be ministered to by special chaplains? What is the evangelistic significance of these matters of "church order"?

There is ample evidence that *"individualism"* in its varied forms is definitely on the decrease in evangelistic thinking. New ways are sought to reach man in his communal relationships and to approach him wherever he lives his life with others. The addressee of evangelism is increasingly conceived in communal terms. In the same way the agent of evangelism is seen in a representative capacity. Even if he be a single person he is part of a corporate personality and he is thought of as the nucleus of an anticipated community. The widespread popularity of the Christian "cell" movements and the ever heatedly discussed possibility of the foundation of "para"-churches as "halfway houses between the Church and the world" are both indications of this trend away from "evangelistic individualism."

The *communal approach* is well known in missionary work among primitive, prepersonal societies. Mass movements in India and elsewhere are only recent examples of this approach to the group where the individual cannot take any decision. The same approach is now advocated in modern postpersonal civilizations, such as the industrial proletariat.

There, where "irreligion is part of the prevailing culture pattern"[2]—and men follow the group in their decisions—individuals can hardly be expected to detach themselves from their milieu. If they would do so, they will inevitably have to "emigrate" from their original sphere of life and to become a "cultural convert" to bourgeois society. This is the reason why most of the "Younger Churches" founded in the European proletariat during the past hundred years have become "bourgeois Churches" in the second generation.

Evangelism is, therefore, in these situations to be conceived as a corporate representation of the Gospel within the group. The Gospel must challenge and eventually permeate the prevailing thought and life forms of the group before any decision can be made. A Christian "cell" should demonstrate the dynamic of the Gospel, patiently and hopefully, before any relevant word can be spoken.

At the same time there should be no pressure to integrate inquirers as quickly as possible into the organized Church. This could only be done at the price of complete separation from their life environment. Inquirers and eventual converts should stay in their milieu, there to *be* the Church, with its own indigenous forms and patterns. The social distance between their "world" and the present form of church life is too great to be covered at once. There should be "halfway houses between this world and the Church," *para*-Churches. The matter of relationship with the already established Church must be looked into at a later stage.

These highly controversial proposals are made in very different parts of the world. It is evident that they do not offer any final solutions. It is equally clear, however, that those who are engaged in evangelism in modern mass society— and this is increasingly a global phenomenon—are pushed in this direction.

[2] J. V. Langmead Casserly, *The Retreat from Christianity in the Modern World,* London, 1952, pp. 106 ff.

Question

Do you know of any fruitful "community approach" in the evangelistic efforts in your country? How would you describe the social distance between the organized life of your church and the various groups of society around it? Is there need of a halfway house? Is the New Testament concept of the "house-church" of any relevance for this view on the para-churches? In New Testament times the "house" was the actual social context in which people lived: what are, in your situation, the life contexts (=houses)?

This leads to another trend which might be termed *the decline of verbalism in the evangelistic approach.*

Partly this may be due to the apparent devaluation of words in general. In many situations a coherent system of reference is so entirely lacking, that words can no longer function as symbols, which transmit meaning. They can only become means of communication again when speaker and audience will participate in a common experience. For evangelism this implies that words can only be used in any significant way within the context of a demonstrated solidarity which creates a common experiential background.

Concurrent with these practical considerations, theological reflection has elucidated that "witness" can never be reduced to a *verbal* proclamation. Biblical witness happens simultaneously through proclamation (*kerygma*), fellowship (*koinonia*) and service (*diakonia*). The life witness of the entire community encompasses and qualifies every spoken word. The proclamation is always situated in a total life context.

This rediscovery of the multiform character of biblical witness has opened the way for new experiments in evangelism along the lines of what, in missionary circles, has been known as the "comprehensive approach."

Question

How much is there of "the language of Canaan" in contemporary preaching? Is it understood? "Your community
life speaks so loud, that we cannot hear your words"—
this was said to a missionary in Africa. Could it be rightly
repeated elsewhere?

What does it mean in practical terms: witness through
proclamation-fellowship-service?

Do you agree with the following statement of somebody
who knows the situation in Europe: "The Christian message is best proclaimed not in words but primarily in
deeds and in shared action, in working quietly shoulder
to shoulder with the actual workaday man in the real
situation with which living confronts him. Out of this,
true solidarity is forged." . . . What does this imply for
the "Apostolate of the Laity"?

As a last, more or less general, trend we note *a reluctance
to deal with abstractions*, such as culture or religious systems. Usually this is not due to a lack of genuine interest in
the currents of thought which frame the minds of men. In
theory a widespread desire is manifest to understand the
whole cultural setting in which people are placed, acknowledging that "the churches have been too often content with
achieving communication on too narrow a front."

This does not mean that a confrontation should be attempted with these systems as such. Controversy, apolo-
getics, an intellectual presentation or argument are pushed
to a secondary place in the evangelistic approach. It is felt
that we have to probe beyond the professed systems of
thought and emotions and begin with a clear affirmation of
man as he is: brother of Christ. Where man defines his situation, even before he adheres to an "ideology" to interpret
this situation, we should attempt to meet him; there we
should try to redefine with him this situation. This trend
will have important inferences for the approach of the ad-

herents of non-Christian faiths. It will be equally significant with regard to the ideologies of a (pseudo-) religious character.

Question

Can we evangelize "ideologies" or "social structures" as well as persons?

What are the practical implications of the identification in service with the others of which Paul speaks in I Cor. 9?

Where does controversy come into your approach?

What is the first word you speak in your approach to adherents of a non-Christian faith; is it a refutation of his faith? Why (not)?

Acknowledging the difference of situations in various parts of the world, we find almost general agreement on the following emerging pattern of evangelism:

Evangelism is the participation of the total Christian community in Christ's mission in the world;

Every single aspect of the Church's life and activities is of evangelistic significance;

In proclamation, fellowship and service, the Church must demonstrate the Gospel in the actual life context of men;

Laymen are on the frontline, served by the ministry whose function it is to equip the people of God for its mission;

Laity and ministry together strive to be of the mind of Him who "emptied Himself" in service to the world.

VI

CONCLUSION

As the reader of this Survey will have noted, the story of evangelism in our generation is one of "mingled yarn"—confessions of failure under awesome divine judgment, side by side with witnessings to the miraculous grace of God at work in the churches, as if we were still in the midst of a belated chapter of the Acts of the Apostles. Both responses, that of penitence and of gratitude, are, surely, right in our encounter with the Church's Lord. We can apply to our time the words of St. Paul to the Christian flock of Corinth: "Now all these things . . . are written for our admonition, upon whom the ends of the world are come." (I Cor. 10.11). The drama of missions and evangelism may, indeed, under God's rule over time and history be only in its infancy. If the Lord delay His Coming because He is "not willing that any should perish, but that all should come to repentance" (II Peter 3.9), our vocation is unmistakable. We are to be Christ's evangelists "while it is day: the night cometh, when no man can work" (John 9.4). Those who stand on the watchtowers of the Church can tell us that our rejoicing over the spread of Christianity throughout the world is often still premature. Scores of millions, in Asia and Africa and elsewhere—in Muslim lands, to cite conspicuous examples—have as yet never even heard the Gospel. The Church of Christ is still today, at home and abroad, "on mission sent."

PREPARATORY COMMISSION II

on

EVANGELISM—THE MISSION OF THE CHURCH TO THOSE OUTSIDE HER LIFE

Members

The Rev. Canon Theodore O. WEDEL, U.S.A., Chairman
*Principal David G. MOSES, India, Vice-chairman
The Rev. D. T. NILES (W.C.C.), Secretary

The Rev. Thomas ALLAN, United Kingdom
The Rev. Bishop S. U. BARBIERI, Argentina
*The Rev. Benö BEKEFI, Hungary
The Rev. J. P. BENOIT, France
*The Very Rev. Dr. Jerome COTSONIS, Greece
*The Rev. Dr. Edwin T. DAHLBERG, U.S.A.
The Rev. Dr. S. E. ENGSTRÖM, U.S.A.
The Rev. Professor J. C. HOEKENDIJK, Netherlands
The Rev. Principal C. H. HWANG, Formosa
The Rev. Dr. Hajime INADOMI, Japan
Professor T. E. JESSOP, United Kingdom
*Mrs. John KAREFA-SMART, Liberia
*The Rev. P. MAHANTY, India
*The Rev. Dr. Jesse Jai McNEILL, U.S.A.
*The Rt. Rev. John S. MOYES, Bishop of Armidale, Australia
*The Rev. Professor H. Richard NIEBUHR, U.S.A.
The Rev. Chandu RAY, Pakistan
*The Rev. Professor H. RENDTORFF, Germany
The Rev. Professor Richard C. SMITH, U.S.A.
The Rev. Canon E. R. WICKHAM, United Kingdom

Consultant

*The Rev. Eric W. NIELSEN (International Missionary Council)

Central Committee Consultants

*The Rev. Dr. E. T. DAHLBERG, U.S.A. (member of the Commission)

* Not present at August, 1953, meeting.

*The Rev. Bishop Ivan Lee HOLT, U.S.A.
The Rev. Dr. Pierre MAURY, France

Substitutes and ad hoc Consultants attending the August, 1953, meeting

The Rev. Dr. O. V. ANDERSON, U.S.A.
Mr. Oliver BEGUIN, Switzerland
The Rev. Dr. A. M. CHIRGWIN, United Kingdom
Mr. Huib van COEVERDEN, Netherlands
The Rev. Professor Ralph D. HYSLOP, U.S.A.
The Rev. Dr. Charles W. RANSON (International Missionary Council)

SOCIAL QUESTIONS—
THE RESPONSIBLE SOCIETY
IN A WORLD PERSPECTIVE

An Ecumenical Survey
prepared under the auspices of the
World Council of Churches

CONTENTS

I

INTRODUCTION

The theme for the Assembly at Evanston is the Christian Hope, and it is one of the assumptions of the special commission which has defined the meaning of this theme, that the Christian must be concerned not only with the hope of ultimate redemption but also with the hope for a better society within history. As the Advisory Commission on the Theme of the Second Assembly stated in its first report:

> It is the task of the Church to show how the Lordship of Christ as the hope for the world is meaningfully related to every aspect of the world situation and the human predicament. . . . To the hungry and the poor, to those in bondage and social disorder, the Church must be the servant of that Lord Who healed all manner of diseases and proclaimed liberty to the captives. As Christians we must support every effort of peoples and individuals to still their hunger, to gain the respect of their fellowmen, and to achieve the full stature of their manhood.

This survey reviews the efforts of the churches and individual Christians to interpret and act upon the economic and social problems of our time.

The three great ecumenical conferences dealing with social questions: Stockholm (1925), Oxford (1937), and Section III of the First Assembly of the World Council of Churches, Amsterdam (1948), have all emphasized two fundamental points regarding the Christian attitude toward society: (1) Christians must work for social justice, and (2) no particular political or economic system can be identified with the Will of God or equated with the Kingdom of God. These have been the keynotes of ecumenical social thinking.

In the conference at Amsterdam they were expressed in

1

the declaration that the "churches in all lands" must work for the goal of "the responsible society," and it was explained that:

For a society to be responsible under modern conditions it is required that the people have freedom to control, to criticise and to change their governments, that power be made responsible by law and tradition, and be distributed as widely as possible through the whole community. It is required that economic justice and provision of equality of opportunity be established for all the members of society.

In relation to the most important contemporary social issues, attempts were made at each conference to suggest the specific implications of these points for action by Christians in society. After the Amsterdam conference the Study Department of the World Council of Churches began an inquiry on *Christian Action in Society* to stimulate further an exchange of views on social questions among the churches, to obtain information about the social issues confronting the Church in different countries and to develop the meaning of the Responsible Society in relation to such issues.

The present Survey attempts to do three things: (1) to give a general picture of the world situation in which the churches have been living over the past few years, (2) to describe the social problems which have faced the churches in specific regions and countries, and (3) to report on the varying attitudes and activities of the churches in relation to these problems. A final section attempts to draw from these reviews some conclusions regarding the tasks of the churches today. Space has not permitted the exhaustive treatment of any of these topics which would be desirable, and it has been necessary in many cases to omit much valuable specific material and to concentrate on certain situations and approaches which may be regarded as typical.

II

THE WORLD SOCIAL REVOLUTION

Christian social responsibility today must be seen against the background of a vast world upheaval marked by the decline of old social and economic ideologies and institutions, the social effects of continued rapid technical change, the complete shake-up of old patterns of life in Asia, Africa and Latin America, the increasing economic and political interdependence of nations, and the effects of the continuing struggle between the communist and noncommunist countries.

One social era is passing away and a new one is being born, and the result is radically new tasks and opportunities for Christian witness and service. The purpose of this opening chapter is to survey some of the basic changes which have taken place in recent decades and which determine the dimensions in which Christian social responsibility must be conceived, today and during the coming years.

A. The Decline of Classical Capitalism

One of the important developments of recent decades is the rapid decline of *laissez-faire* capitalism as the dominant economic conception of the Western industrial countries. By this is meant not a decline in capitalistic techniques or in the practical importance of privately owned commercial and financial institutions (for indeed in Western Europe and the U.S.A. these have actually grown in size and importance), but rather the displacement of the *laissez-faire* idea that economic activities should be regarded as autonomous activities. As one writer has said, "The twentieth century . . . is witnessing on a widespread scale the disappearance of the economic

3

autonomy of the capitalist era." We are eyewitnesses to "a great reversal of all the tendencies which made for the independence of economic activity from the total demands of society and from ethics."[1] Increasingly during the last several decades economic activities have been subordinated to non-economic requirements.

Various motives have led to the subordination of the free market system—economic justice, the restoration of responsible community life, and the desire of people to be in control, as far as possible, of the social and economic conditions in which they live.[2] There has been an enormous change in recent decades in thinking on the duty of the community in relation to economic life. The community has had to intervene to protect the rights of weaker parties; moreover, the formulation of natural rights which are regarded as conditions of well-being in modern life has come to include the right to subsistence, to health, security and housing, and to employment.

The responsibility of the democratic state to provide as a matter of right for its citizens security against unemployment, sickness and old age, and to control and plan the use of national resources so as to maintain work for all and ensure a fair distribution of income between different sections of the community, is a principle which is accepted in one form or another in almost all the industrial nations of Western Europe and North America.

What questions does this development raise for the churches of the ecumenical movement? In the past they have consistently challenged certain tendencies in capitalist economic thought and organization, rejecting the liberal ideology of the harmony of interests underlying it, and rejecting also the tendency to view production as an end in itself rather

[1] V. A. Demant, *Religion and the Decline of Capitalism,* ch. 1. See also Denys Munby, "Moral Problems in the Economic Situation Today" (mimeographed), a document published by the Study Department, World Council of Churches, 1952, 32 pp.

[2] V. A. Demant, *op. cit.,* p. 27.

than as a means to serve man. The report on the Economic Order, prepared at the Oxford Conference on Church, Community and State (1937), pointed to dangers in capitalism— the concentration of wealth, the growth of the large urban masses which in industrial society were the victims of irresponsible economic power, the tremendous waste of productive power in business depressions, the treatment of "human labor as a commodity, to be bought at the lowest possible price and to be utilized to the greatest possible extent."[3] The "enhancement of acquisitiveness," the "inequalities," the "irresponsible possession of economic power," the "frustration of the sense of Christian vocation" due especially to unemployment, all these were cited as "points at which the Christian understanding of life is challenged [by the capitalist economic system.]"[4] There are areas of the world where these criticisms still apply, but in many countries these specific social evils have been substantially alleviated through social reform. In thinking about economic issues today the Church must face issues of a different order.

It will be one of the main purposes of the survey to see how the churches are redefining and reinterpreting their function in society in relation to the new social conditions which arise from the decline of capitalism and the growth of tendencies in the direction of the social welfare state.

B. The Reformulation of Socialism

A second new factor in the social situation today, closely related to the first, and which also radically alters the problem of Christian social thought and action, is the "de-Utopianizing" and the "de-Marxizing" of socialism. This development is important in view of the extent to which Christian attitudes to social problems have in the past been formulated,

[3] *The Churches Survey Their Task*: Report, Oxford Conference on Church, Community and State (1937), Allen and Unwin, London, 1937, pp. 100-102.
[4] *Ibid.*, pp. 104-9.

especially in Europe, specifically either in opposition to or in sympathy with the ideals and the program of socialism. On the one hand, the movement toward Christian political parties and Christian trade unions, at least on the continent, was in large part based upon opposition to the atheism and materialism of socialism. On the other hand, in many countries the movement for Social Christianity has frequently been based upon the idea that socialism was the practical expression of Christian faith.

At Oxford and at Amsterdam the churches consistently opposed the contention of socialist theory that socialization of property would inevitably solve all problems. Thus in the report of Section III at Amsterdam it was stated:

> In the light of the Christian understanding of man we must . . . say to the advocates of socialisation that the institution of property is not the root of the corruption of human nature. We must equally say to the defenders of existing property relations that ownership is not an unconditional right; it must, therefore, be preserved, curtailed or distributed in accordance with the requirements of justice.[5]

Today, however, socialist thinking largely accepts this view.

The extent to which basic principles are being reconsidered is illustrated in reports published by various socialist study groups especially in Britain but also in Europe and Asia. One such group in Britain has referred to the "central belief . . . that through some form of collectivism the just and good society would be established" as "a Creed of Yesterday."[6] It is acknowledged that the assumptions of economic determinism and the inevitability of progress have been seriously weakened by the events of two great wars and the experience with totalitarian governments.

In general we have seen that a desire for power for its own sake may have a greater influence on social change than economic inter-

---

[5] *The Church and the Disorder of Society*: Report of Section III, First Assembly of the World Council of Churches, 1948.

[6] *Socialism, a New Statement of Principles*, Socialist Union, London 1952, pp. 13-14.

ests. The influence which unscrupulous politicians can exercise over the masses obviously rests on more elusive and complicated psychological factors than can be accounted for by a rigid economic interpretation of history.[7]

Although democratic socialists still draw their inspiration from a faith in the capacity of the human will and social conscience to liberate men from exploitation and other social evils, they are radically revising their views of the fundamental human situation. One of the leading theoreticians of the British Labour Party writes in *The New Fabian Essays*:

The evolutionary and revolutionary philosophies of progress have both proved false. Judging by the facts, there is far more to be said for the Christian doctrine of original sin than for Rousseau's fantasy of the noble savage, or Marx's vision of the classless society.[8]

[7] *Ibid.* p. 19.

[8] *The New Fabian Essays,* ed. by R. H. S. Crossman, with preface by the Rt. Hon. C. R. Attlee, Turnstile Press, London, 1952, p. 8. Author's italics.

Only British socialist thinking has been cited, but in many other countries socialist groups are rethinking their basic principles. Cf. the Declaration of the Socialist International meeting in Frankfurt/Main on July 3, 1951, on *Aims and Tasks of Democratic Socialism,* in which it is argued that socialists can base their concern for social justice on religious beliefs and need not be Marxists.

The Planning Committee of the Netherlands Socialist Party has published a report, *De Weg naar Vrijheid* (*The Road to Freedom*), Amsterdam, 1951, which outlines the objectives of the party in the coming years in terms which suggest a recasting of fundamental theory similar to that which is taking place in Britain.

A similar, though less striking, development is reported in socialist thinking in Germany and Sweden. A German Marxist writes: "We no longer have one-track minds in explaining social events. We have realised that social forces are not all derived from a single primary force, but that they are interdependent. . . . So today it is no longer possible to explain the course of history in such a way that the development of the conditions of production is the only decisive factor for determining the course of social life in history." (From a statement on *Sozialismus und Marxismus,* by Dr. Gerhard Weisser, (mimeographed, 1947).

And Mr. M. M. Thomas has shown that in Asia also socialism as an ideology is undergoing a transformation attempting to hold on to what is true in liberalism, Marxism and Gandhism, and rejecting what is false in them. ("The Responsible Society in India," by M. M. Thomas, *Indian Journal of Theology,* Nov., 1952.)

The new emphasis of socialists on preserving the creative freedom of the individual and on the responsible use of power in the modern state, and the felt need for a new theory of the place of man in society represent a great change in socialist thinking compared with the years before the war. It means a new opportunity to confront such groups with the Christian understanding of man and society, provided Christians can translate their insights into language of social and political thought and action. How does this opportunity present itself in different countries and what is the response of the Church?

C. The Inadequacy of the "Isms": New Dimensions of the Social Problem

The decline of *laissez-faire* capitalism and Marxist socialism[9] does not mean the end of the need for social change. On the contrary, there is at present a desire for fundamental change in social conditions which is deeper and more far-reaching than at any previous moment in world history.

The struggle for justice in Europe, Asia and Africa is increasingly conceived today not in terms of economic or political ideologies but in terms of such goals as respect for the individual, fellowship, equal sharing of burdens and opportunities, the abolition of unjustified privilege and the correction of various social evils which are no longer regarded as unavoidable necessities.

[9] The term "Marxist socialism" as used here refers mainly to the socialist movements in Western Europe and in Anglo-Saxon countries, not to the Russian communist system as such. The socialist movements of the West very frequently were Marxist only in the sense that they made use of the Marxist view of progress and social determinism. Disenchantment with the Russian communist system as the basis of the hope for a better society is very widespread in the West, and has undoubtedly contributed to the disillusionment with socialist theory generally. Those hoping for radical social change see Russian communism as the perversion of the social revolution rather than as a means to implement it. See, for example, *The Christian in the World Struggle,* by M. M. Thomas and J. D. Mc-Caughey, a Grey Book of the World's Student Christian Federation, Geneva, 1951.

The desire for a fundamental rethinking of the goals of political and economic life is characteristic especially of the situation in Europe. Something more decisive than the construction of a socialist or a capitalist Europe is at stake. Many people have lost confidence in the national state dominant in the past. There is a search for a new Europe. What is being sought is a society which expresses through its institutions a concern for the individual man and which affords him both the security and the freedom for responsible living. Everything is being judged according to whether or not it serves these ends.

But it is not only the depth but the breadth of the social change which is significant today. In a way not known in the past the consideration of social responsibility today involves thinking in world terms. A United Nations "Preliminary Report on World Social Conditions" emphasizes that:

To an extent which might have seemed inconceivable even fifty years ago, there has come increasing recognition that 2,400 million people have somehow to contrive to live together, and share together the resources of the earth; that the general impoverishment of any area is a matter of concern to all areas; and that the technical experience and knowledge acquired in rapidly changing industrialised societies have somehow to be made available to those communities that are less advanced and less well-equipped. That this has come to pass is an historical and inspiring fact. Indeed, it has been suggested by a distinguished historian that in the broad sweep the 20th Century will be chiefly remembered in future centuries not as an age of political conflicts or technical inventions, but as an age in which human society dared to think of the welfare of the whole human race as a practicable objective.[10]

The economic and social condition of the underdeveloped countries has raised the need for radical social action on a world-wide scale. The countries of Africa, Asia, the Middle East and South America together comprise two thirds of the

[10] *Preliminary Report on the World Social Situation,* United Nations Economic and Social Council, April, 1952, p. 1 (mimeographed edition).

world's population and the vast majority of the world's oppressed and impoverished peoples. Radical improvements in health, food, work, housing and education are needed, and these involve not only new economic and political institutions, but a radically new understanding of individual and social responsibility and a new conception of human relations in the home, the factory, the village and the city.

Success in the creation of new societies in Asia, Africa, the Middle East and Latin America is vital for the welfare of the world. As an expert on Asian problems has written,

The struggle for a new society in Asia is undoubtedly *the* great issue which confronts humanity in this decade. A fire has been started in Asia which will either burn or warm the whole world in the second half of this century. The problems are economic and social as well as spiritual and political.[11]

The revolutionary situation of the underdeveloped countries is especially a challenge to old patterns of Christian social concern. In the past Christian social thinking has not given adequate attention to the social problems of the non-Western world, in consequence partly, perhaps, of a curious division of functions between "missions" and "social action" in the development of the different branches of the ecumenical movement. But it is obvious today that this division is intolerable and that efforts to develop a united missionary, evangelistic and social witness must be speeded up. How urgently do the churches see this problem?

D. The Concern of the Churches with Social Problems: Some General Remarks

Speaking generally of the Church around the world, it is now more widely accepted than in the past that the Christian ought to be concerned with social issues and that the guidance of Christian thinking in relation to them ought to

[11] De Vries, "The Churches and the Economic and Social Problems of South and South-East Asia," in *The Ecumenical Review*, April, 1953.

be one of the central concerns of the Church. For Christians in many countries the experiences of the last two decades have irrefutably confirmed the views of the Ecumenical Conference on Life and Work at Oxford in 1937 that "the Church and the world are indissolubly connected," that "it is part of the very essence and mission of the Church to carry responsibility for the welfare of man," that the churches must develop "a common body of Christian criteria and assumptions on social questions" to be able to meet the challenge confronting them in the modern world.[12] More and more today the argument on the social witness of the Church is not, as in the past, *whether* the Church has a responsibility in society, but *what* precisely that responsibility is, and *how* it can best be realized.

The greater awareness of Christian social responsibility must, however, be considered in relation to reports from certain countries which indicate widespread apathy toward social questions. The following report describes an attitude which is probably typical of the situation in many churches:

Speaking generally, it appears that the rank and file of Christians here are not actively concerned with the contribution to be made by the Christian faith and ethics in the development of the free and responsible society. Many are not even aware of the issues. Some are opposed on principle to the Church's taking any responsibility in the wider community because they feel her concern is wholly with the spiritual life of her members and with strictly ecclesiastical matters. . . . Official bodies and spokesmen of the churches have given leadership, cautious but often far-seeing and well-considered. If the laity has been content to relegate responsibility to the clergy this is probably because the positions taken by men with time and training to consider these matters are too far outside the usual range of thinking of the general membership, and effective means have not been devised to bridge the gap and to explain and justify the Church's concern with such matters.[13]

[12] *The Churches Survey Their Task.*

[13] This and other quotations not otherwise specified are from the unpublished reports submitted for the preparation of this Survey.

It is explained, however, that this attitude manifests not only the traditional apathy and indifference of many Christians. It is due also to the fact that the crucial issues which gave rise to Christian social concern in the past have, especially in Western countries, been mitigated by reform. The achievement of a high degree of economic prosperity and stability in many Western industrial countries in the postwar years has undercut efforts to arouse concern for social issues.

The general acceptance of the Christian social objectives of the past coupled with disillusionment about certain aspects of the welfare society has led to the "slackening of intensity" in Christian concern for such issues and has even brought about the "collapse" of the Christian social movement in some countries.

The most significant new thinking about the task of the Church in society may, in the future, come from the Church in Europe, in the communist-dominated countries and in the underdeveloped countries of Asia, Africa and Latin America. In all these countries the Church is living in the midst of great social pressures and dangers, and it is in varying degrees responding to its opportunities and duties with new courage and inspiration.

The development of the Church's social witness has been especially significant in some countries of Western Europe, so much so that there is ground for reversing the historic contrast between the American and the European churches with regard to social concern. The new "activism" of the European churches was noticed by some observers at Amsterdam and judging by the reports for this survey it has continued to develop since. It was put most clearly by Reinhold Niebuhr in a report on the Amsterdam Assembly:

The old contrast between American activism and continental quietism has disappeared completely. The European churches awakened to their social responsibilities in the last tragic decade. In doing so they have become considerably more radical than most American churches. With this radical (generally socialist) political conviction they combine an eschatological note, an insistence on the final triumph of Christ over sin, evil and death, no matter what may happen in the next year, or decade, or century. This note of New Testament faith was found very baffling by many Americans who thought it connoted irresponsibility toward the pressing problems of the world. Indeed it was expressed in words which seemed to suggest the possibility of human beings achieving a kind of timeless serenity, which had no concerns with this world. Yet the same men who baffled us with such words insisted that the Church was much too sentimental in dealing with problems of political justice. It found some of the Anglo-Saxon devotion to such matters as the human rights declaration of the United Nations quite irrelevant in the light of the more pressing decisions confronting the world.[14]

In the following chapters there is an attempt to show the new patterns of the churches' response to the problems of the social order in particular countries and regions.

[14] *Union Seminary Quarterly Review*, Nov., 1948, p. 14.

III

TRENDS IN GREAT BRITAIN

The most important fact about the social teaching of the churches in Britain is that social changes brought about in the years since the war have largely fulfilled the objectives for which Christians worked for many years. The social movement which many people in Britain would associate with the name of Archbishop William Temple has seen its aims to a great extent achieved by the welfare state and the postwar reforms. This general acceptance by society of the ends which Christians had set before themselves has led to uncertainty and doubt as to the future of the social teaching of the churches.

The uncertainty which characterizes the political situation is thus described in a report from Britain:

The election of 1950 marked the end of an era of reforms. The success of the Labour Party in putting on to the statute book a series of radical reform measures as promised in 1937 and further affirmed in 1945 ended an epoch, both of socialist thinking and of clearly marked ideals. By 1950 the shame of inter-war history in Britain had been finally wiped out by measures which decisively consolidated the wartime changes and enacted a number of long necessary reforms, such as the nationalisation of the railways, public utilities and coal-mines, some of which had long existed in other countries. For those not blinded by wishful thinking or traumatic experience of pre-war days, a new period was to be entered upon, with no clear moral choices and no easy victories to be gained by redistributing income or making use of unemployed resources.

The same report points to the role of the Church in relation to the political situation created by the "end of an era of reforms":

14

The new period is . . . accompanied by the narrowing of the divergent policies of the two political parties, and the narrow electoral difference between them. Thus the apparently bitter political skirmishing hides an incapacity to think out fresh policies appropriate to the times, a disease of both political parties. The great need is for rethinking of fundamentals in politics, and the Church could (in theory) be a great stimulus, and is provided with a tremendous opportunity.

How far is the Church meeting the new situation and the new opportunities? On the one hand, many of the old bodies that were influential in creating the social movement are no longer entirely appropriate to the new situation, and feel themselves in somewhat of an impasse. Thus Maurice Reckitt, one of the leaders of the "Christendom Group," which has had a great influence on the social thought of the Church of England, summing up the present influence of the group writes, "But we are now in the fifties, and the picture is very different [from the twenties]. . . . [We have failed] to respond to the needs of the latest age . . . and to meet with a new initiative the very different postwar circumstances."[1] The same might be said about some others of the formerly important centers of Christian social thought and action.

There is an increasing realization of the need to strengthen the foundation of belief as a basis for rethinking Christian social theory and Christian discipleship in social and economic life in Britain. With some this takes the form of direct evangelism, a proclamation of the Christian Gospel in terms familiar to the Church but seeking new and more effective techniques. Others are seeking a fuller understanding of the new social and economic issues which have arisen from the industrial, social security and welfare measures enacted since the end of the war, with a view to discerning the religious and theological factors involved and thereby beginning afresh the working out of Christian social ethics. There has also

[1] M. B. Reckitt, "Challenge and Response," in *Theology*, June, 1953, p. 212.

been a significant move in responsible groups in industrial life seeking the guidance of Christian people and of the Church in grappling with their new problems of purpose for industry and motivation for work.

A. THE EMPHASIS ON THE LAITY

In formulating Christian ethics in relation to particular issues the emphasis is increasingly on the experience and insights of laymen as the basis of a realistic and relevant ethic. This approach involves the co-operation of laymen and theologians but the pattern for such co-operation has not yet been fully developed.

Moreover, the organized churches still have too slender a contact with working-class organizations, with industry and political movements, and, in consequence, there is too little systematic discussion between theologians and those who are immersed in political and economic life. This need is outlined as follows in one of the reports received:

What is needed is both elucidation of the fundamentals of our political and economic life and detailed analysis of the proximate steps to be taken and concrete things to be done. Both parts of the analysis can be undertaken only in relation to study and understanding of the complex situation in which we find ourselves. . . . What is wanted is not merely greater concern with social issues, though that is always welcome, but the proper organisation of that concern to make the best use of experts and theological minds.

The churches have been more successful in grappling with certain types of social problems of a practical nature. They have been actively concerned with a variety of issues, especially where the responsibility of Christians in local community action is involved or where problems of personal ethics are concerned.[2]

[2] Some of the publications issued by the churches and Christian movements indicate the range of interests. The Church of England has issued important reports on atomic energy, and on new housing areas; the Church of Scotland, among others, has produced a Christian critique of

In the discussion of the larger problems of modern political and economic life, individual Christians have made a substantial contribution to the discussion which has had great influence both inside and outside the Church.[3]

Some of the new and promising steps taken in Britain to meet the circumstances outlined above are:

(a) The establishment of groups of laymen who occupy positions in which they can exercise some influence on their own professions or occupations or localities. In the Christian Frontier Council, for example, set up with the agreement and blessing of the churches but responsible to none of them, this method has also produced books and papers for the guidance of a wider public.

(b) Work with laymen by virtue of their function in society. One example of this is the work of the YMCA in England and Wales with industrial and commercial technicians.

(c) Efforts by certain groups to find ways of integrating the theological, liturgical and sociological activities of the Church, making social concerns an integral part of the normal life of the local church. Also there is a revived interest in biblical theology in the search for a more adequate theological basis for social ethics than was provided by the "social gospel" as it was known in Britain.

(d) The assumption of chaplaincy duties in industry and

---

communism; the Congregational Union has published a report on European Unity; the Methodist Church has given serious thought to problems arising in the Welfare State and in industry, as have other bodies; the British Council of Churches has issued important statements on "Christian Responsibility in Industry," "Christians at Work," "Strikes and Lock-Outs," and "Married Women in Industry." These are only a few examples, but they indicate an alertness in the churches and among Christian groups and movements which needs to become more widespread as well as more profound.

[3] The writings of two British historians may be cited to illustrate the searching rethinking of the meaning of Christian faith for society: H. Butterfield, *Christianity and History*, and G. Kitson Clark, *The English Inheritance*.

commerce by the clergy, bringing them into a closer connection with people in their work.

(e) The Iona Community. This is an association of ministers and laity in the Church of Scotland, who live according to a simple common rule, and spend part of the summer together on the island of Iona working at manual tasks and taking part in discussions and conferences; it has a deep concern for social matters and in particular for the working class.

(f) The establishment of colleges and training centers by both the Anglican and free churches seeking to give theological training to those laymen who are engaged in various aspects of social work in an attempt to create a theologically literate laity, and in addition developing shorter courses and schools for personnel managers and welfare workers in industry.

B. ATTITUDES ON SPECIFIC SOCIAL ISSUES

It is difficult to summarize the tendency of Christian thinking in Britain on specific social issues. As already noted above, the churches and Christian groups are engaged primarily in exploring the situation resulting from the type of social welfare society which has developed in Britain after the war. There seems to be general agreement that modern technical society inevitably involves a large degree of planning. For example, the report on *Personal Freedom in a Planned Society* issued in 1950 by the Committee on the Church and the Community of the Presbyterian Church of England declares that:

The interdependence of modern technical civilisation makes planning not only desirable, but possible; and the satisfaction of social justice makes it necessary. These broad principles all parties and shades of political opinion accept; they part company only on the point where the line shall be drawn.

The report also points out that:

Freedom and planning are not necessarily opposites, for planning may be itself the way to freedom. Quite plainly the Welfare State delivers many people from the pressures and anxieties of poverty to develop their free personalities; and full employment, which is the foundation of freedom for working men, cannot be secured without planning. A wisely planned state is the true alternative to totalitarian control. Any return today to *laissez-faire* would swiftly produce such chaos that men would gladly surrender power to the dictator who promised to put things straight. Christians, therefore, will welcome that measure of planning which is consistent with fundamental freedom, and will gladly recognise in many of its achievements a Christian valuation of men, and an approximation to the just social order for which the Old Testament prophets pleaded in the name of God.

Judging from the trend of discussion, the main social problems confronting people in Britain are to develop further the meaning of community life at the local level and between social classes, to preserve the responsibility of the individual and avoid the overconcentration of power in national governmental agencies, to increase the efficiency and productivity of industry and to avoid the "evident tendency of the Welfare State to make us all preoccupied with security and cosiness."[4]

Also more than in the past there is a recognition that the welfare of the British peoples cannot be separated from the welfare of other peoples. Stimulated partly by pamphlets published by the parliamentary group of Christian socialists there has been a growing consideration in the churches of the social conditions of the underdeveloped countries.

[4] A. R. Vidler, "The Welfare State from a Christian Point of View," in *Theology*, Dec., 1952, p. 448.

IV

SOCIAL THOUGHT AND ACTION IN THE UNITED STATES

In the United States the rapid changes in economic and political life have led to the need for rethinking the relation between Christian faith and social action and also the Church's responsibility in society.

In the years before the war Christian social thinking was motivated largely by the ideas contained in the statement known as "The Social Ideals of the Churches" (first published in 1908, and revised in 1912 and 1932). This statement, although its principles are compatible with a variety of theological positions, may be regarded as an epitome of the thinking of the American churches which developed during the ascendancy of the so-called "social gospel" movement,[1] and of both the contributions and inadequacies of that movement. On the one hand, it was the social gospel which delivered the American churches from a very individualistic interpretation of society and of Christian responsibility. It also brought the churches together on a pragmatic approach to certain social problems which enabled them to move beyond traditional theological quarrels into areas of common responsibility. In both these respects all American Christian social thought and action today is the heir of the social gospel.

On the other hand, however, the inadequacies of the social gospel have become apparent in recent years. The social gospel

[1] The "social gospel" was not really one movement, but a whole constellation of movements. Any interpretation of the social gospel as a whole is, therefore, necessarily very general, and would not always apply accurately to every phase of the movement.

20

has been challenged in a number of ways. In the first place, it has been undermined by history, by political and economic developments which have brought most of its hopes (as represented, for example, in "The Social Ideals of the Churches") into reality, thus taking much of the "bite" out of its social witness. The rethinking of the social gospel has coincided with the transition in America from *laissez-faire* capitalism to what is sometimes called "welfare capitalism" which has closer similarities to the economic developments in Britain than is usually realized on either side of the Atlantic.

The social gospel has also been undermined ideologically, by theological movements which have challenged its Pelagianism, its easy optimism, and its tendency to make too direct an identification of certain social goals with the whole of the Christian Gospel. These movements, which reflect similar theological trends all over the world, have been largely spurred on in the U. S. A. by such thinkers as Reinhold Niebuhr and by the ecumenical conferences on social problems at Oxford, 1937, and Amsterdam, Section III, 1948.[2]

The process of rethinking Christian social responsibility has been complicated by other changes in the political and economic scene as a whole, in which the churches and church people have themselves been involved. Most notable is the tremendous shift over the past twenty years in the attitude toward the social welfare activities of government. No major political group would now dare to advocate the repeal of the major New Deal social legislation. In actual practice, most of the major goals of the "welfare state" are now wholeheartedly accepted, even by those groups which constantly attack the concept of the welfare state.

Against the background of this general shift toward the left in action, if not in thought, in the country as a whole, there

[2] See John C. Bennett, *Christian Ethics and Social Policy* (1946), John A. Hutchinson, ed., *Christian Faith and Social Action* (1953), Paul Ramsey, *Basic Christian Ethics,* (1951), Walter Muelder, *Religion and Economic Responsibility* (1953), and Reinhold Niebuhr, *Christian Realism and Political Problems* (1953).

is a new awareness of the dangers involved in the increase of
the power of the Federal government. Accepting in the main
the achievements of the past twenty years of increased government activity in economic and social affairs, American public
opinion is now concerned that the centralized power of government should not be expanded indefinitely. At the same
time, the new social power wielded by organized labor makes
it necessary for the churches to avoid the uncritical support of
labor that was characteristic of many social gospel crusaders,
and yet to realize that labor needs to be sympathetically interpreted to the middle-class constituency of the churches.

Another result of this shift has been the appearance of relatively small but extremely vocal groups supporting the kind
of highly conservative point of view which no longer finds any
expression in the programs of either major political party.
These groups have become increasingly noticeable within the
churches themselves. The situation has been described as
follows:

> The social gospel emphasis on the application of Christian ethics
> to social life tended, particularly in the 1930's, to become rather
> uncritical of collectivist answers to our questions. Now there has
> developed in our Protestant churches a very extreme type of in-
> dividualism which wants to go back to an absolutely unrecon-
> structed capitalism.[3]

Faced with "the one-sided tendency toward collectivism" and
"a one-sided tendency toward individualism," the churches
have found it necessary to build a better foundation for thinking about the Christian witness in relation to economic and
political issues.

To explore the relevance of Christian thought for the increasingly complex issues in American economic life the
National Council of Churches has a Department of Church

[3] Statement of Prof. John C. Bennett, University of Chicago Round
Table (NBC Radio Discussion) on the Goals of Economic Life, March 1,
1953. For a discussion of Protestant right-wing and left-wing groups,
see Ralph Roy, *Apostles of Discord* (1953).

and Economic Life which includes representatives of major elements in the economy as well as professional economists and theologians. The organization of this department stemmed from the Federal Council's conference on the Church and Economic Life, held in Pittsburgh in 1947. The continuous co-operative study promoted by this department on such issues as industrial relations, inflation, agriculture, etc. has been of great significance in finding the way toward a Christian approach to economic questions. Its nation-wide conferences (the National Study Conference on the Church and Economic Life, Detroit, 1950, and the Conference on the Christian in his Daily Work, Buffalo, 1952) have received wide attention and have exerted powerful influence in the thinking of the churches on these questions. The most ambitious project of the Department to date is the study and research program begun in 1949, which has resulted in the publication of the six-volume series on "Christian Ethics and Economic Life."[4] These volumes do not represent official declarations of the National Council of Churches but are for study and discussion and will be used in a nation-wide program of consultation in the churches.

The work of the denominations through their various departments in the area of social education and action has continued, and in the case of several denominations has greatly expanded. The Methodist Church in 1952 established a Board of Social and Economic Relations. The Protestant Episcopal Church's Department of Christian Social Relations has been expanding and at the same time re-evaluating its work. It has recently completed a thorough survey of "what the Church has done and is actually doing" in the field of social education and action.

[4] The titles of the volumes are: *Goals of Economic Life, The Organisational Revolution, Social Responsibilities of the Businessman, American Income and Its Use, The American Economy and the Lives of People,* and *Ethics and Economic Life* (New York: Harper & Brothers, 1953).

The recent developments concerning the Council for Social Action of the Congregational Christian Churches illustrate the points at which such work is being challenged today. In view of various criticisms of the work of the social action body, the Congregational General Council appointed a Board of Review to make an appraisal of its work. The Board's report includes criticisms of the Council for Social Action for being too one-sided in its point of view, but recommends the continuation of the Council and of its program of social action, in a way which will take more account of opposing opinions.

A few independent and ecumenical social action groups still remain. Among groups having particular social concerns may be mentioned the Religion and Labor Foundation, the Fellowship of Reconciliation, and the Fellowship of Southern Churchmen. Perhaps the most important is Christian Action, which was formed in 1951 from a coalition of several smaller movements and a number of individuals.

It ought also to be mentioned that the various youth and women's organizations of the churches, while not organized specifically for the purpose of social study and action, are often among the most active and effective groups working in the area.

A new trend in the social thinking of the American churches is the increased interest in political questions. Several informal groups have been giving attention to political problems over the past years, and increasing recognition is being given to them in the official programs of the denominations and of the National Council of Churches. The annual Churchmen's Washington Seminars, sponsored by the National Council, have been widely attended by representatives of all denominations, and the National Council is now in the process of forming a permanent Department of Christian Citizenship, which will in the future provide for study of political problems comparable to that which the Department of Church and Economic Life has given to economic questions.

In this connection, particular mention ought to be made of

the increasing concern of the churches in the whole area of democratic freedom. This problem has become particularly crucial in relation to investigations of communism and communist influence in public life. Individual church leaders have made strong and influential statements on this subject, as have some of the denominations and the National Council of Churches. The National Council has recently established a Committee on the Maintenance of American Freedom whose specific task it is to interpret developments in this area.

It is in these varied ways that the churches in the United States are seeking to deal with the new problems in Christian thinking about social questions which have been created by recent economic and political developments.

The Social Teaching of the Churches

It is extremely difficult to interpret and summarize the trend of American church opinion on social issues, particularly because of the disparity which is known to exist but is difficult to measure, between the statements of church bodies and the actual positions or working hypotheses taken by the church constituency itself. Some things, however, can be said, at least about American church opinion in its ecumenical expression.

On economic questions, Christian opinion emphasizes that there can be no sanction for one-sided support of either economic individualism or economic collectivism.[5] It has been noted that the outstanding difference between the conception of social responsibility held by business men and that implicit in Protestant pronouncements on economic affairs is in the attitude toward the capitalist system itself.

The business man, accepting it as inherently desirable, may see the need only of a more persuasive 'selling job', whereas Protestant thinkers are likely to be much more skeptical of capitalism undiluted. The idea of the 'mixed economy' with large measures of

[5] Cf. "The Church and Economic Life: Basic Christian Principles and Assumptions," a statement adopted by the Executive Committee of the Federal Council of Churches of Christ in America, Sept., 1948, p. 5.

social control and social ownership, seems much more acceptable to Protestant thinkers than to businessmen.[6]

The greatly expanded role of organized economic groups such as farmers, workers and industrialists has led the American churches to stress the responsibility which is laid upon such groups. "The problem of making organized groups responsible overshadows all other economic considerations."[7]

The churches have been particularly alert to the responsibility of the United States for the economic well-being of the whole world, and especially of the economically and technologically underdeveloped countries. The Detroit Conference summarized this responsibility in ten points, covering domestic economic policies in relation to their international consequences.[8]

In the study of the implications of the responsible society for political life there is an effort to avoid doctrinaire positions of either the "right" or "left." Such questions as the meaning of freedom, the function and limits of the state, the role of the Christian citizen, the stand against totalitarianism and the role of the Church in political life are being approached in this way.

Finally, it must be noted that, in relation to the subject of communism, the churches in America have repeatedly affirmed their opposition to totalitarian communism, but at the same time they have been concerned about the dangers to freedom inherent in irresponsible anticommunism. Many pronounce-

[6] H. R. Bowen, *Social Responsibilities of the Businessman* (1953), p. 41.

[7] "The Responsibility of the Christian in an Interdependent Economic World." Statement and Reports of the National Study Conference on the Church and Economic Life, Detroit, Feb. 1950, p. 16.

[8] *Ibid.*, pp. 22-25. See also "The Message to the Churches on Christian Faith and International Responsibility," from the fourth national Conference on the Churches and World Order, held under the auspices of the National Council of Churches in Cleveland, Oct., 1953. This report strongly emphasizes the need for economic policies favorable to world trade and for various forms of economic aid to the underdeveloped countries.

ments of church bodies including the National Council of Churches have expressed this concern. The most vigorous statement by any such body was written by President John A. Mackay of Princeton Theological Seminary, the Moderator of the General Assembly of the Presbyterian Church (U.S.A.) and adopted by the General Council of that Church. After calling attention to the ways in which Congressional investigations have threatened the freedom of American citizens, this Presbyterian statement says:

A great many people, within and without our Government, approach the problem of Communism in a purely negative way. Communism, which is at bottom a secular religious faith of great vitality, is thus being dealt with as an exclusively police problem.

As a result of this there is growing up over against Communism a fanatical negativism. Totally devoid of any constructive program of action, this negativism is in danger of leading the American mind into a spiritual vacuum. Our national house, cleansed of one demon, would invite by its very emptiness the entrance of seven others. In the case of a national crisis this emptiness could, in the high-sounding name of security, be occupied with ease by a fascist tyranny.

V

THE NEW CONCERN FOR SOCIAL PROBLEMS IN THE EUROPEAN CHURCHES

There has arisen in Europe in the postwar years a new awareness of the task of the Church in society and a remarkable development of groups and organizations to implement this concern. During the war the churches of Europe discovered at a deeper level their function in relation to society. They discovered the extensive paganization of European culture, the meaning of Christian freedom from the total claims of all political and economic systems and, at the same time, the points in the social system with which Christians must be concerned as part of the spiritual battle. It has been shown in many studies how as a result of this period of discovery for the churches, "some of the narcotic effects of their silent alliance with the world were at last shaken off. The realities of the situation became clear. The churches found out that they had to fight or die. . . ."[1]

In the postwar period this process of renewal has continued. The "partly static and partly dynamic" spiritual situation of Europe has led to a conflict in the Church "between the forces of conservatism which sought to return to the ways of the good old days, and the forces of renewal which realized that the churches were called to newness of life, to reformation of all that had become deformed in the course of their history . . ."[2] There has been a new realization that to survive at

[1] W. A. Visser 't Hooft, "Europe: Renewal or Survival," an essay published in *World Faith in Action*, ed. C. T. Leber, 1951, p. 78.
[2] *Ibid.*, p. 79.

all Europe must be renewed in its spirit, in its purpose for living, in its conception of right social relations in its own body, and right relations between the community of Europe and the rest of the world. This has led to a fundamental re-examination of the Christian tradition in European society and an effort to take seriously the political struggles of the present.

Today these lessons of the war and postwar years are being verified by the new struggle of the churches in Eastern Europe, and more particularly in Eastern Germany, where the battle by the Church with totalitarian communism has been largely a spiritual battle.

A. THEOLOGICAL RENEWAL AND SOCIAL CONCERN

The new concern of the Church for the world evident in Europe is thus not only a reaction to a political situation of change, but is based also on a renewal of theology, especially on the theological discoveries which churches in Europe have made during the last two or three decades. The renewal of European theology began in the twenties and thirties but it was in the experiences of war years that its full effects were felt. The European theologians most prominently associated with this theological renewal are Karl Barth and Emil Brunner, although many other theologians have made important contributions. Mention should be made in particular of certain developments in Lutheran interpretations of the Two Kingdoms (in Sweden and in Germany), which have resulted in a new concern for social problems.

The characteristics of this theological renewal are rediscovery of the Bible as a living message, the preaching of that message to a world in spiritual distress, and the recovery of the prophetic quality of Christian faith which enables people to see clearly the alternatives between faith in the God revealed in Christ and the claims of contemporary ideologies. On the basis of these ideas the reconstruction of Christian social theology in Europe is being achieved. It has not been carried through without confusion and disagreement. (Witness, for example, the argument whether Professor Barth has or has not tended to put an absolute Christian sanction on a particular political position.) Nevertheless, this theological renewal is showing how biblical insights can illumine the spiritual issues involved in contemporary political problems. This has been especially true for the Christian confrontation of communism.[3]

Laymen have contributed significantly to a new approach to social issues by challenging the theologian to explain the relation of biblical faith to their own experience in society.

There is much to be done before this theological renewal penetrates into the life of the Church and the thinking of Christians in many European countries. It is stated, for example, in the report from Sweden that "theological thinking has given very little help in approaching the ethical problems involved in concrete economic and political problems. . . . the decisions on social questions of today have been left to laymen." Moreover, while there is much theological writing on such subjects as Church and State, etc., the problems of democracy and of political ethics have not been thoroughly treated from the Christian standpoint. "The fundamental problem with all treatment of Christian social ethics seems to be to build the bridge that connects ideas formed on principles with a realistic programme of action."

These and other questions have yet to be squarely faced. Nevertheless, in the process of working on different problems and in experimenting with different methods the European churches are laying the foundations for a stronger social witness in the future.

[3] See, for example, the book by Prof. H. Gollwitzer, . . . *Und Führen Wohin du Nicht Willst* (Munich, 1952). Title of English edition, *Unwilling Journey*, SCM Press (London, 1953).

B. The Social Problems of Europe

The social problems which confront the European churches today are massive and complex, and three aspects need to be considered:

(1) *Social Justice in National Life.* Most Western European countries have recovered from the devastation of the war and have equaled if not exceeded their prewar economic prosperity. In the process of rebuilding some of them have discovered ways of overcoming old tensions between social classes, especially between workers and employers. But in others there are grave social problems and issues. Particularly in France and Italy there are serious conflicts regarding the right social policy to deal with unemployment and housing, higher standards of living for workers, social security, inflation, and rights of workers in industry. Most of these countries have developed elaborate schemes for social security but not all are successful in making them work. The Korean war and the rearmament of Europe which followed brought new economic difficulties. In many countries poverty is still very widespread and class tensions and conflicts drain the vitality of the community while antidemocratic groups are able to take advantage of the weakness of governments. Everywhere great changes affecting economic, industrial, and political life are likely in the future. The churches have much to do if they are to help to determine the goals of social policy and show the meaning of responsible living in this situation.

(2) *The Search for the New Europe.* It is clear that the renewal of Europe depends not only on a correct and energetic policy within the countries themselves but on the possibility of achieving some kind of political and economic union between them. Individually they are too weak to effect their own economic and political renewal or to guarantee military security. Their economic welfare depends on obtaining the advantages of production for a larger market and greater specialization in industrial life. The development of supranational insti-

tutions is, however, still at an early stage and it is already clear that it involves a revolutionary transformation in the economic and political thinking of people in Europe. This development is a challenge especially to those European churches which have generally been dominated in the past by an exclusively national pattern of organization and interest. It requires a fundamental re-examination of the Christian tradition in relation to the whole of European society.

(3) *Europe between East and West.* The problems cited above must be considered in relation to the role of Europe in the present world struggle. The separation of Eastern and Western Europe, the constantly recurring fear of a "showdown" between the Western powers and the Soviet Union, the fear of war, and the hope for a *modus vivendi*—all these are factors which constantly influence the method and the psychology of approaching many social problems in Europe. Can Western Europe achieve the necessary unity without increasing the gulf between itself and Eastern Europe and without becoming the pawn of American power? Many people in Western Europe are anxious to show that a united Europe is not necessarily an ally of the U. S. and an enemy of Russia, but an independent force which Russia need not fear and which invites neighborly relations with Eastern Europe. Also there are a considerable number of people, particularly in France, who are convinced that the present world struggle is an ideological conflict between Russian communism and American capitalism, and that Europe should be absolutely neutral between them. This issue has inevitably raised an intense debate about attitudes toward Russian communism, about the role of Europe between East and West in which the churches in almost every country have been heavily involved.

In relation to these problems, many European churches have urged their members to take their political and social duties seriously, not with the hope of creating some ideal

"Christian society," but as a fundamental part of living their Christian faith in the world.

To implement this concern, and to guide Christian thinking in view of all the complexities of contemporary social problems, there has developed in many churches on the continent an exceedingly comprehensive and substantial organization of study and action groups and Christian social institutes, dealing with the vast range of social issues and problems which confront European countries today. Laymen and youth are being mobilized to participate in this work because it is strongly felt that in dealing with social problems the practical experience and the technical *expertise* of laymen must be added to the contribution of the theologian.

C. The Churches and Social Justice

Up to World War II, the churches had been concerned primarily with Christian social service and charity, leaving to independent and unofficial social action groups the concern for the fundamental structure of the economic and social order. Since the war the European churches have given practical and constructive help on a large scale to refugees and displaced persons, and they have greatly enlarged and strengthened their social diaconate. But in addition to these practical efforts for social welfare, the churches are seeking to define their approach to the larger problems of developing responsible economic and political systems.

Speaking generally, Christian opinion in Europe tends to support a measure of state intervention in economic life as a social necessity. On this point, for example, the report from Sweden states:

. . . there are diverging opinions among the different parties, and thus also among Christians. There is no disagreement about the fact that interventions by the state are necessary to a certain extent. Besides, a change can be observed in the present political debate on interventions by the state. The main question is not nationalisation or not, socialisation or not, but to what extent the state ought to control and to regulate.

A recent report on *The Changes in Society and State and the Church's Call for a Responsible Society,* prepared under the auspices of the Social Commission of the Dutch Ecumenical Council, declares that the "welfare state" is based on the idea of greater responsibility in social and human relations:

Thanks to the dynamics of social development and the impossibility of allowing *laissez-faire* to continue, the state has found itself obliged to accept a share of responsibility for the process of production, for labour affairs and for the protection of individual man. . . . If we look back on the history of the last half-century in the West, the institution which we now call the welfare state is seen to be dominated above all by (a) the protection of the weak by authority; (b) the campaign to achieve a juster economic order; (c) an effort to do away with the causes of defects in the economic structure.

The Dutch statement concludes that the Church in its concern for strengthening and deepening the meaning of responsibility in society

must no longer resist but must, in its own fashion, co-operate with those forces in society which regard the *laissez-faire* principle as untenable, and which seek to replace it by that of a system serving spiritual freedom—though it is important to keep a sharp look-out lest this concept conceal a collective egoism.

In Germany, also, where the official economic policy is aimed at establishing a new type of free enterprise system, it is generally agreed that the issue is not "capitalism versus socialism," but how to find the right combination of freedom and control in economic life:

It is taken for granted that this combination is not achieved by a policy of *laissez-faire.* The criticism of the socialist opposition . . . raises one main objection, that inadequate planning has resulted in a lack of balance between production and distribution. On the other hand, the advocates of a more liberal economic policy stress the dangers of a centralised administration, which nobody wants. But in practice the difference does not consist in rejecting state intervention of every kind. No state can govern today without a whole series of controls, but opinions differ (a) concerning the extent of such state intervention, and (b) concerning the form it should take.

There is a considerable body of Christian opinion which, remembering the Nazi regimentation of economic and social life, regards the growth of state power with apprehension, as opening the way to new totalitarianism and a new threat to personal dignity and freedom. Bishop Berggrav of Norway, in an address on "State and Church Today" before the Assembly of the Lutheran World Federation (Hannover, July, 1952), has strongly criticized the totalitarian tendencies in the modern state, but in speaking about the "welfare state" in this connection he says:

The welfare state as such does *not* belong to this category, and it need not develop in this direction provided the Church and individual Christians exercise their influence. We should recognise the God-given tasks of the state and assist it in all its worthy endeavours.

Bishop Berggrav emphasizes four "legitimate demands which the Church may direct to the welfare state":

(1) The Church must demand the undiminished freedom to proclaim the Word of God and to exercise Christian love in the service of men. The Church dare not be satisfied with the assurance that freedom of worship is guaranteed. An attempt by the state to sterilise the social welfare work of the Church would constitute a frontal attack upon the freedom of the Gospel.

(2) The Church must not allow itself to be exploited by the state for political purposes. The Church must not become a tool of power politics.

(3) The right to determine the education of the children belongs to the parents. The free time of children and youth must not be monopolized by state agencies.

(4) The state must force nothing upon anyone, whether child or adult, that is contrary to God's clear commandments. A state which

arrogates to itself the right to determine what is good and what is evil must logically think of itself as an institute of salvation, and this is equivalent to the deification of the state. Christians must be allowed to have their own religious convictions; this right is one of the basic rights of man, even in states where practising Christians form a minority of the population.[4]

D. Efforts to Overcome Tensions between Church and Workers

Another illustration of the new social concern of the European churches is the new attitude toward workers. It is stated in the report from Germany that "the greatest handicap of Protestant Christianity in Germany has always been in its bourgeois (often petit-bourgeois) character, and its hostility to the socialist workers." A report from Sweden also emphasizes the carry-over of misunderstanding from the old conflict between the Church and the workers' movement. In the years since the war the churches in many parts of Europe have made a great effort to span the "almost unbridgeable gulf which had arisen in the second half of the 19th century between the churches, defending the ethos and morals of pre-industrial society, and the workers living in the technical and impersonal world of great industry."[5] The churches have realized their responsibility for the alienation of workers from the Church, and the workers are modifying the materialistic philosophy of their socialist tendencies, which makes it possible to begin breaking down old prejudices on both sides. Through conferences and discussions with socialists, the churches (including independent Christian groups) in Holland, Germany and Scandinavia have been able with some success to overcome the former hostility. For example, in the spring of 1953 a conference on the relation between socialism and religion, organized by the secretariat of the Socialist International, was held at a Christian institute in Holland. The conference provided

---

[4] Similar requirements are made of the state by Bishop Dibelius in his book *Die Grenzen des Staates* (Furche-Verlag, 1949).

[5] W. A. Visser 't Hooft, *op. cit.*, p. 87.

an opportunity for Christians to question the anticlerical and antireligious attitudes of socialists, and for socialists to inquire about the socially conservative views of the Christians. Referring to similar efforts in Germany, a report tells us:

The Church's relation to socialism has changed considerably. There are a number of reasons for this. The effects of the movement for religious socialism, which grew up after the first world war, are still felt. More important is the common resistance of the Protestant Church and of liberal socialism to National Socialism. The Protestant Church has no social programme of its own; it endeavours rather to listen and to learn. It tries to loosen fronts which have become rigid, and to overcome the dogmatism which is so typical of political discussion in Germany, even today. Moreover, during the last decades the Socialist Party in Germany has changed considerably.

Through its new approach, and by its endeavor to create a friendlier atmosphere with socialists, the Church, while not ignoring certain fundamental problems of socialist ideology, is endeavoring to show that it is not "preoccupied with one class to the detriment of the others." In the relatively few instances where the leaders of the Church have spoken on specific social issues, they have supported the passage of legislation which was of vital concern to workers.

E. HUMAN RELATIONS IN INDUSTRY

There has also been much discussion in European churches of the threat to human values in "modern mass society," with particular attention to the spiritual and moral problems of work in the technical mass environment of modern industry. This has led to a consideration of the ways by which industrial work could be made a vocation in the Christian sense and the changes needed in the structure of industrial life to realize this. In Holland, Germany, France and throughout Scandinavia, new patterns of relations between workers and employers are being developed and Christian study groups and churches have begun to define Christian attitudes in relation to these

developments. There is space here only to mention some of
the points which have received the most attention:

(1) the social responsibility of industrial management and
owners, and the need for a wider distribution of property
rights in industry;

(2) the need for greater participation by workers in determining the structure of industrial relations and the issues
involved in the various proposals for achieving this (*Mitbe-
stimmung* in Germany, *comités d'entreprise* in France, etc.);

(3) the role of the trade union, i. e., the problem of increasing trade union responsibility, the role of Christians in a trade
union dominated by a secular ideology or a political party, etc.;

(4) the development of industrial planning and organization so as to avoid the mass character of life in industrial community (efforts to avoid large urban industrial concentrations,
etc.).

F. The Churches and European Unity

It is becoming clear as a result of the developments in
European life that the churches must not only make their witness in relation to the developments of each nation, but bear
witness together concerning the social and economic trends
affecting the whole of European society.

In 1950 an unofficial group of laymen formed a committee to
explore the responsibility of Christians for European questions. This group, now called the Committee on the Christian
Responsibility for European Co-operation, is composed of politicians and economists from most of the countries of Western
Europe, and meets twice yearly to discuss European issues.
It has prepared a number of reports on the possibilities for
constructive action by Christians on these issues,[6] and it has
sought to ask questions of the different countries, to help each

[6] See Reports of the Committee on the Christian Responsibility for
European Co-operation (formerly known as the Ecumenical Commission
on European Co-operation).

to see its responsibility more clearly and to clarify many points where there is disagreement and misunderstanding.

The Committee has stated its views of the Christian responsibility as follows:

This [European] situation represents a challenge to the European churches. For, as has become clear . . . the question of European unity is not merely a tactical political problem, but at the same time a moral and spiritual issue of decisive importance. If it is true —and we believe it to be true—that no responsible society can be built in European nations unless the area of cooperation is greatly enlarged, then the churches must take this question very seriously.

They can exert a creative influence, and help governments and peoples to face facts, to accept sacrifices and to seek the common weal, instead of selfish and local interests. They can help to build that indispensable foundation of common conviction concerning the place of man in society without which European unity can have no permanent and stable basis. So far the European churches have done very little to discharge this responsibility. There is today a great deal of cooperation and contact between European Christians, but these new ecumenical relationships have not yet borne fruit in constructive common thinking about the problem of European common life.[7]

In the opinion of the Committee, "it is essential that the sphere of the supranational European institutions be extended as quickly and effectively as possible."

The Committee is agreed that European unity must not be conceived in such a way as to solidify the isolation of Western from Eastern Europe. "The Europe . . . we want to construct is not a Western Europe but a free Europe. There must be room for all those who at present either cannot or do not wish to participate." The Committee also has stated that the renewal of Europe must include a new relationship with the nations of Asia and Africa. The European nations must understand that

[7] From the Report of the Committee, published Jan. 1951.

the time is past when they could have unilateral relations with the nations of Asia and Africa. . . . Europe still has a great responsibility to fulfil in Asia and Africa, namely to help the countries of these continents in their economic development and to aid them, on the basis of European experience, in solving their social problems.[8]

In these ways the Committee has tried to point out to Christians in Europe that an entire new world of Christian service and action is opened to the churches in the present European situation.

[8] From the statement on Germany and European Cooperation, Jan. 1952.

VI

THE CHURCHES AND THE POLITICAL
AND SOCIAL UPHEAVAL OF THE
UNDERDEVELOPED COUNTRIES

The social changes taking place in Asia, Africa and Latin America confront the churches in these countries and throughout the world with the need for social thinking and action in an entirely new framework. The lives of people in these areas are being completely changed by movements for political independence and self-determination in economic matters, by industrialization and the organization of economic and social life on functional rather than on traditional lines, by the spread of new convictions about the nature of the universe and the meaning of human life and by the revolt against enslaving and exploiting institutions. There is a need for rapid change, and social developments which have taken centuries in the West have to be accomplished in decades in these areas and all at the same time. Competent observers agree in their description of the chaos which threatens in consequence of the lack of an agreed basis for swift social improvement.

Scores of millions in South and South East Asia drift helplessly in an ocean with dangerous currents. The area is wide open to all ideologies and philosophies; people are eager for a change, without knowing where to go or how to start. Modern nationalism, unknown to a village society or an absolute monarchy, has a grip on the masses, easily fed by resentment against foreign imperialism and economic penetration. It gives national governments the possibility of achieving real progress through an appeal to patriotism. But it also closes many doors to foreigners. Yet the nations are more than ever interdependent, and international cooperation is unavoidable, to say the least.[1]

A report on social conditions in the Middle East concludes:

At the present time, the Middle East is in the grip of a social upheaval the causes and ingredients of which are varied and complex. . . . The byword in many quarters is change, though there is little unanimity on what change is desirable, or how it is to be effected, or at what pace.[2]

And from Latin America a correspondent writes:

We are living in a total revolutionary situation into which many other factors enter, principal among them being the almost total political breakdown in these countries with the collapse of liberal democratic movements and the almost complete lack of an alternative to Communism, which leads the most sensitive people . . . to despair or Communism. . . . We are sitting on the top of a volcano which might erupt at any moment.

A rise in the standard of living, expansion of the necessary social services, and the improvement of educational and health facilities are needed, and these depend upon the ability of the countries concerned to devise social and economic policies and programs for overcoming the various causes of their economic weakness. This means in most cases better and more efficient use of the land, reorganization of village life, improvement in the means of transportation and communication, industrialization, efficient government administration, etc. It also requires social understanding of the highest order, a sense of direction regarding the goals of social change and a will to share the responsibility and the sacrifices involved in achieving

[1] E. de Vries, "The Churches and the Economic and Social Problems of South and South East Asia," in *Christ—The Hope Of Asia,* Papers and Minutes of the Ecumenical Study Conference for East Asia, Lucknow, India, Dec. 27-30, 1952 (Madras: The Christian Literature Society, 1953), p. 57.

[2] *Preliminary Report on the World Social Situation,* United Nations Economic and Social Council, April, 1952, p. 372.

a better society. It is these intellectual and spiritual resources which need to be discovered and developed:

Governments can only support and never replace the efforts of the nation as a community of responsible citizens. But can these governments expect their citizens to act that way? Hardly—it is one of the tragedies of Asia that opportunities are only by a hairs-breadth separated from defeat and disaster. The same forces which made Asia free from foreign domination are apt to destroy it from within, unless channelled and directed in the right way. It is here that the real responsibilities of the churches in Asia begin: building communities of responsible citizens of free nations.[3]

The demands being made upon the human spirit are overwhelming. In some countries within a generation or two people are making the transition from primitive seminomadic, pastoral and hunting communities to the complex life of modern industrial society. The economic change cannot be stopped. An African missionary writes:

It is useless to gird at this process of industrialization. Africa needs the wealth which, it seems, only the addition of industrial development can supply. For good or ill, the African is caught up in the modern world of industry and commerce.[4]

To deal with this revolution in economic life, the rapid growth of big cities in Asia and the dissolution of village communities, some common views and standards are needed for guiding the introduction of new techniques and new institutions which will guard against their being used to destroy rather than to enlarge the possibilities of man for self-realization.

The experiences with industrial development in underdeveloped countries indicate that when industrialism is pursued irrespective of the person, the challenge to the human person may be as great if not greater than in the preindustrial society. The same African missionary writes that there are

[3] E. de Vries, "The Churches and the Economic and Social Problems of South and South-East Asia," *op. cit.*

[4] R. K. Orchard, *Africa Steps Out,* London, 1952, p. 18.

two contrasting social organisations in Africa today,—the collectivism of the traditional tribal society, and the individualism of the industrial and commercial societies which the West has brought into Africa. In neither of them can the African find a full personal life.[5]

The fight to maintain personal integrity comes to a decisive engagement in, particularly, the field of African family life:

The change from a barter to a money system, from a subsistence to a cash economy, from a strongly communal to a markedly individualistic society . . . all these and many other social and economic changes now sweeping through Africa have their most far-reaching and devastating effect on family life. The greatest single threat to the future of Africa is the absence of a recognised and accepted framework within which the life of families can grow strong and vigorous.[6]

How do the churches express their concern for these and many other issues and questions confronting people in countries undergoing such rapid change? The churches have a vital interest in the foundations of the new societies and in the problems which their social environment presents to their members, especially to youth.

A. THE NEW STAGE OF CHRISTIAN SOCIAL THOUGHT IN THE CHURCHES OF ASIA, AFRICA AND LATIN AMERICA

Reports from Asia, Africa and Latin America indicate that the churches and missions are being awakened to a new understanding of Christian social responsibility by the impact of social upheaval and unrest in many of these countries. The rise of political movements for national freedom and the attainment of national independence in many countries have made it necessary for Christians to define the Christian conception of the goals of society which are relevant to the situation of these countries.

[5] *Ibid.*, p. 35.
[6] *Ibid.*, pp. 38-39.

It would be presumptuous to characterize this new development of Christian concern for society as more than in its preliminary stages. "The churches as a whole," says a report, "have not yet realized that Christian social thinking is needed, nor have they recognized that it is their duty to encourage and inspire such thinking . . ." They are too preoccupied by the struggle "for self-existence in the narrow sense." Nevertheless, even in the most pessimistic reports it is stated that "attempts are being made by certain groups to promote thinking on social problems."

The churches and missions are beginning to realize that they must make a witness in relation to the vast changes in economic and political life, especially since these changes are in part the perhaps unconscious consequences of Christian teaching on the dignity of man. Indirectly, through their emphasis on education and social service, Christian missions have contributed to the revolutionary ferment in Asia and Africa. As Bishop Newbigin of the Church of South India has observed:

Because education for the past hundred years in India has been dominated by ideas derived from Christianity and often by the figure of Jesus himself, no form of popular government is possible which does not in some sense accept the idea of the welfare state. . . . Because Christianity puts into men's minds a divine discontent with things as they are and a conviction that society ought to be justly and rationally ordered, the way is open for the tremendous appeal of Marxism.[7]

The leaders of movements of national freedom and social change, even when consciously anti-Christian, have been intellectually and spiritually reared by Christian missionary institutions. The consciousness of the intimate relation between the Gospel and the ideas and ideals that inspire the revolutionary urge of the peoples of Asia and Africa is beginning to

[7] "The Background of Church Life in South India," in *The Frontier*, Nov., 1952, published by the Christian Frontier Council in Great Britain.

make Christians in these lands aware of the further contribution which the indigenous churches can make to stabilize and revitalize the social goals which people seek.

As a result of the work of Dr. Merle Davis,[8] the missionary movement began some years ago to place increasing emphasis on the economic and social environment in which the missionary endeavor is set. His studies especially helped the missions to have a new conception of the mission in rural Asia. He brought worship, preaching, education, health service, rural and industrial service, etc., into an integrated whole, with the aim of developing a community which responds to the hopes and fears of the ordinary individual. This conception still remains a valid one and one may find the consequences of it in the results of the recent Eastern Asia Christian Conferences at Bangkok (1949) and Lucknow (1952), which speak of the "revolutionary significance of the local congregation," living under God as a community bringing to bear upon all personal and institutional relationships the light of Christian faith, hope and love. Today, however, these ideas are being applied in the wider context of the nation, and even of whole regions.

Events in China especially have helped Christian missions to see their social responsibility in larger perspectives. While frequently the reaction to these events has been to whip up negative anticommunist propaganda, it has had some positive results also, in awakening the missions, and through them the "younger" churches, to the need to be concerned with social matters. The following quotation is typical of many which may be culled from missionary bulletins:

It is no longer good enough to open dispensaries, hospitals, orphanages and schools, colleges and universities, to attract pagans to the Church. While you are caring for their bodies and cultivating

[8] See his studies for the International Missionary Council especially "The Economic and Social Environment of the Younger Churches" and Vol. V of the Madras Series.

their minds, social forces are working against you. The preaching of the Gospel must be accompanied by the proclamation of social justice.[9]

B. New Approaches at the Ecumenical Level

The Eastern Asia Christian Conference held at Bangkok, 1949, under the joint auspices of the International Missionary Council and the World Council of Churches, gave a lead in showing the relation of the Gospel to social justice in Asia. In view of "the revolutionary ferment" at work in Asia, the Bangkok meeting stated that it was "the responsibility of the Church to rediscover and proclaim both to its own members and to those outside the basic truths declared in the Bible about the life of men in society and in the state." It declared that "the proclamation of the Word of God, with a profound sense of its relevance to the ideological and political conflicts of the Orient, is therefore the central task of the Church in Asia," and it called on the churches to help "those within their fold and outside, especially youth, to understand the true nature of the social crisis in which they are, and in a positive way to accept its challenge. . . ." The churches were asked to train new types of "evangelists who will identify themselves in a costly way with the day to day struggles of the labourer and peasant for justice." The Bangkok Conference pointed out that "a true social democracy" might be an effective answer to communism in certain countries and urged the churches to help provide democracy with a moral and religious backbone so that it can become truly social.

In 1950 the International Missionary Council "in view of swift sharpening of the political, social and religious crisis, involving the world in general and the World Christian Movement in particular" issued a *Summons to Immediate Action* calling the churches and missions to join in a special program

[9] Statement of Mr. Gerard Filion, a Catholic layman, editor of the newspaper *Le Devoir* (Montreal) and delegate to the Peace Conference in Peking, Oct., 1952, quoted in the *China Bulletin* (Far Eastern Joint Office, Division of Foreign Missions, NCCC/USA, No. 8, April 20, 1953).

of study and consultation to formulate a crisis strategy to deal
with three questions which included "the witness of the Church
in relation to Communism." Under the program a series of
consultations of missionaries and church workers were held
throughout the Middle East and East Asia to discuss Christian
social witness in these areas. These meetings were held under
the leadership of outstanding theologians and Christian social
thinkers, and they aroused widespread interest.

In December, 1952, the World Council of Churches in preparation for the Evanston Assembly sponsored an Asian Study
Conference at Lucknow, and one Commission of the Conference dealt with the "Responsible Society in Asia in the Light
of the World Situation." The purpose of this Commission was
to relate ecumenical social thinking to the specific social and
political problems of Asia within the perspective of the world
situation. The report of this meeting indicates the views of
Christians on specific social questions such as land reform and
industrialization, and emphasizes the need for political action
in support of these and other goals of the responsible society.
Moreover, it stated the churches' social witness in a manner
intelligible to those outside. A quotation will serve to
indicate the trend of the thinking of the Asian churches on
these issues:

> We are concerned with social justice, that is to say with the
> development of social conditions in which human dignity and free-
> dom can find their expression as befits the nature and destiny of
> man as a child of God. Communism has awakened and challenged
> our conscience to see the need for action. It is not, however, pri-
> marily the fear of communism but our concern for our brother
> for whom Christ died, that should impel us to fulfil our social
> obligations. But a positive programme for social justice will help
> to meet the challenge of communism. . . .[10]

The statement goes on to stress the need for land reform,
for nationalization of certain basic and key industries, together

[10] "The Responsible Society in East Asia in Light of the World Situation," in *Christ, the Hope of Asia, op. cit.*, p. 27.

with the development of large- and small-scale private industries. Christians are called upon to play their role in the development and maintenance of healthy political institutions.

C. NATIONAL AND LOCAL APPROACHES

In connection with the parliamentary elections of 1953, the General Assembly of the National Council of Churches in Indonesia sent a letter to the churches calling their attention to their political responsibility, and suggesting particular stress on the development of political understanding and action among church members. The Assembly also expressed a desire to see Article XVIII of the Declaration of Human Rights incorporated into the Indonesian Constitution, and spoke of the need for a clearer definition of the church-state relationship.

The East Asia secretariat of the IMC and WCC are following up the stimulus of Bangkok and Lucknow through regional conferences and visits, and a volume on "Christianity and the Asian Revolution" is being prepared.

A Conference on Christian Social Action in North India, held in May, 1953, discussed problems of Indian political life. Speaking of the Welfare State, the Conference said: "As Christians we are bound to support this determination to build social justice into the fabric of Indian society." Consideration was also given to the major Indian political parties and the place of Christians in them. The conclusion was, "When everything has been taken into consideration we are left with Gandhism and socialism as the two real choices for the Christian. . . . It should not be beyond the power of Indian Christianity to provide both . . . with those elements which are lacking in the ideology of each. . . ."[11]

Organizations like the Economic Life Committees of the National Christian Councils, the great agricultural institutes, schools of social work, organizers of rural and other service projects under Christian auspices as well as movements like the Christian Ashram Movement of India make a vital con-

[11] Report of the Conference, p. 11.

tribution in solving specific social issues, but their contribution in terms of social thought has not been sufficiently developed and the relation between social service and social action needs working out in the light of an adequate theology of society.

Some of the significant contributions to Christian social thought in the churches of Asia, Africa and Latin America have come from small groups like the Youth Christian Council of Action in South India, the Christian Fellowship for Social Education and Action in North India and Japan, Schools of Sociology held in Ceylon, study groups of professors and students of social science in Tokyo, and study conferences of the Student Christian Movements of Latin America.

One of the most hopeful signs in the situation is the number of books, pamphlets and articles that are now being written on the need for rethinking Christian strategy in connection with the social situation, especially in Asia and Africa. For instance, the Federation of Philippine Christian Churches prepared a *Primer on Communism* which was used as the basis of study in twenty regional conferences during the summer of 1951, as a means of orienting Christians with respect to communism which is in their midst.

In India the Christian Institute for the Study of Society, established in 1950, which has a close relation to the churches and other Christian bodies as well as with the United Theological College in Bangalore, and the Committee for Special Literature on the Indian Church and Social Concerns, related to the National Christian Council of India, have real potentialities for becoming growing points of the Christian social thought for the churches in India. They may very well become also a pattern of formulating and expressing Christian social concern in a changing society for other countries in the area of the "younger" churches.

The development of social departments and commissions of churches such as that of the United Church of Christ

(Kyodan) in Japan and the Study Commissions of the NCCs are worthy of mention because they represent a formal recognition by churches and missions of the necessity of Christian social study, thought and action. Theological schools in many of these countries are also including the study of Church and Society in their curricula.

It is to the credit of the churches and mission boards that in these and other projects they show that they have begun to take seriously the question of Christian responsibility for social and political life. However, with a few exceptions this new concern has not yet become real in the life and work of the churches. It is, of course, an important fact that the Church *is* in Asia and Africa and *is* involved in the revolutionary situation, and that it has grown in self-sufficiency and in responsibility for, and influence on, the community. But it is also true that the Church is not yet penetrating to the level at which the character and action of society are really determined. Nor have the churches as churches shown enough awareness of the urgency of prophetic social witness. No doubt there are an increasing number of groups who are concerned with such witness, and they and their thinking are winning growing recognition by the churches. But if it is true, for example, as is said of the Church in Africa, that in the present situation "it is expected to provide Christian leadership and service for a wholly new pattern of life on a continental scale,"[12] then the churches there must orient themselves in that direction both in terms of structure and of thought. Whether as a result of failure in policy at high levels or of the momentum of a past tradition, all the available reports indicate that the churches are developing their social witness at a relatively slow pace, while social changes are occurring with unprecedented rapidity.

[12] R. K. Orchard, *op. cit.,* p. 58.

VII

THE CHRISTIAN WITNESS IN COMMUNIST COUNTRIES

As a result of the expansion of communist power in Eastern Europe and in Asia in the years following the war a large body of Christians now live in countries under communist régimes. How do Christians in these countries understand and express their responsibility for society? What is the significance for ecumenical social thinking of their experience with the communist system?

A. THE CHALLENGE OF COMMUNIST IDEOLOGY

It is difficult to generalize about the specific tasks of the churches in communist countries, because circumstances vary greatly. In certain countries communism has become dominant through internal political action, in others through military occupation. In certain countries it is associated with a strong indigenous communist party, and in others it has few roots in the native soil. In certain countries it has brought far-reaching social reforms, and in others it has thwarted democratic social reform movements. In some it came with the collapse of a bankrupt régime with no available alternatives, and in others it destroyed such alternatives. In some the churches have had experience in dealing with a totalitarian situation, and in others they have not.[1]

Nevertheless, all the churches in communist lands must deal with the challenge to the Christian view of man and society resulting from communist ideology. The points of conflict between Christian faith and communist social theory

[1] See "The Responsible Society in a World Perspective," a memorandum published in *The Ecumenical Review*, Oct., 1953, p. 86.

and practice are indicated in many reports and may be summarized as follows.

(1) *The claims of a total ideology, which aims at changing the consciousness of the population to correspond with a Marxist society.* This involves the remoulding of the entire school curriculum on Marx-Leninist dialectical materialist principles, and the examination of students on their points of view as well as on their knowledge; it means also control of the channels of public information by the same ideology, the schooling of the whole population in factories, farms, offices and neighborhoods. The main problem here is what this means to the school child or student from a Christian family. The whole question of truth and sincerity is involved. Must he lie in order to remain at his school or university or must he bear witness to his faith and take the consequences?

(2) *The claim of total power which the state makes and its means of exercising it.* The communist conception of justice is completely different from that held under other régimes. The interests of the party and state are paramount, and where the state and the individual clash the former is always right. It follows that the state feels justified in using whatever methods may be found effective to subdue resistance.

(3) *The changes in the economic and political structure which result in the tendency to treat individuals and families as productive units.* This proceeds partly according to the "class war" formula of the communists, whereby property is transferred to public ownership, and positions are awarded to peasants or workers by the elimination of "landlords" or "capitalists" rather than by due process of law. It proceeds also by the total planning of the economy from the top. In collectivized industry and agriculture, personal, family and vocational life is changed by compulsory schooling and thought control, by controlled wages and by compulsory activities embracing large portions of free time.

B. The Christian Hope in Communist Society

What is the witness of the Church in face of these pressures? The Church is able to bear witness only through the courage and fortitude which comes through a deep renewal of faith. The Church lives in this situation only as it understands that it has a new opportunity, given of God, to witness to the truth of the Gospel. The great joy with which many Christians in communist countries welcome the test of their faith is well illustrated by the words of a young pastor who was imprisoned for a period during the "church struggle" in Eastern Germany in 1953. He writes:

Let me say clearly to start with, it is a good and precious thing to preach here in the East, that Jesus Christ alone, Lord and Saviour, refreshes the weary and the suffering, and that He has found the lost and the strayed; no one can snatch them from His hands or take from them the peace which their Almighty Father gives. . . . The man who has a light in the darkness of night is well established. Many wanderers will join him because they see from afar that "there is light, guidance, security." As Hitler came to power, all the stars of the bourgeois world lost their brilliance one by one, and many a citizen discovered with amazement the little light of the Gospel. Here among us in the East the old stars never came out again. A new (communist) religion, claiming the whole universe as well as the inmost conscience of men, is being proclaimed from the rooftops and in the smallest rooms. Yet the . . . years we have been hearing it have only been able to make us more sure of the truth of God, and more sustained by it. . . . It is our growing experience that God's word is like a hammer which smashes the greatest rocks. Who can but rejoice at the chance to be there!

Most Christian thinking in this situation starts by affirming a theological basis which strongly emphasizes hope because the historical action of God is so important. It takes as its starting point the Lordship of Christ over history and over the Church; this makes the Church free from all concern for earthly position or power, and critical of all ideologies. It recognizes the judgment of God in the events which led to communist rule, the importance of concrete repentance, and of accepting Christ in this new society. This does not imply acceptance of the system. The way of Christ is to follow a Lord who took the sins of the world upon himself, who suffered and rose again. But opinions differ regarding the way in which this theological conception of the basic Christian hope is to be applied to the actual developments in communist countries. It is not possible here to survey all the different views but two may be cited.

C. Communism as a Judgment upon Pre-Communist Society

There is the view which holds that pre-communist society, because of its spiritual emptiness, its social and economic injustice, and its failure to meet the challenge of the rising masses, collapsed completely before the revolutionary force of communism. This collapse is regarded as evidence of the total judgment of God. The new economic and political society of communism is seen as the first step toward the classless society, which is a provisional hope which Christians also can affirm. Professor Hromadka of Czechoslovakia, who holds such a view, emphasizes that the prophetic response of the Christian to communism must not be a plain "No."

We must meet . . . the challenge of Marxism and what it represents. First of all, we have to understand the real effort of the Marxists to reconstruct our social order, to raise the working class to a level of active participation in the shaping of human conditions, to establish a society in which all class differences and injustices would disappear. We must understand *why* it is precisely the Marxists who have taken over the historic role of socialising our countries. Moreover, Marxism is a special challenge to the Christian churches because it is being taken seriously by its followers, while Christians are largely guilty of having no burning convictions. Many churches have degenerated into empty conventions and institutions.[2]

[2] J. L. Hromadka in *The Ecumenical Review,* Oct., 1952, p. 57.

And a young Christian theologian in China writes:

Many young Christian men and women are considering the ministry and church work as a way for them to serve God and the people. Today, Christian ministers are working within an environment of moral health and vigour. They can carry on their moral and spiritual tasks with consciences at peace because today they have the freedom to come all out for peace, democracy, liberty, human dignity and all those things which the Christian faith demands of a human community.[3]

Those Christians who believe that Christians must affirm the fundamental liberating forces in the communist social revolution emphasize the progress inherent in the social changes taking place in communist countries.

The Church, and each Christian, is called to participate in the building of the new society, to build up an atmosphere of trust between church and state, to prove that Christians are not imperialist or reactionary.[4] The Church must help explain and gain approval for the measures of socialization, and of the "battle for peace." Christians may not become ideological communists, but according to this view their place is in the mass organizations, perhaps even in the Party. The Christian tries at the same time to humanize the social revolution. He may protest or set right the incidental injustices of it. He must help all those in need. However, there may also come a time when, as Professor Hromadka has stated, the Church must say "No" to the state, "if someone tries to lead her away from God's authority and to subject her to a human authority."

D. CHRISTIAN RESISTANCE TO COMMUNIST IDEOLOGY

Another viewpoint claims to base a thoroughly practical realism about the forces at work in the world on the Christian hope. It discerns the judgment of God on the old society and on the Church without making sweeping denunciations

---

[3] K. H. Ting in *China Monthly Review*, July, 1953.
[4] This view is expressed in a report for this Survey from the Ecumenical Study Commission of the Hungarian Churches.

of it, and without illusion as to the character of communism. It sees in communism the attempt of another total ideology, a false faith, to press human beings into its mold, and to wield total power in the world. According to this viewpoint, the task of the Christian is to analyze the forces of society in the knowledge that God in Christ is their Lord and judge, who has prescribed their true functions; to judge the policies of the government with sober empiricism, according to whether they serve the needs and preserve the freedoms of human beings; to act in whatever range God grants, in responsibility for one's neighbor in His Kingdom, without too much strategy, without too much hope for success or fear for the consequences. These are the logical consequences of the Christian hope. This viewpoint is well illustrated in a statement by a pastor in Eastern Germany:

We have to learn how to accept the limitations of the position in which God has placed us, and to limit our responsibility to the tasks He gives us. Christians in different places and times have had different ranges of potential influence and knowledge. Ours is very small. We have a little power in our immediate surroundings, but very little. We must reckon with prison where we will have less. We have some understanding of the issues at stake in the world situation, but it is one-sided and scanty. We are tempted always to become impatient with these limits, to imagine that our power or our knowledge is greater than it is, and that therefore the total trend of society is our responsibility. . . . We are called to much more modest strategies and more direct responsibilities—to bear witness to the truth where we know it, to work for a bit of justice or humanity wherever a way opens, to know our Bible (and next to it our Marx-Leninism) better than the communists, in order that we can understand, love and help the people with whom we live.

For Christians who believe it is necessary to resist the communist ideology at specific points with spiritual power, four examples indicate the possibilities of social action:

(1) The very existence of the Church as a parish fellowship in love of free men bound to one another in Christ,

hearing and carrying the Word of God into their daily lives, is a social act. The Church is the only voluntary fellowship in society. Therefore, these Christians exercise and defend the broadest possible scope of church activity and privilege. Freedom not to register church meetings with the authorities, the right to own land, the right of religious instruction in the schools, all of which in a normal state would be matters for compromise, become here points on which the Christian stands against the state's total claim. The mutual confidence and love and the freedom from fear which grow in a church meeting or conference, the economic community based on free co-operation which can be built on church farmland as in Eastern Germany, and the witness which intelligent religious instruction can bear to all truth, are living challenges to mass organizations based on fear, forced economic planning and ideological education. For example, as a means of resisting the totalitarian claims of the state, the churches in communist countries have discovered the fruitfulness of Christian philanthropic, mission and social work, supported entirely by voluntary contributions from church members.

(2) Social action in this situation is also the Christian's personal encounter with his neighbor, backed by the counsel and support of the congregation and the pastor. The communist is thus encountered whenever a Christian refuses to participate in some mass demonstration—petition, parade, election, joining an organization, etc.—and has to answer for this refusal. He then has the opportunity to explain biblical commandments in their practical applications, and to draw communists out of their ideological shell. Other men are encountered in their bitter hatred against the regime, and need the Gospel of Christ if they are to go on living in this society.

The following account of conversations between Christians and Marxists in Eastern Germany is a good example of the way in which the Christian through his personal encounter with his neighbor bears witness to the power of God, and helps his fellow sufferers and the victims of totalitarian ideology to rise above hate and resentment:

Two young communists are talking with us. They are trying to persuade us to take part in the voting for "peace." They make the usual statements about "peace." When they have finished, we begin to ask about the nature of their struggle for peace in relation to the teachings of Lenin. They say: "Peace means not a condition of peace between nations, but peace in the classless society, which will be achieved through revolution, the collapse of capitalist power and the dictatorship of the proletariat."

"So this plebiscite is directly connected with belief in the truth of scientific socialism?" "Oh, yes." "But you see, we don't believe that it is the truth!" It nearly takes one's breath away to see how the two react to this unexpected conclusion. "Then what have you got instead of this belief?" And so begins a three-hour talk about obedience to God's law, and other aspects of Christian faith. One of them, who is married, asks, "How can God be real if He has no substance? For nothing can exist without substance." "Is the love and confidence between himself and his wife real, and on the other hand can he prove that it has substance?" He agrees that his conception of what is real is inadequate, even for the relationships between people. He reflects and then puts a surprising question. "But supposing I am lying when I say that love and confidence are a reality between two people?" "Then your marriage must be a very unhappy one!" Then his human side comes to the fore. "You are right; life would be awful without that." We ask other questions: has Marxism any answer to the question, what is the death of the individual? Without it can there be an answer to the question, what is man? We men exist only as dying men. Has communism any answer to the reality of evil in us? When he took his leave he said, "I tell you frankly, that is my first encounter with the Christian faith. You have said things that I can't forget."

(3) The Christian can, so far as his knowledge goes, witness to a truth and an order in society which is based on the Kingdom of God. His faith makes him free from communist interpretations, to see scientific facts and human relations more clearly. Recognizing that God ordains political order

and justice and an economic system to serve the needs of men, he will co-operate with even a communist state when a practical useful task needs to be done. He will also be free to resist state power or evade it, when only by this means can he serve his neighbor or remind the state of its true function. The Church itself has resisted the state in East Germany on occasion, in official statements on land reform, on elections, on lying in propaganda and education, and the police threat behind it, and on attacks on the Church and its youth in 1953. There are centers of social influence such as socially necessary professions (doctors, engineers, science professors, etc.) which give opportunity for effective Christian witness, and even in the more controlled ones there are opportunities. Economic freedom from the state becomes, in this connection, a treasure to defend for its value to this witness.

(4) All Christian action in society in communist lands must reckon with the possibility of loss of employment, or imprisonment. The acceptance of this suffering as a vocation, when it comes, is a supreme act of responsible obedience. It breaks the hold of fear, which is the greatest single social illness in a communist state. Thus it makes creative action and truly objective thinking possible. It carries responsible society into the heart of a system which does not believe in an ultimate responsibility to God—into its prisons, courts and concentration camps. Even there the possibilities of Christian action are present. There are neighbors, and there is the power and grace of God.

VIII

CONCLUSION

In the light of this survey what are the most important social questions to be discussed by the churches meeting at Evanston? In approaching specific problems to what extent can the churches make use of previous ecumenical thinking about the Christian witness in society and to what extent must they discover new approaches? What old strategies for social action have proved most effective in various situations, and where do new channels need to be explored? With reference to the main theme of the Assembly how can the Christian hope be expressed in ways relevant to contemporary social issues? These are some of the questions raised by the survey which can be dealt with only in a summary way in this concluding section.

To the extent to which the Church has learned to accept its responsibility for the conditions of society, and to avoid identifying the Christian faith with particular economic and political institutions, it is possible to point to a great advance of Christian social thinking in the last twenty-five years and more particularly in the last ten years. Churches and Christian groups have made great progress in discovering the need for Christian witness in relation to the spiritual and moral issues in political and economic life and for expressing this concern in the language of social and political thought and action. It is also evident that the ecumenical movement has been instrumental in helping the churches to see their responsibility for society and to find the right means for expressing that concern. There is no considerable body of Christians who would challenge the conclusions of Section III at the Amsterdam Assembly, that the Christian churches should

61

avoid the identification of Christianity with any economic system, and that in relation to political and economic problems, "it is the responsibility of Christians to seek new, creative solutions which never allow either justice or freedom to destroy the other."

Nevertheless, it is apparent that there is also great apathy and indifference in the Church concerning social issues. Everywhere the churches have much to do to demonstrate to the world that the Christian faith "delivers us from enslavement to worldly projects and institutions" and also "summons us to responsible action in God's own service in and for the world." On the basis of the scanty information which has been received it is not possible to speak precisely about the cause of this apathy but three factors play an important role in almost every country.

(1) *The Lack of a Vital Faith*: there is a need in many countries for a renewal of faith, for new theological insights regarding the spiritual dangers in modern society. Christians are not prepared to interpret the great social catastrophes of our time and cannot help peoples who are "overwhelmed by them and perish spiritually in their confusion." The Christian concern for social renewal which is evident in some countries today is due not only to the challenge of social conditions but is based on a discovery of theological insights and a quickening of faith.

(2) *The New Social Situation in Most Countries*: it is clear that in the years since World War II, changes have crystallized in economic and political life which confront us with quite new problems in Christian social thinking. *Laissez-faire* capitalism, communism and socialism are outdated categories in most countries. In many countries people have found ways around these extremes and the social issues they are facing are more subtle and complex than in the past, therefore new approaches are required. In some countries, patience and a sacrificial spirit are required while new economic and political systems are developed. In other countries great imagi-

nation is needed to discard traditional approaches and to visualize entirely new relationships at every level of community life.

(3) *The World Dimensions of Social Problems*: the great disparity and the bewildering variety of social problems today baffles and confuses many people who have lived and still do live in conditions of relative stability and security. Half the world is in a state of complete social revolution and the other half in a condition of rapid social evolution. The different degrees and stages of social change taking place make it difficult to pinpoint the common social issues for ecumenical discussion. Moreover, it is now impossible to speak about the meaning of the responsible society in any country without considering world needs. It is this interdependence of the local, the regional, and the world needs and issues which makes for a great feeling of impotence and irresponsibility and which baffles many churches.

Tasks for the Churches

This description of the new situation suggests certain tasks which the churches everywhere must take seriously:

(1) *Developing Common Convictions Regarding the Structure of Political and Economic Life.* Christians can express their solidarity in the world through their common witness on political and economic issues. But to make this possible Christians must think together more than they have done in the past about their convictions concerning the structure of political institutions, the function of the state in economic life, the goals of economic life, and the Christian criteria for measuring the desirability of social policy at many levels. To speak about the Responsible Society in a World Perspective means not only to develop schemes for economic and political co-operation but a common ethos, common convictions concerning the destiny of man and his relation to society. The churches have much to do to fulfill this responsibility in relation to the many new conflicts and divisions about the right pattern of economic and political life.

(2) *The Role of the Church in Society.* The churches have perhaps too often been guilty of supposing that all that was required of them was to develop certain positions on social issues and then to use conventional means for making these positions known and to engage in certain remedial social work. With the increasing complexity of social problems and social structures in the world, it is becoming clear that the churches need to re-examine the ways in which they have tried to deal with social issues in the past. They need also to look carefully at the nature of the political and economic forces with which they have to deal, and to try to determine how their convictions can best be translated into responsible influence on public opinion and public policy. The pursuit of this responsibility will require expert knowledge, imagination and the determination to hold in balance the Church's calling to minister with effectiveness as well as with good intention in the world, and at the same time to remain loyal to its witness to the truth which is not of the world.

(3) *Demonstrating the Basis of Our Hope.* It is clear that the world needs not only more freedom, security, justice and the social and economic institutions for realizing them, but the faith which gives these terms meaning and which gives people hope in the midst of overwhelming evil and widespread despair. Where will the churches find the spiritual resources which will enable them to interpret this hope as the real answer for men without hope? In this connection, this survey suggests that the churches around the world have much to learn from the experiences of Christians in communist countries who have discovered what it means to live by the ultimate hope in Jesus Christ, and who have also discovered the powerful help from the Holy Spirit which comes to those who fearlessly proclaim the will of God.

(4) *The Responsibility of the Churches and the Social Revolution in the Underdeveloped Countries.* Perhaps the most important single social problem confronting the churches today is their task in relation to the economically and tech-

nically underdeveloped countries. It was said in the Second Report of the Commission on the Main Theme for the Second Assembly that:

We cannot worthily proclaim to men the Gospel of the resurrection of the body to eternal life, unless we are at the same time ready to rush to their help in every predicament of body as well as of soul even to the sacrifice of our own lives. The cry of half the world's people in the present day for bread enough to sustain life in their bodies must be heard by the Christian as the cry of Christ. He who spoke the parables of the Last Judgment and of Dives and Lazarus will surely not leave us without condemnation if we are content to eat sumptuously while millions starve.

PREPARATORY COMMISSION III

on

SOCIAL QUESTIONS—THE RESPONSIBLE SOCIETY IN A WORLD PERSPECTIVE

Members

Professor John C. BENNETT, U.S.A. ⎱ Co-chairmen
Dr. C. L. PATIJN, Netherlands ⎰
The Rev. Paul R. ABRECHT (W.C.C.), Secretary
The Rev. John W. TURNBULL, U.S.A., Assistant Secretary

Dr. Walter BAUER, Germany
Mrs. L. CHEVALLEY-SABATIER, France
Mr. Tilford E. DUDLEY, U.S.A.
°Mr. John EDWARDS, M.P., United Kingdom
°The Rev. John GARRETT, Australia
°The Rev. Bishop Gerald KENNEDY, U.S.A.
°Dr. John MATTHAI, India
°Mr. Irwin MILLER, U.S.A.
°Mr. Charles C. PARLIN, U.S.A.
°The Rt. Rev. Bishop J. PETER, Hungary
°Professor Andre PHILIP, France
°Professor Mikio SUMIYA, Japan
°Dr. A. M. TAMBUNAM, M.P., Indonesia
Mr. M. M. THOMAS, India
Professor H. D. WENDLAND, Germany

Central Committee Consultants

°The Rt. Rev. Bishop A. FJELLBU, Norway
°The Rev. H. J. LAZARUS, India
°The Rev. E. C. URWIN, United Kingdom

Substitutes and ad hoc Consultants attending the August 1953 meeting

Mr. Edwin BARKER, United Kingdom
Professor Pierre BURGELIN, France

°Not present at August 1953 meeting.

Mr. Eugen MARTI, Switzerland
Mr. Denys L. MUNBY, United Kingdom
Mr. Jim PRICE, U.S.A.
Mr. Charles P. TAFT, U.S.A.
Professor E. DE VRIES, U.S.A.
The Rev. Charles C. WEST, U.S.A.

INTERNATIONAL AFFAIRS—
CHRISTIANS IN THE STRUGGLE
FOR WORLD COMMUNITY

An Ecumenical Survey
prepared under the auspices of the
World Council of Churches

CONTENTS

iii

I

INTRODUCTION

The Second Assembly of the World Council of Churches has attempted to come to grips with the responsibilities of "Christians in the Struggle for World Community." This Survey was prepared to provide the Section on International Affairs with relevant source material on what the Churches have said and done on international issues since the First Assembly. A brief appraisal of such experience is included, but the document is essentially a factual report.

During recent years a wider recognition of Christian responsibility for the promotion of peace and justice in the world of nations has led to numerous efforts to bring a Christian influence to bear on international events. The World Council of Churches and International Missionary Council, their joint organ, the Commission of the Churches on International Affairs, and several national Christian agencies have provided means for corporate action and for stimulating individual Christian action. The convictions expressed by the Churches at the national level have provided ground work for international action and also reflect the distinctive national settings of many problems.

In this review, attention is focused on the work of the Churches for world order since Amsterdam. The statements of the First Assembly and of earlier ecumenical bodies are here perforce largely omitted, but have been summarized separately in the October, 1953, issue of *The Ecumenical Review*. For such information as has been made available on work at the national level during the past five years, the help of National Commissions of the Churches on International Affairs and of special correspondents is gratefully acknowledged.

1

Chapter II gives, as background for the later chapters, a very brief outline of the world situation. The need for such background is more fully met by a special study of the world situation prepared for the Second Assembly by the C.C.I.A. This chapter also deals with the question of Christian responsibility in international affairs, which underlies the more specific issues of Christian witness.

Chapter III constituting the major portion of the Survey, reports convictions expressed by international and national Christian agencies in seven areas of world concern: the need for international order, the tensions arising from the clash of rival social and power systems, the conditions necessary for disarmament, the plight of refugees, the claims of dependent peoples, technical assistance and other forms of international economic co-operation, and human rights.

Chapter IV attempts to analyze methods by which Christian convictions have been brought to bear upon the complex and often elusive problems of international relations. This is all the more necessary because organized Christian effort in this field is relatively new.

Chapter V seeks to appraise the extent to which objectives have been realized, to identify areas where added emphasis is needed, and to explore new issues on which Christian witness is called for.

In reading this Survey it is essential to keep the modest contributions here recorded in proper perspective over against the profound and menacing character of the contemporary crisis. A review of Christian experience in this field can serve a useful purpose if it helps to discipline Christian conscience and commitment. But these matter most. What is needed from Evanston is not so much a new set of generalizations, but a renewed faith and determination, expressed throughout the world-wide fellowship in responsible action for peace and justice.

II

THE WORLD CRISIS AND
CHRISTIAN RESPONSIBILITY

A. The International Situation

The years since Amsterdam have witnessed vast changes in the world scene. Some of these are accomplished facts of the political and international order. Others are tendencies of thought or policy which are effecting, or will in due time effect, such changes. Of the actual changes the most important perhaps have taken place in Asia, particularly the entry of China into the communist camp. The war in Korea has occurred during this period. Fighting in Malaya and Viet-Nam still continues.

These years have witnessed also an intensification of the struggle between the two great blocs of world powers, with little or no easing of their relations of mutual suspicion. Their rivalry has been carried into the portals of the United Nations, which has thus lost to some extent its character of an impartial arbiter in international affairs. Fear of the use of atomic and other weapons of mass destruction has raised in a still more intense and urgent form the question of possible disarmament.

Concurrently, the human need of the less developed peoples has come under close examination, followed by action. The world's food supplies, the health of mankind, conditions of labor, the spread of education—in a word the raising of the standards of living everywhere—are now questions of international importance, and through the machinery of technical assistance make their claims upon the resources of the nations. This program is sometimes regarded, as indeed it is,

3

as an effective reply to communism, but for Christians at least it has its own intrinsic merits.

In the Western world, one of the foremost problems is the immense defense program carried to a certain level only by American aid, at the cost of substantial outlay. Europe cannot yet show a treaty of peace with Germany, and the unification of that country is as yet unaccomplished. Great Britain continues her loose association with the nations of Western Europe, but refuses a formal connection. Meanwhile, efforts are being made for an economic and political integration of Western Europe. America has maintained and increased her prosperity, but many Europeans fear the extreme anti-communist trend of some of the most vocal American leaders, lest such attitudes should hinder the achievement of peaceful coexistence. The exporting countries, particularly Britain, are beginning to experience the rigors of the fierce struggle for markets which they must win or die.

In this period, the nations which have newly won their independence have been struggling to develop their national life. This has led in some cases to extreme national sensitivity. The modern world presents the sharply contrasting pictures of intense national pride, and yet persistent desire to develop the influence of international institutions.

Among the free societies, the promotion and practice of basic human rights, social, racial, economic and religious, have become a public concern. The pursuit of their fuller attainment has brought into stronger light the obvious fact that there are too few commonly accepted principles of international conduct and morality.

This in brief is the world in which the ecumenical movement has pursued its international witness. Prior to a survey of the substance of this witness, some consideration must first be given to the question of Christian responsibility in international affairs.

B. Christian Responsibility

The question of personal and corporate responsibility of Christians in international affairs has been treated in successive ecumenical conferences. It remains of general concern.

Major attention has been devoted to Christian responsibility among the European Churches, and particularly in Germany. The Evangelical Church of Germany (EKD) in May, 1949, emphasized the importance of Christian laymen taking an active part in the tasks of political life. The Bishop's Conference of the United Evangelical Lutheran Church (VELKD) in March, 1952, sought to remove misunderstanding of the doctrine of the two realms, pointing out that the earthly order has a responsibility before God. Christians working within the earthly order must bear this in mind.

A working party on issues related to this Survey stated that because God loves the world, Christians must work for peace and world order, avoiding black and white distinctions because of our common guilt before God, and avoiding Utopian and idealistic illusions which mislead. The issue for the Christian is a better, as over against a worse, world order. The protection of peace rests basically on trust and justice, and power means, in the Christian view, only enhanced duty. In another paper, the working party rejects the idea that world peace is a technical or organizational problem. Nevertheless, Christians must help to hold the world together and to secure recognition of the rights of the weak and oppressed, and to prove their trust in and obedience to God's will by co-operating in the tasks of state and society. Christians must help those who work for the establishment of freedom and justice in the world, for this is God's will and command, even though such efforts are not a means to "Christianize" the world and its institutions.

1. *Conditions of Effective Witness.* If the witness of the Church is to be both distinctive and effective, certain conditions must be fulfilled. The Eastern Asia Christian Confer-

ence of December, 1949 (Bangkok), sponsored jointly by the W.C.C. and the I.M.C., stated:

The prophetic witness of the Church in the social and political order depends on the Church being truly a community of persons rooted in the Word of God, that is, worshipping congregations in which human worth and mutual responsibility are acknowledged and realized, and from which love goes out in work of service to the neighbourhood.

The C.C.I.A. Executive in 1951 stressed the same point:

Christians can witness convincingly to peace only if they and their churches, in their relations with one another across all frontiers, put loyalty to their common Lord above any other loyalty.

2. *The Responsibility of Power.* Among American Churches during the past five years, the question of the responsibilities of power has been a major topic. In April, 1949, the Federal Council of the Churches of Christ in America stated:

As Christians we believe that this nation holds its power under the providence of God, to whom all nations are subject. We seek that our nation shall resist both the temptation to use its power irresponsibly and the temptation to flee the responsibility of its power. . . . The corollary of all power is responsibility. Power can corrupt. So, too, it can be made to serve worthy ends. . . . Power is a trust for which we are accountable to God.

Later, laying the burden of responsibility upon the individual Christian, the Council said, "Each one of us, in whose name our government acts, has a personal moral responsibility for the direction and consequences of our foreign policy."

3. *Responsibility for Peace.* The Hungarian Ecumenical Commission, stressing the importance of a Biblical orientation, stated that Christians are bound as a Church, in which the children of the various nations are united in one Body, to work for a relaxation of present tensions, and the peaceful co-operation of the nations. Churches in Japan have empha-

sized the importance of spiritual transformation as a basis
for peace. The National Christian Council of Japan said in
March, 1952: "We Christians believe that the foundation of
world peace rests on the spiritual awakening of every nation." The relationship between peace and justice was underscored in the report on "The Church and International Disorder" presented to the Synod of the Reformed Church of
France in June, 1950. Pointing out that there can be no peace
without justice, and no justice without peace, the report said
that peace will be the work of justice (Isaiah), while the
fruit of justice is sown in peace (James).

4. *Contribution to an International Ethos.* Another aspect
of Christian responsibility, that of contributing to the building up of an international ethos, has received increasing
attention in recent years. At Madras, the statement had been
made that "in the Gospel men must seek the spiritual and
moral basis for ordering national life and international relations." The Oxford Conference asserted that Christians have
a duty "to do all that in us lies to bring Caesar—the traditions and practices of government—to the recognition of his
duty to God." But the lack of a common foundation among
the nations of moral and spiritual principles has become increasingly evident in recent years. The Conference on the
Foundations of International Law convened at Bossey in
April, 1950, pointed out that whereas classical international
law developed "among a plurality of equal nations all acknowledging much the same binding tradition," new large
blocs of powers face one another with "hardly any common
ethos binding them to one another."

In this connection the British Council of Churches have
stressed "the overseas service of the Churches . . . to proclaim the Gospel and lay the spiritual foundation on which
alone a just and peaceful order of society may be established." The Congregational Union of England and Wales
said in May, 1951, that "there can be no world peace until
both East and West acknowledge the existence of a law

higher than that prescribed by their own emphases and interests." The Hungarian Ecumenical Commission, on the
other hand, argues that no international ethos is needed for
international reconciliation (i.e., for a "temporal, relative and
provisional reconciliation"), for the cross of Jesus Christ has
provided all the necessary conditions. The Commission also
points out that God may use for His own ends those that
do not know Him.

III

CHRISTIAN WITNESS IN
INTERNATIONAL AFFAIRS

A. INTERNATIONAL ORDER

The need to bring the tangled relations of nations under the rule of law has remained a major concern of Christian groups. While little has been said on the subject of world government or the problems of international law, a number of statements stress the obligation of nations to pool part of their sovereignty in international organization. The idea of any surrender of sovereignty is criticized by the Hungarian Commission: "The end of this road . . . would be that the smaller, weaker, poorer nations would come under the subjugation of the richer, better armed countries." The Bossey Conference on the foundations of International Law in April, 1950, urged the churches to "rouse the nations and their governments to a consciousness of their duty to establish a just and lasting code of international law."

1. *The United Nations.* While much consideration has been given by Christian leaders to substantive issues before the United Nations and its related agencies, and beneficial contacts have been established with international officials and government representatives, less attention has been given to underlying questions of postwar international organization.

Within the ecumenical movement, the strongest support for the U.N. has come from the American Churches. The U. S. National Council, while not pressing the case for any pooling of sovereignty in the U.N., has given increasing attention to the problem of collective security, and has urged the widest possible use of Peace Observer Commissions. Similar concern

9

about strengthening the U.N. has been manifested in the deliberations of churches in Great Britain, Australia, Canada, and elsewhere. European Churches, on the other hand, have paid less attention to the U.N., for a number of reasons.

In a statement entitled "Christians Look at the United Nations," the C.C.I.A. Executive Committee in August, 1953, stressed the substantial contributions of the U.N. despite the handicaps under which it is forced to operate, such as the difficulties of co-operation among sovereign states, the abuse of the veto, the tendency of representatives to look at international questions on the basis of national or ideological interest rather than merit:

Nevertheless, the United Nations, as well as related agencies including the International Court of Justice, provides the nations with an instrument for the development of international law, the just regulation of common interests of nations as well as for the peaceful settlement of disputes, and the discouragement of threats to peace. It also provides a world forum for the interchange of thought between diverse cultures and viewpoints. Through such cooperation these institutions offer now an effective means of developing conditions essential to the rule of law in the world.

Moreover, the United Nations offers the best means for coordinating the activities of the nations for human welfare. Through its related organizations it is rendering valuable service in combatting ignorance, want and disease, especially in underdeveloped territories. It is helping to create a common mind on the subject of human rights, and to provide those services essential for refugees and migrants.

Therefore, the United Nations needs and deserves the discerning and active support of Christians. The valid purposes of the Charter can be served neither by Utopian illusions nor by irresponsible defeatism, but only by the constructive support of all people of good will. The tremendous task of developing effective international machinery cannot be performed within a few years, but only by the patient and cumulative effort of generations. To aid in this task is a Christian duty.

The question of Charter revision, scheduled for discussion in the General Assembly in 1955, has received increasing attention. The C.C.I.A. Executive in August, 1953, called for Christian alertness to guard against steps which would weaken the Charter or to encourage revisions which would strengthen it. The Executive stressed the need for a new confidence and a sound moral foundation for any fundamental revision. It also stated:

> The present structure is flexible enough to permit more adequate procedures if public opinion can be sufficiently informed and aroused. The growth of the United Nations requires fuller cooperation on the part of member states in honouring their common commitment.
>
> We therefore call on Christians everywhere to study, pray, and work for a better fulfillment of the purposes of the United Nations Charter.

2. *The Christian and War.* A specific issue of international order on which Christians remain divided is that of participation in the use of armed force. While there is agreement and common effort to help prevent war and promote the conditions that make for peace, little headway can be reported in this area, particularly with regard to a re-examination of underlying theological issues.

Representatives of the "Historic Peace Churches" issued in July, 1951, a symposium entitled *War is Contrary to the Will of God.* "Our conclusion," states the latter document, "is that the Church must reject war, not merely because of the disorder, waste or suffering which it causes, but far more because it is contrary to the will of God."

The W.C.C. Central Committee, on the other hand, in July, 1950 (with two dissents on pacifist grounds), commended the United Nations for its prompt decision "to meet this aggression (in Korea) and for authorizing a police measure which every member nation should support." At the national level, the report of the Dun Commission of the Federal Council of Churches (U.S.A.) in November, 1950, on "The Christian Conscience and Weapons of Mass Destruction" may be quoted:

There can be no justice for man and no responsible freedom without law and order. . . . The law which gives any just order must be sustained by power, and, when necessary, by coercive power. . . . Can we extend the beginnings of this order in the United Nations, if we do not undergird it with effective power? . . . In the last resort, we are in conscience bound to turn to force in defence of justice even though we know that the destruction of human life is evil. There are times when this can be the lesser of two evils, forced upon us by our common failure to achieve a better relationship.

B. The Prevention of War

In the face of the mounting international crisis, Christians have been obliged to consider not only broad objectives of international order but also concrete issues which threaten the peace.

1. *The Dominant Conflict.* The massive conflict which has dominated international life since World War II, and the danger of a global holocaust have been constant concerns of the ecumenical movement in the period under review. This conflict has been seen as a clash of ideologies, a confrontation of social systems, and a struggle for power. In 1949, a special conference on existing tensions was convened at Bossey, and its report, as emended by the C.C.I.A. Executive Committee, included the following judgments:

i. The Amsterdam Assembly refused to equate the Christian cause with any of the political or social ideologies or systems.

ii. Communism creates a specific problem for the Churches because it claims to provide a complete answer to all questions of life. . . . The first answer of the Church to communism must be the renewal of the Church itself. . . .

viii. The Church must resist the danger of exploitation for political and propagandist purposes by both sides.

ix. Every possible effort must be made to maintain the ecumenical fellowship between the Churches in the areas under different political systems. . . . Through the unity of the Church, God speaks to a divided world.

The Central Committee of the W.C.C. in July, 1949, condemned totalitarian doctrine and methods in blunt language:

> Justice in human society is not to be won by totalitarian methods. The totalitarian doctrine is a false doctrine. It teaches that in order to gain a social or political end, everything is permitted. It maintains the complete self-sufficiency of man. It puts political power in the place of God. It denies the existence of absolute moral standards. It moulds the minds of the young in a pattern opposed to the message of the Gospel. It sanctions the use of all manner of means to overthrow all other views and ways of life.

In similar fashion, the Bangkok Conference distinguished between "the social revolution which seeks justice and the totalitarian ideology which interprets and perverts it."

While condemning totalitarian ideology, the ecumenical agencies have sought to curb the menace of a new general war, stemming from the clash of social and power systems. The idea that war is inevitable, and even more the idea of a preventive war, have been condemned. It has been argued that the ideological conflict cannot be settled by war, and that the clash of interests need not and must not. On the other hand, attempts to extend domination and tyranny have been equally condemned. Thus the C.C.I.A. Executive in 1951 stated:

> As Christians it is our duty to seek both peace and justice. We no less than others detest war, and we shall do everything in our power to prevent present tensions and limited conflicts from leading to a third world war. Yet we must neither purchase peace at the price of tyranny nor in the name of justice look on war as a way to justice or as a ground of hope.
>
> We stand opposed to every form of oppression and aggression. We condemn any extension of oppression, carried on behind a façade of propaganda for peace. We condemn equally the proposal of a preventive war, or the use for aggressive purposes of atomic weapons.

Major emphasis has been placed on keeping open the doors of negotiation. The W.C.C. Executive Committee in February,

1950 appealed for "a gigantic new effort for peace" and urged "the governments to enter into negotiation once again."

Many National Councils of Churches (e.g., in Great Britain and the U.S.A.) have stressed the importance of patience and perseverance in negotiations with the Soviet Union. The Hungarian Ecumenical Commission, pointing out that the root of the word *eirene* means "to speak again with each other," states: "This is the way of peace; speak again, speak repeatedly with each other until a settlement is reached." The Netherlands Reformed Church in July, 1952, said that for the sake of freedom, the nation chooses the side of the West, without unreservedly accepting all the ideologies and practices of the West. But ecumenical ties all over the world must be maintained, and the Church must insist on a spirit of reconciliation among the nations.

2. *Korea*. When war broke out in Korea, the W.C.C. Central Committee at its Toronto meeting in July, 1950, was outspoken in its condemnation of aggression, and supported the action taken by the United Nations, though this evoked a number of strongly worded protests from groups in such countries as France, Hungary and China. The Committee attached outstanding importance to the role of the U.N. Commission in Korea as a means of identifying the fact of aggression. The Committee also stressed the need for efforts to secure "a just settlement by negotiation and conciliation." The Bièvres letter issued by the Executive Committee in February, 1951, expressed gratitude that "through the United Nations, the lines of negotiations have been kept open and that it continues to seek an honorable and generally acceptable reconciliation."

The W.C.C. has persistently opposed any extension of the war in Korea. When the Korean truce negotiations became deadlocked over the prisoner-of-war issue, the Director of the C.C.I.A. put forward "A Plan for Deferred Action on Prisoners of War in Korea." The resolution approved by the U.N. Assembly in December, 1952, and used in subsequent negotiations included principles stressed in this memorandum. Finally, when it was feared that prospects for a truce might founder on misunderstandings between the government of the Republic of Korea and the U.N. Command, the C.C.I.A. Director flew to Korea for consultations with leaders in church and government circles, including President Syngman Rhee and Mr. Walter Robertson, in the interests of mutual understanding and agreement. In its first meeting after the conclusion of a truce, the W.C.C. Executive Committee stressed the "critical problems of political unification and effective rehabilitation by processes of negotiation and reconstruction."

3. *Germany.* The problem of a divided Germany, while of broad ecumenical concern, has been for the German Churches an insistent issue bound up with the mounting tensions among the Great Powers. In April, 1949, the Fellowship of Christian Churches in Germany declared:

Behind the divisions of power politics there are conflicting philosophies, the one making freedom an idol, the other collective society. In this age we have to strive for the right middle way between anarchy and tyranny, but not for any of these idols.

In October, 1949, the Synod of the EKD stated:

We are not able to prescribe to the responsible politicians the decisions they have to make, nor to take these decisions from them. But we ask them not to leave any way untried which may lead to reconciliation, nor to create any further facts by which the division of our nation with its disastrous consequences for the whole world threatens to become established forever.

In April, 1950, the Synod of the EKD said:

We urge all members of our nation to avoid the spirit of hatred and enmity. Don't let yourselves be made instruments of a propaganda by which enmity between the nations is promoted and war is prepared, nor instruments of any peace propaganda, which in fact is sowing hatred and making for war! Don't be led into the illusion that our distress could be removed by war.

4. *Japan.* The Churches of Japan have likewise been pre-occupied with problems of a peace settlement. In 1951, representatives of the National Christian Council presented an expression of their views to the U.S. Ambassador at Large, stressing the importance of the Japanese constitutional renunciation of war, and the economic plight of postwar Japan. In the U.S.A., the Council of Churches in June, 1949, pressed again for "an early peace settlement with Japan" and in June, 1951, urged prompt U.S. ratification of the Treaty of Peace with Japan. The C.C.I.A. Executive supported the "quality of reconciliation" embodied in the draft Treaty.

5. *The Near East.* Recognizing the tension that exists in the Near East as an aftermath of the Palestine War, the Beirut Conference in 1951 expressed its conviction that a satisfactory solution to the Arab refugee problem could only be found within the framework of an international settlement of Near East problems. It urged the repatriation or resettlement of the refugees, the speedy release of "frozen" assets, the prompt payment of compensation, and more adequate and effective international guarantees of frontiers. In the absence of any satisfactory political solution, tension between Arabs and Jews continues to mount. The C.C.I.A. Executive in August, 1953, stressed again the importance of just over-all political and economic solutions, if the problems of Arab refugees are to be met.

6. *Regional Arrangements.* The growth of regional pacts against the background of international tensions and insecurity has asserted a claim for attention. In April, 1949, the U.S. Federal Council of Churches expressed the view:

Regional pacts can add to the total of common security if they are genuinely within the universal framework of the United Nations; if they are based upon a natural community of interest and are in fact designed and operated to preserve and to promote the general welfare of the participating nations. Such pacts can on the other hand add to insecurity if their words conceal what is essentially a military alliance which might validly appear to others to be aggressive.

The main focus of attention has been upon various efforts to develop West European or European unity or union, and an unofficial group of Christian laymen from some twelve European countries has met as a Committee on Christian Responsibility for European Co-operation to study these issues. The British Council of Churches included European unity as one of the seven objectives in its statement on "Christians and World Order," while the Church and Nation Committee of the Church of Scotland has more than once referred to the importance of close relations. The Ecumenical Council of Churches in the Netherlands has stressed the role of the churches in the life of Europe today, so that Europe may be inspired afresh with the living faith that is her heritage, and thus reach deeper levels of unity.

The Philippine Federation of Christian Churches has spoken of its interest in a Pacific Union, while the Federal Council of Churches of the U.S.A. in 1949 urged the importance of U.S. co-operation with the U.N. Economic Commission for Asia and the Far East.

C. DISARMAMENT

Both on grounds of principle and in view of existing tensions Christians have been impelled to press for a genuine international reduction and regulation of armaments though often without a thorough analysis of the problems involved. Numerous churchmen in Eastern Europe have urged the necessity of international outlawry of atomic and bacteriological weapons. The Synod of the French Reformed Church in 1950 called for disarmament, progressive and complete, under rigorous international controls, beginning with atomic and bacteriological weapons. In February, 1951, the Rhenish Evangelical Church raised the question whether German rearmament would serve the cause of peace, as it would result in two hostile German camps. The same month, the W.C.C. Executive Committee at Bièvres expressed the urgent Christian concern that "armaments, whatever their necessity, do not dominate the whole life of national and international society" and pressed for "the objective of bringing all national armaments under international control."

In the U.S.A., not only the "Historic Peace Churches" but several of the larger denominational agencies as well have maintained an active concern in disarmament, often linked with opposition to compulsory military training. In February, 1948, the Federal Council declared:

In present conditions of international anarchy, where international law and international police power are lacking, national military strength is necessary, while we continually strive for the multilateral reduction and control of armaments through the United Nations.

Other Churches (e.g., in Great Britain and the Philippines) have adopted resolutions on the subject of disarmament. In Japan, church leaders are wrestling with the problem of rearmament at the expense of revising the postwar "peace constitution." The Ecumenical Study Conference at Lucknow in December, 1952, reflected the thinking of many church leaders in East Asia:

Large-scale rearmament reduces the capacity of the more developed countries to help the underdeveloped economies of East Asia. At the same time world tensions force the countries of East Asia to spend a disproportionate amount of their budget for defence and thus reduce the resources available for social development.

In similar terms, the W.C.C. Executive Committee at Bièvres in February, 1951, stated that "one of the gravest dilemmas the nations are in consists in the danger that rearmament will itself drain the vigour out of social reconstruction."

1. *Essential Conditions.* The ecumenical agencies have continually stressed the importance of taking moral and political factors into account, if the technical problems of disarmament are to be solved, and also of building mutual confidence and trustworthy collective security as essential conditions for the reduction and control of armaments. Thus the C.C.I.A. Executive stated in 1950:

The outlawing of atomic weapons is not enough; peace requires a workable means of restraining every aggressor, no matter whether he uses atomic or other instruments of destruction, or measures of coercion or infiltration. Any plan to outlaw atomic weapons must be based upon effective measures of inspection, and any system of inspection must provide for *continuous* international supervision.

Similarly the statement "Christians Stand for Peace" reads:

We do not believe that peace will come merely by new pacts or disarmament. There must first be sufficient mutual trust and good faith between nations to ensure that agreements will be honoured. Peace and disarmament will follow from mutual trust; they will not automatically create it.

In 1950, the W.C.C. Executive Committee, meeting at Bossey, warned of the "crescendo of warfare which has changed war . . . to a mass murder of human life." It urged governments not only to take the initiative in inaugurating international consultations for the international control of armaments, but to give tangible evidence of their sincerity and good faith. They should be prepared both to take reasonable risks in order to secure international agreement, and to delegate their sovereign authority to international agencies as required for effective multilateral control of armaments.

While the ecumenical agencies have not attempted any specialized study of disarmament, the C.C.I.A. Officers in February, 1951, put forward provisionally certain conditions as necessary for the progressive reduction and eventual abolition of national armaments. They looked forward to the day when an "international combined force" under the U.N. would safeguard any state against aggression, and enforce international law. Progressive reduction of armaments to that end could be inaugurated. As an interim measure, the U.N. might assess by international inspection the existing level of weapons and fighting forces and of potential production of armaments. In addition states could agree on partial and occasional measures for the reduction of available armaments, thus building up mutual confidence in place of distrust. Any disarmament measure presupposes effective and continuous inspection and control under the U.N.

At the Sixth Session of the U.N. General Assembly, the C.C.I.A. Director stressed the claim that "the reduction of armaments is not an arithmetic proposition but a political and, above all, a moral problem." He said:

If there is to be provision for verified assurances that atomic weapons will not be used, there must also be provision for verified assurance that powerful nations will permit peoples in all countries freely to choose their own forms of government, to determine their own policies, and to bring about changes by peaceful means and with the preservation of freedom.

2. *U.N. Observer Commissions.* The value of the U.N. Commission in Korea in identifying an act of aggression led the Officers of the C.C.I.A. in August, 1950, to propose to church leaders in Member States of the U.N. a plan whereby the U.N. General Assembly should set up a system of International Observer Commissions, to provide teams of Observers for all areas which constitute a special and urgent international responsibility, and to make such teams available upon the request of any government which fears aggression of any kind. The response to this proposal was reflected in representations made to several governments. The main elements of the plan were subsequently incorporated in the "Uniting for Peace" resolution approved overwhelmingly by the U.N. General Assembly on November 3, 1950. The section on the Peace Observation Commission was approved unanimously.

In the Bièvres letter of February, 1951, the W.C.C. Executive Committee stated that "U.N. Peace Observer Commissions ought to be placed at every danger spot," while in July, 1952, the C.C.I.A. Executive urged "governments to make use of the services of the U.N. Peace Observation Commission, both as a possible deterrent to aggression, and in the event that aggression occurs, as a means to subordinate to international judgment the decision to take defensive military action" and authorized "representatives of the C.C.I.A. to encourage the establishment of additional Sub-Commissions (besides that in the Balkans) as appropriate and necessary."

D. REFUGEES AND MIGRATION

Long before its formal establishment in 1948, the World Council of Churches was grappling with the spiritual and material needs of those uprooted by war. In July, 1949, the Central Committee called upon member Churches to use their influence on behalf of continued and increasing national and intergovernmental action for refugees. The relief activities of the W.C.C. Department of Inter-Church Aid and Service to Refugees and of other Christian agencies fall outside the scope of this Survey, but their humanitarian work gives substance to the Christian appeal for intergovernmental action on a problem whose long-term, if not permanent, character is now accepted.

At the Willingen meeting of the I.M.C. the Committee expressed the general point of view of the ecumenical agencies on the subject of the refugees in the following terms:

The Churches should continue alert to the needs of these persons and to the responsibility for introducing them to new faith as well as new homes and neighbours.

In April, 1950, the Netherlands Reformed Church, in addition to urging prayers for D.P.s and other refugees, appealed for homes for older refugees, while the Norwegian Institute reports that the churches there are trying to make a contribution to the solution of the refugee problem. British church bodies have stressed the necessity of giving high priority to cooperation in regard to refugees. The C.C.I.A. has lent its support to measures for sustaining the work of the U.N. Children's Fund (UNICEF).

1. *The High Commissioner*. In July, 1950, the Central Committee reminded "all Christian people of their inescapable obligation to stand by those who through no fault of their own

have lost home and country," and protested against national policies which are steadily increasing the number of innocent citizens uprooted and set adrift. It called the refugee problem "a judgment upon our whole society."

At this meeting the Committee urged the C.C.I.A. to seek such modifications in the arrangements for the office of the High Commissioner for Refugees as would enable it to deal with refugees who are homeless but not stateless; to accept voluntary contributions to its budget; and to tackle the whole refugee problem, with all forms of discrimination on grounds of nationality removed. Changes in the draft statute reflected a number of the improvements sought by the C.C.I.A.

At the Sixth Session of the U.N. General Assembly in 1951-52, the C.C.I.A. Officers endeavored to strengthen still further the powers and authority of the High Commissioner. The Seventh Session of the Assembly expressed hope for further contributions to the fund for emergency aid for refugees and reiterated its appeal for giving refugees "every possible opportunity in and benefit from projects to promote migration."

The Department of Inter-Church Aid, the Lutheran World Federation, the Y.M.C.A. and the Y.W.C.A. were designated among the first operating agencies through which the Voluntary Fund has been used to help meet refugee needs.

2. *German Refugees*. The German Churches have been preoccupied with the staggering problems of German refugees, expellees, war prisoners and internees. In April, 1950, the EKD issued a plea that the prisoners and internees be returned from Russia. A Conference on the German refugee problem held in Hamburg in February, 1949, under the auspices of the W.C.C., and attended by representatives of the Occupying Powers and German governments as well as of the Churches, initiated certain concerted actions of a remedial character.

3. *Palestine Refugees*. In November, 1949, the C.C.I.A. expressed to the fifty-nine delegations at the U.N. Assembly its concern for a solution of the Palestine refugee problem and urged adequate financial support for their relief. The Assembly

voted to secure fifty-four million dollars for this purpose. In May, 1951, the Department of Inter-Church Aid and the I.M.C. convened a Conference at Beirut, which requested the C.C.I.A. in co-operation with National Commissions of the Churches to consult with governments and the United Nations, with a view not only to an adequate service of relief to the refugees, but also to a just and satisfactory solution to their problem. It urged, also, that the activities of the U.N. and of the voluntary agencies should be correlated. The C.C.I.A. subsequently gave its support to a three-year plan presented by the Director and Advisory Committee of the Palestine Relief Agency, as being in line with the Beirut recommendations. The plan was approved by the General Assembly.

The C.C.I.A. has continued to urge that the U.N. with full support of Member States should provide financial resources for a program of resettlement and reintegration, and that, without prejudice to any ultimate solution of the problem, adequate provision should be made for continuing relief services. As a result of the Beirut Conference, the contributions of member Churches to the relief program have been quadrupled, thus enabling the NECC Committee for Refugee Relief to expand its activities.

4. *Korean Reconstruction.* Liaison has been maintained by the C.C.I.A. with the U.N. relief and reconstruction agency in Korea pending the achievement of conditions which would allow a planned and integrated civilian relief program. In January, 1953, officers of the C.C.I.A. visited Korea to consult with officials concerning the churches' contribution to that program. In August, 1953, the W.C.C. Executive urged upon the member Churches "their obligation to participate fully in all intergovernmental relief measures, and themselves to support through Christian liberality the Relief Committee of the National Christian Council of Korea in making its vital Christian contribution to the work of national reconstruction."

5. *Migration.* Through its adviser on refugee problems, the C.C.I.A. has played an active part in intergovernmental and

non-governmental conferences dealing with the complex problem of migration. The Churches in the U.S.A. have also been occupied with this question. In 1952-53 leaders of the National Council joined with leaders of other religious bodies in successfully championing emergency legislation to complete the Displaced Persons Program by the admission of more than 200,000 persons. Also in 1952 the National Council urged that revision of U.S. immigration and naturalization laws "conform with our democratic tradition and with our heritage as a defender of human rights." The C.C.I.A. Executive in August, 1953, expressed the hope that "governments of countries of immigration will provide, either by special legislation or priority selection, more adequate opportunities for the resettlement of refugees in their countries."

E. THE ADVANCEMENT OF DEPENDENT PEOPLES

One of the most significant factors in the present world situation, and one that is fraught with the greatest potentialities for good or evil, is the recent acquisition of political independence by nations hitherto under the control of one of the Western powers or under some form of mandate or trusteeship. The Bangkok Conference of December, 1949, found both good and evil potentialities in the revolutionary situation in Asia. It noted "tendencies to nihilism and totalitarianism," as well as creative elements. It said: "The struggle for and the attainment of political freedom has awakened the hitherto submerged peoples of East Asia to a new sense of dignity and historical mission."

1. *Political and Social Advancement.* The ecumenical agencies have given increasing attention to the problem of promoting both the political advancement and the well-being of subject peoples. At Chichester in 1949 the W.C.C. Central Committee reaffirmed the findings of Section IV at Amsterdam:

We oppose aggressive imperialism—political, economic or cultural—whereby a nation seeks to use other nations or peoples for its own ends. We, therefore, protest against the exploitation of non-self-governing peoples for selfish purposes; and retarding of their progress to self-government; and discrimination or segregation on the ground of race or colour. . . .

On the same occasion, the Chairman of the C.C.I.A. stressed the fact that more than the question of self-government was involved. Each nation must be encouraged to develop its own talents and gifts, and be protected against abuses and against unchristian methods and feelings of superiority on the part of individuals as well as of groups and states.

The W.C.C. Central Committee at Toronto in 1950 noted how easy it was for the "resentments of subject peoples" to be exploited by postwar totalitarianism, and stated that action to overcome the injustices and disorders so exploited was "the most important means of rendering the world morally impregnable to totalitarian penetration."

The Ecumenical Study Conference at Lucknow in December, 1952, emphasized the same general principles:

1. As members of countries which have struggled for freedom and self-determination, the Christian in East Asia is bound to support the genuine movement of national freedom and social justice. Therefore it is necessary to demand that the Colonial Powers recognize unequivocally the right of these nations to self-determination, and to set up machinery for the transfer of power satisfactory to the democratic conscience of Asian peoples and within the structure of international law.

2. There is an obligation for the Colonial Powers to see that national liberation is achieved in a democratic framework, without the movement falling into the hands of Communism.

3. The peril of the present military situation is that on the one hand defence against Communism might become a means of suppressing the movement of national liberation and social justice in the country, and on the other hand the national liberation movements are in danger of being exploited by world Communism and abusive tyrannies.

The Hungarian Ecumenical Commission, on the other hand, asserts that the appeal of communism to oppressed and struggling peoples is "established by the logic of facts." The Commission maintains that all peoples are "entitled to *full* human dignity, that is, national independence, autonomy, freedom and freedom from want."

In line with its Charter objective, the C.C.I.A. has followed closely the work of the U.N. Trusteeship Council and the General Assembly's Committee on Information from non-self-governing Territories. On the issue of the international status of Southwest Africa, the C.C.I.A. supported reference of the question to the International Court of Justice. In the U.S.A., the Churches have been primarily concerned that the U.S. should demonstrate sympathy for, and solidarity with, the aspirations of non-self-governing peoples. The importance of the U.N. Trusteeship System has also been stressed by the U.S. Churches.

2. *The British Commonwealth.* The Churches of the United Kingdom have devoted more attention than those elsewhere to the problems of dependent peoples. In the statement on "Christians and World Affairs," the British Council of Churches urged as an objective: "to support and apply the principle of partnership in all relationships, official and personal, with other members of the multiracial Commonwealth to which we belong." In reference to the South African claim to the three High Commission Territories, it has stated that there should be no transfer except with the consent of the inhabitants. It regards the new scheme of Central African Federation as a test of good will. Much, it says, depends upon how the plan is operated. Good intentions should be demonstrated through the removal of discriminatory legislation. The International Department has recommended the sending of a mission of fellowship to the Churches of Central Africa.

3. *Indonesia.* The Synod of the Netherlands Reformed Church has given much attention to the question of relations with Indonesia. In its letter of September 22, 1948, to the Council of Ministers, it said "a solution of the problems by means of arms would inevitably become a source of many

difficulties in the future" and that "the spiritual damage has now been done." Again it stated: "We confess that we as Church and People in our relationship with the peoples of Indonesia have pursued our own profit rather than loving them as our neighbors." The Netherlands people and the Netherlands government must make every effort "to restore confidence." We profess "our oneness with the Churches in Indonesia, who profess the same Lord and Savior."

4. *French Overseas Territories*. The French Reformed Church has taken an active interest in the status of the local inhabitants in Madagascar and Indo-China, as well as in Morocco and Tunisia. In watching political developments, it is following carefully the interests of the peoples concerned.

5. *The Near East*. The leaders of the Orthodox Churches in the Near East have for generations championed the cause of national independence, or the right of the Christian minorities in Muslim lands. In Cyprus today the church leaders are active in the movement for union with Greece. Arab Christians, while apprehensive of Muslim rule, have joined in the protest of their fellow countrymen against the policy of the Western powers in Palestine and the Near East countries.

F. ECONOMIC AND TECHNICAL CO-OPERATION

Independence alone cannot meet the needs of dependent peoples. Action on the economic and social front is equally important. Speaking of the "vast upsurge of peoples," as an explosive element in the situation, the W.C.C. Executive Committee in February, 1951, said:

Over 700 million people formerly dependent have recently attained independence. Other peoples are still seeking independence. At the same time the widespread and rightful demand for equality of personal status and for release from poverty and economic oppression remains unmet. Little wonder that the offer of civil rights and freedoms loses its appeal when people are wholly obsessed by the daily struggle against hunger and want.

1. *Technical Assistance.* The sharing of technical knowledge and skills has long been an element in the missionary work of the Churches as well as in the policy of some colonial powers. The concept of technical aid as an intergovernmental function and obligations is relatively new. It has now become a major concern of the C.C.I.A. which maintains consultative relations with the Food and Agriculture Organization, UNESCO, and the technical assistance agencies of the United Nations.

The part that Christians, individually and corporately, can play in this field of technical assistance has been indicated by the ecumenical agencies. The enlarged meeting of the I.M.C. held at Willingen in July, 1952, spoke of "the duty of Christians everywhere to encourage and assist the governments concerned in programs for raising the standards of living of the hungry and under-privileged areas of the world." It urged governments and other agencies offering technical assistance:

1. To recognize the fundamental rights and the cultural heritage of the peoples served.

2. To give attention, in selecting technical experts, not only to professional qualifications but also to the moral and spiritual requirements of the work they do.

3. To cooperate with nations already engaged in working for technical and welfare services, and to foster their training and development.

4. To concentrate effort upon those fundamental improvements which will enable the people to help themselves.

5. To include in the capital estimates for any given project an item for the provision of needed welfare services.

6. To avoid any confusion of long-range technical aid with mutual obligations for defence.

In similar terms, the C.C.I.A. Executive in July-August, 1951, said:

Perhaps the chief task of Christians and Christian agencies is to help create and sustain the favourable moral climate necessary for sound technical assistance programmes. A further task in the more developed countries is to help qualified laymen to find vocations and to accept employment in this field. We urge Christians and Christian agencies to study the implications of the new undertakings for their own life and work, as well as for the advancement of a positive peace strategy.

The W.C.C. Central Committee at Lucknow in January, 1953, defined the function of the Churches as follows:

Churches all over the world must ask how they can help the people of Asia in their efforts to obtain a standard of living which meets basic human needs, and in their search for a more just social and economic order. The Church in Asia has the crucial task of helping to provide the true moral and spiritual dynamic for the peoples longing for social justice and peace. Without this dynamic their longing cannot be realized and may easily be betrayed by false hopes.

The Churches in the more developed countries must urge their peoples and Governments to do everything possible to strengthen programmes of technical assistance, without which such efforts in Asia cannot succeed.

The Norwegian Institute for Inter-Church Relations reports that church authorities wholeheartedly support the plan launched by the Norwegian Parliament, whereby a fund of 20 million crowns for technical assistance in India is being raised both by government grant and voluntary contributions. The Philippine Federation reports appreciation of technical assistance and the help of the Specialized Agencies. Reports from India reveal that projects under Christian auspices are making a large contribution to development plans, whose challenge and scope concern the churches very closely.

2. *Specific Proposals.* The C.C.I.A. Executive Committee in July, 1952, in its statement on "Christian Concerns in Food and Agriculture," referred to the need for safeguards of social welfare, just solutions of problems of land tenure and debt; the availability of labor-saving technological processes; fundamental education; the promotion of voluntary co-operation; expanded production; and the conservation, reclamation and improvement of the soil. The Committee also pointed out that

"resources now available are insufficient to meet the immense needs" and urged better integration of projects at the field level; a longer-range evaluation of program planning, the greater use of literature, and a more adequate procedure for consultation and co-operation between U.N. technical assistance agencies and non-governmental agencies.

The U.S. Churches have devoted more attention than others to the subject of aid to underdeveloped countries as "a positive program for peace." In the spring of 1950, a special conference was convened to consider the question of voluntary co-operation of Christian agencies with the technical assistance programs. Similarly in Great Britain the Council of Churches urged support to efforts to give social and economic assistance to the peoples of Asia and Africa through colonial development schemes and the Colombo Plan "even if it means reducing standards of living in this country."

The C.C.I.A. Executive in August, 1953, emphasized the need for better integration of multilateral and bilateral assistance schemes, the further development of the resident representative system to provide co-operative centers at the field level, full co-operation with local inhabitants, and more serious efforts to provide the financial support for the sound and steady growth of technical assistance programs "urgently needed as an earnest of the world's concern for social reconstruction."

3. *Economic Assistance.* The U.S. Federal Council of Churches gave its support to the Marshall Plan as a potential affirmation of "faith in the curative power of freedom and in the creative capacity of free men." It warned against any hampering of European co-operation or East-West trade. Christian agencies in the U.S. have consistently supported the Reciprocal Trade Agreements Program. Mention may also be made here of the National Council's action in January, 1951, urging emergency food aid to India "on such terms as may be mutually acceptable to the two governments."

The Ecumenical Study Conference at Lucknow in December, 1952, made a number of proposals for reform of land tenure, the development of unutilized land, and the provision of credit to counteract the power of the moneylender. It also recognized the need for family planning and national and international redistribution of population. In regard to problems of economic assistance, the Conference said:

In the first place, people in industrial countries must realize that their economic assistance to the underdeveloped countries on an adequate scale is a matter of social justice i.e. arising out of a concern for man in his needs wherever he lives and as a response to human solidarity. In order to encourage the flow of foreign private capital it will be necessary for the governments of East Asia to agree on a principle of proper compensation in case of nationalization.

The C.C.I.A. Executive in August, 1953, supported "adequate planning for international financial assistance for economic and social development, particularly when its aim is to help establish conditions in less developed regions which will enlist expanding capital investment, both private and public, both domestic and foreign."

G. Human Rights

In the present international situation world community presupposes the coexistence of a wide variety of cultures, just treatment of minority groups, and the observance without discrimination of basic human rights. So clear was the consensus of opinion of the churches on this subject that it provided the main initial basis for the work of the C.C.I.A. Since Amsterdam, the C.C.I.A. has continuously sought to bring a Christian influence to bear on the recognition of international standards of human rights, and also on specific situations where such rights are violated. The Declaration on Religious Liberty, adopted by the World Council and the International Missionary Council in 1948, continues to guide efforts in this field.

1. *The Commission on Human Rights*. With the support of its parent bodies, the C.C.I.A. has followed closely the work

of the U.N. Commission on Human Rights. It has favored
the giving of the widest possible publicity to the Universal
Declaration of Human Rights. It has supported the new
article on freedom of thought, conscience and religion in the
draft Covenant as well as the draft provision to ensure the
right of parents in determining the education of their children and especially their religious education. It has pressed
for the maintenance unimpaired of the rights of the individual to change his religion or belief. It has urged the need
of some international machinery to protect human rights,
and upheld the right of individual and group petitions. It
has expressed the opinion that international covenants should
be prepared to include economic, social and cultural, as well
as political and civil, rights. And it has supported other measures within the terms of reference of the U.N. Commission
for advancing the observance of human rights through international and national action.

A Study of "Religious Freedom in Face of Dominant
Forces" presented by the C.C.I.A. to the W.C.C. Central
Committee in 1950 called upon the churches to examine
critically their own practices to ensure that they did not conflict with the requirements of religious freedom, and pointed
to the strong position held by the churches in pursuing the
cause of religious freedom by their understanding of the
Gospel and their close-knit world fellowship. It encouraged
a continuing program of education on religious liberty
throughout this world-wide constituency especially at the
parish level, and urged closer consultation with leaders in
other religious communities. It suggested that greater use
might be made of the Universal Declaration both by governments and by church officials. In cases of discrimination, the
report suggested as remedial measures self-scrutiny and self-
improvement, research and report, appeal to religious leaders,
direct appeal to government, friendly intervention by government, intergovernmental action, and publicity.

2. *Specific Cases.* A number of cases involving actual or potential denials of religious freedom and other basic rights have come before the C.C.I.A. and its parent bodies for special consideration. Among them may be mentioned the need for protecting religious interests and activities in Palestine; support for the repatriation of Greek children; representations at the intergovernmental level on behalf of German prisoners of war still held in Eastern Europe; concern over the situation of the Indian minority in the Union of South Africa; and the inclusion of adequate safeguards of human rights in the peace treaties with Japan, Germany and Austria. The C.C.I.A., its parent bodies and several national church groups (e.g., in Great Britain, the U.S.A. and Norway) have made charges of violations of basic rights of Evangelical Christians in Colombia. Regret has been expressed that the governments of Bulgaria, Hungary and Rumania have refused to co-operate in the examination of charges against them of suppression of human rights contrary to the terms of the Peace Treaties. More recently world attention has been called to interference with normal church activities in the Eastern Zone of Germany.

One subject which has received special consideration by the W.C.C. has been that of the treatment of conscientious objectors to war. The Toronto meeting of the Central Committee set up a special subcommittee to study and report on provisions for conscientious objectors in various countries, and replies to a questionnaire have been received from over 40 churches. Several church bodies have called for more humane treatment of C.O.'s.

Among some of the "Younger" Churches, struggling to survive in a hostile environment, as in parts of Asia and Latin America, human rights constitute the one overriding issue for Christian action. In Pakistan, Christians have expressed urgent concern over a reported omission from the draft Constitution of a provision for the right to "propagate" one's faith. Joint Protestant-Roman Catholic representations have helped to secure modifications of the rules governing schools in East Pakistan, in the interests of religious freedom. In India, the National Christian Council has been in touch with the Central Government in regard to the disabilities resulting from a change of faith. In Indonesia, Christian leaders have been pressing for constitutional safeguards of a citizen's right to "change" his faith. In Egypt, both the Inter-Mission Council and the Committee of Liaison between the Communities have frequently intervened with the authorities when legislation was contemplated or passed, or when administrative action was taken, which threatened religious freedom, especially in the field of education. The Philippine Federation reports that any encroachment on religious freedom by the dominant religious group is denounced in the press.

In 1950, the Council of EKD issued a strong statement condemning the Iron Curtain and concentration camps, and saying that the unity of Germany cannot be bought at the price of human worth and freedom. At the same time, the Foreign Department of EKD proposed several changes in the text of the draft of the U.N. Covenant on Human Rights, and pointed out that human rights are grounded in God's grace, and that it is for secular authorities to recognize and protect them. Later the Council of EKD denounced anti-Semitism, and made a plea for amnesty and pardon for those still involved in the war trials. In East Germany the courageous witness of the Junge Gemeinde (Young Church) has helped to win a modification of Communist policy.

In Norway, church leaders have supported a bill to remove the regulations which prohibit the entrance of Jesuits into the country. In Holland, the General Synod of the Netherlands Reformed Church, in a call to prayers for all Christians, made special reference to Protestant churches in certain totalitarian countries, the curtailment of religious freedom in some Latin countries, and the "grief and indignity" so often felt by non-European people in South Africa.

In connection with the European Convention on Human

Rights, the International Department of the British Council of Churches has pressed for the recognition of the right of parents to determine the religious education of their children. In December, 1950, concern was expressed by the B.C.C. at the grave oppression of the Roman Catholic Church in Poland. Very considerable publicity has been given by Christian bodies in the U.S.A. and Canada to denials of human rights and particularly of religious liberty. Some U.S. church leaders, in close touch with the C.C.I.A., have been engaged in consultations with certain Roman Catholic leaders with a view to establishing the facts regarding charges of violation of human rights in Colombia. The National Council has taken great interest in the drafting of the U.N. Covenants on Human Rights, and has urged the importance of supporting the Universal Declaration with vigorous educational programs. In an extensive statement on "The Churches and Human Rights" issued in 1948, the Federal Council stressed the relation between right and responsibility in the Christian view.

IV

METHODS OF CHRISTIAN ACTION
FOR WORLD COMMUNITY

The preceding chapter has indicated contributions which Christians are seeking to make, or are actually making, in the struggle for world community. The present chapter summarizes procedures which have been regarded in recent years as effective and in accord with the character of the Christian witness. Inevitably it has been found that differing situations both at the international and national level call for differing methods of approach.

A. METHODS AT THE INTERNATIONAL LEVEL

The fact of the ecumenical fellowship is itself a potent factor in bridging the gulf of national and regional differences from which international tensions often arise. A common faith offers not only a common standard for the interpretation of problems, but also a spirit in which solutions can best be sought. Through the proclamation of the Gospel and by programs of education and service Christianity has touched the lives of vast numbers, among whom are many who serve their governments in official capacities. This fact undergirds efforts to bring a Christian influence to bear on international decisions.

The C.C.I.A. has fashioned a general procedure which may be described as a two-way line of communication. On the one hand, it maintains continuing relations with its worldwide Christian constituency, securing advice and transmitting information through the members of the Commission itself, officers of National Commissions, leaders of the constituent Churches and Church Councils, and special correspondents.

36

On the other, it maintains continuing contact with governments, receiving extensive documentation, attending important intergovernmental meetings, and conferring with official delegates and secretariat. It is in close touch with the United Nations, and has consultative relations with the U.N. Economic and Social Council, and with Specialized Agencies, such as UNESCO and FAO. By informal as well as formal means, it is able to submit at the time and place of political decision recommendations from the Churches or their agencies.

For some months prior to the meetings of the U.N. General Assembly the C.C.I.A. endeavors to secure up-to-date information regarding actions taken by its Christian constituency on questions likely to appear on the Assembly's agenda, and a memorandum is then drawn up, summarizing the background history of relevant items on the agenda, and the position taken by the C.C.I.A. Some of these items form the subject of consultation between National Commissions or member Churches and their local governments, as well as between the C.C.I.A. staff and individual delegates to the General Assembly and the U.N. Secretariat. The memorandum is made available to heads of delegations and others interested in the views expressed. Through such means, constructive proposals and points of view are submitted, and support is sought for decisions which the Churches consider of vital importance.

The business of representing the ecumenical movement on international issues is both serious and delicate. Fidelity to the Gospel and to the judgments of a world-wide constituency must be combined with a technical competence which will command the respect of those in official positions. Methods must be tested in the hard school of experience and continuously subjected to criticism. The experience of the past seven years has made it possible to identify certain situations in relation to which particular procedures have been found helpful.

1. *Representation on Agreements.* In cases where a large measure of agreement is evident among Christian leaders on the interpretation of a problem and the procedure for its solution, C.C.I.A. representation can reflect a common mind. Thus, on the question of religious freedom, the C.C.I.A., on the basis of the WC.C.-I.M.C. Declaration on Religious Liberty and a further study in which Christian leaders from many parts of the world participated, was able to make a fairly precise representation.

The initial draft outline for the article on religious freedom, prepared by the U.N. Secretariat, read:

There shall be freedom of conscience and belief, and of private and public religious worship.

The article finally incorporated in the Universal Declaration reads:

Everyone has the right to freedom of thought, conscience and religion; this right includes freedom to change his religion or belief, and freedom, either alone or in community with others and in public or private, to manifest his religion or belief in teaching, practice, worship and observance.

2. *Admission of Disagreements.* There are many international problems on which Christians are divided as to the best solution. In such a case, a frank admission of the different points of view is a service to intergovernmental agencies which tends to increase respect for the reliability of representation. Thus, when the U.N. was drawing up plans for the internationalization of Jerusalem, it soon became apparent that there was no common mind among Christian leaders, and this situation was made known to the U.N. Trusteeship Council to which the planning had been entrusted. What the C.C.I.A. could do was to stress the points on which there was agreement, namely, the need for the guaranteeing of the right of access to the Holy Places, the protection of religious property, and the safeguarding of religious freedom in the current work of the churches.

3. *Exchange of Christian Views.* The judgment of Christians in any particular country is liable to be colored by the national environment, and by the influence of local channels of publicity such as the press and radio. The value of an international Commission of the Churches is that it can help to raise Christian thought to a broader perspective. An example is the visit of the C.C.I.A. Director in June, 1953, to confer with church and governmental leaders in Korea on the desirability of an early armistice on honorable terms.

When the Netherlands used military action in Indonesia, the C.C.I.A. invited representatives in the two countries to draft separate memoranda on the political issues, keeping in mind the Christian communities and responsibilities in both countries. These memoranda were circulated among certain church and political representatives, and indicated a valuable type of Christian action, whether or not a constructive influence was actually exerted on the successful Round Table Conference at The Hague in the Autumn of 1949.

Similar efforts have been undertaken by national Christian groups. Thus a major concern of the Commission on International Affairs of the Protestant Federation of France has been the Franco-German Fraternal Council bringing together French and German churchmen. The British Council of Churches and the U.S. National Council have committees to arrange interchange of preachers, and have recently set up groups in the two countries to correspond on problems vexing Anglo-American relations. The U.S. and Japanese Councils are proposing a similar procedure. There have been exchanges on a Far East settlement between the Australian Churches and those in the U.S.A. and Japan. In 1951, British Friends sent a mission to Moscow to meet with religious and secular leaders. A considerable number of church contacts have been maintained across the Iron Curtain.

Procedures of this kind may prove to be of great value when tensions arise among countries in which there are influential Christian communities. Unfortunately in many areas of tension, substantial Christian communities are lacking.

4. *Simultaneous Impact on Governments.* Occasions arise on which two or more governments are in process of shaping joint policy, and though there may be no immediate danger of conflict, there is urgent need that their common policy be rightly formed. In such circumstances it is possible to suggest simultaneous action by the Churches in relation to their respective governments. At a critical point in the conflict in Korea, through the help of the C.C.I.A., church leaders in the U.S. and the U.K. were able to make similar and concerted representations to their governments, urging policies of patience and restraint immediately prior to a conference of the heads of government. This procedure is of special value in helping to minimize risks of serious dissension among nations which have an established basis for collaboration in common traditions and outlook.

5. *Evidence of Christian Concern.* Beyond the values found in such procedures there are additional values in the presence of church representatives at intergovernmental meetings. Delegates have tangible evidence of Christian concern and those who share our faith became aware of the Christian fellowship even when dealing with political issues. The observer is a reminder of the principles for which the churches stand and an indication of the churches' concern for Christian vocation at the political level. His presence, moreover, often provides opportunity for informal discussions of religious questions and of the work of the ecumenical movement. The importance of such indirect methods of Christian witness should not be underestimated, for the moral climate of international conferences helps to shape their decisions.

B. Methods at the National Level

Most of the National Commissions are in touch with the governments of their countries for purposes of information and of formal or informal representations. In some cases, these contacts are fairly extensive. The Netherlands Commission, for example, met with representatives of the various political parties to discuss the position of Netherlands New Guinea. The British Department is in close touch with various branches of the Foreign and Colonial Offices. The Department of International Justice and Goodwill has frequent contacts with various Executive bureaus, has consultative status at the U.S. Mission to the U.N., and is often authorized by the National Council to testify before Congressional Committees.

The normal approach of a national church agency is to the government of its own country. There are, however, occasions on which representations have been made to the government of another country. Thus in 1950, the EKD sent a statement on war crimes to fourteen governments. The Japanese Council made representations on the draft peace treaty to the U.S. Ambassador-at-Large. Various Christian agencies have lodged protests over the persecution of Protestants with Ambassadors of Colombia. Procedural questions are raised in such cases, which have not yet been fully explored.

More still needs to be done at the national level to bring a Christian influence to bear at the time and place of political decision. Of course, in many countries the resources of the Churches are sadly limited. A Middle East correspondent reports, for example, that the Churches in his country consult government officials only on local problems, have little access to media of public information, and have no actions for world order to report. Nevertheless, many Churches and Christian agencies have not begun to use the resources at their disposal. Many churchmen appear to think that a resolution standing in their minute books constitutes Christian action.

1. *National Commissions on International Affairs.* One of the features of recent years has been the continued growth of National Commissions of the Churches on international affairs. These are specialized agencies, normally including experienced Christian laymen, to give continuing attention to

international problems and to advise the National Christian Councils and the international ecumenical agencies. Some 21 such commissions now exist and co-operate with the C.C.I.A.

They are organized in various ways. The older established departments, as in the U.S. and U.K., have a wide range of responsibilities. Others are at the initial stage. In South Africa, the International Affairs Group must carry on consultations by correspondence. In the Near East, where the Christian communities are unable to maintain separate commissions, there is a regional commission. Despite the many limitations which hamper efforts at the national level, there have been encouraging signs of growth since Amsterdam.

Mention should also be made of the important work carried on by a number of denominational bodies for social education and action.

2. *Education and Evangelism.* There are many ways in which Christian evangelism and education contribute to Christian world order strategy. The preaching and teaching ministry play a fundamental role in providing the broad groundwork for Christian witness in this field.

Some Churches are striving to develop more specific forms of education for Christian action in international affairs. Such efforts include attempts to train members for the responsibilities of Christian citizenship, to help prepare qualified laymen for public service, to inform public opinion through the secular media. Much benefit has been derived from conferences for the briefing of local church leaders, and in the U.S. by national study conferences, which bring together church leaders for a week's discussion of some main issues of foreign policy.

3. *Intercessory Prayer.* The Christian act of intercessory prayer, the turning to God, through whose grace alone can any acts of peace and justice succeed, is the beginning and ending of Christian efforts for world community. True intercessory prayer is a listening as well as a beseeching, a com-

mitting of oneself to God's will which issues in Christian action.

Many Christians have responded to ecumenical or national calls for prayer for peace and justice, as on United Nations' Day on October 24 and Human Rights Day on December 10. There have also been special calls to prayer for refugees and those suffering persecution. In December, 1950, the Synod of the Netherlands Reformed Church, in view of growing mutual distrust among the nations and the terrifying race in arms, called upon all Christians to pray for peace, especially at Christmas, when God gave peace to the world.

V

THE PRESENT SITUATION AND
THE ECUMENICAL TASK

Ecumenical work in international affairs since the Amsterdam Assembly cannot yet be evaluated, and what follows has the dangers as well as the gains of self-criticism. It is the general approach that must first be reviewed.

A. CHRISTIAN WITNESS SINCE AMSTERDAM

The major advance, namely, the continuous review of selected world issues, has been achieved through the establishment of the C.C.I.A. and National Commissions. The latter have been in a position to furnish prompt and accurate information so as to enable policy to be decided and action pursued. This allows international decisions to be anticipated and recommendations made before the event, instead of protest after. Christian witness has become more relevant; responsible laymen have found guidance; and non-Christian statesmen have appreciated a new Christian contribution to these tangled problems. The work has thus been practical and immediate.

But there is this danger: Has this Christian witness perforce paid a price in breadth and depth? Have the foreground obstacles obscured the perspective, and the petty goals obstructed the greater end? It is hard to say. It may, indeed, be true that efforts successful at the time have created the illusion that world community is not very far off. If this is so, it must be deplored. The C.C.I.A. lacks resources even to tackle the day-to-day tasks and has had severely to limit its responsibilities. Regional organizations, such as the Council of Europe or the Iron and Steel Community, have not had sufficient attention. Many urgent matters at the U.N. have been passed over, and consultative relations with some Specialized Agencies deferred.

On the other hand, the policy of advancing slowly but solidly has led to a modest reputation for thoroughness and sound judgment which is an important asset for the Churches in this field. Increasingly, of late, attention has been given to follow-up work, discussion with government representatives, submission of informal suggestions to overcome impasses, and contacts of a kind too miscellaneous to be described. In the nature of the case, much must be in the hands of few and mobile persons, but every effort is made to consult and inform responsible church leaders.

In retrospect, experience has shown that the following criteria must be applied to the selection of issues claiming attention from ecumenical agencies:

1. Is the problem inherently urgent?
2. Is there a clear Christian concern about it?
3. Is there a substantial consensus of world-wide Christian opinion on the line to be followed?
4. Have those who have to handle the problem been able to acquire a real competence in it?
5. Is there a reasonable possibility that a contribution may be effective, or an overriding imperative for Christian witness?

To some of the issues which have been handled accordingly we return below. Before doing so, however, attention must be called to at least three conspicuous gaps in the total program.

B. RESPONSIBILITIES THAT CHALLENGE

First, the C.C.I.A. itself is not a theological commission, Consequently, little work has been done on the relationship between specific proposals in international affairs and the basic principles of world order. The difficulty of retaining a balance between Christian action for peace and justice and Christian judgment on the predicament of man and society has hardly been grappled with. Most important of all, the Christian obligation to seek the establishment of an international ethos as a common foundation of moral principles for the world community has not been met. It is urgent that thought be given on how this challenge can be faced and by what agency of the Churches.

Second, there is pressing need for education for world-wide community on a world-wide scale, and this means much money and imaginative minds. Christians do not yet see international responsibility as a part of the total field of Christian witness. They are often perplexed about the issues and their relative importance. There is no obvious connection between their churchmanship, their citizenship, and the attitude of their political representatives to international questions. These seem remote from the parish and congregation, and it is only when the bombs fall that such questions suddenly light up. Moreover, many Christians are as much swayed by radio, television, and press, as by the Bible. They suffer the same frustrations as other men at the apparent pigheadedness of the nations. They have, too often, a local or at best a national, but not an ecumenical and international, outlook. They need the stimulus of a Christian approach based on the truths of their faith.

Third, there is equal need for sound and active National Commissions on International Affairs—not names on paper but minds at work. The advance made here in recent years is most encouraging but it is not enough. It is these commissions that make a specific Christian impact on the foreign policy of a single country. It is they who must inform and advise the C.C.I.A. and indeed correspond with one another directly—and when friction grows, immediately. It is one of the most regrettable facts that the responsible officers have been unable to travel, to visit, and by personal presence, conference and stimulus, develop a livelier pattern of local action, adapted to the varied situations and traditions of the Christian communities and their common needs.

C. THE PRESENT STRUGGLE FOR WORLD COMMUNITY

We must look summarily at the specific issues which have already found their place in these pages. They are very far indeed from settled. The struggle for world community continues. Every advance creates the demand for further effort. Every defeat must evoke fresh prayer, thought, and action.

Efforts to restrain *perilous tendencies toward a new world war* have helped to preserve the fragile and tattered fabric of peace, although the dangers remain and indeed mount. At least, in Korea the conflict was not enlarged by impatient and immoderate military action, and now that a truce has been achieved, there remains the achievement of a peaceful settlement.

Christians are committed to reconciliation. As a first step —and it is only that—the conditions of peaceful coexistence must be explored and fulfilled. Two major goals of policy, to oppose the extension of tyranny and to restrain tendencies toward a "preventive" war, claim immediate attention.

The churches must also wrestle with the pacifist and non-pacifist issue. Exchanges of views have been sought, but it does not appear that the three broad positions of Amsterdam have been sufficiently re-examined and reformulated to justify extensive discussions. Pacifist Christians have not faced sufficiently the charge that they make an absolute of peace at the expense of justice. Non-pacifist Christians who hold the concept of a "just war" have not sufficiently examined the implications of the new mass-destruction weapons for the idea of just means. And those non-pacifist Christians who hold that modern war "can never be an act of justice" have failed to make clear the grounds on which participation in war "in particular circumstances" may be still a Christian's duty. The deeper theological issues in those positions have hardly been touched, and a more thorough and profound ecumenical study is needed as a prerequisite to effective discussion.

In the present world crisis, tensions among the opposing power blocs is unabated and distrust and fear abound. The desperate competition in mass-destruction weapons grows. Neither international regulation and reduction of armaments, nor a U.N. combined police force are any nearer. Yet, in their approach to disarmament, men have to recognize the importance of moral and political factors more widely. It is meanwhile disappointing that nations fear to use the U.N. Peace Observer Commission lest their request precipitate aggression. The Balkan Sub-Commission has served a restraining purpose, but one side has denied it entrance.

It is the *Declaration on Human Rights* that has furnished a valid standard of essential rights. It will be influential to the degree that nations understand and maintain it. It has already influenced four international treaties and five national constitutions. It has stimulated the growing sensitivity to violations of fundamental freedoms which has switched the hot glare of publicity on to gross violations as in Colombia and East Germany. As for the draft Covenants, the belief has grown, particularly in the U.S. Government, that the basic agreement on which they must effectively rest does not exist, and much work has yet to be done—a task in which the churches must clearly co-operate.

Meanwhile, specific situations continue to command attention, although inadequate resources for field investigations and remedial measures hamper the effectiveness of ecumenical action in this area. No international guarantees for religious interests in Jerusalem have been given. In the Balkan countries, in spite of the peace treaties, rights are trampled; pastors are still imprisoned and Greek children have not been repatriated. In the Union of South Africa the people of Indian origin have been unable to improve their situation, and the problem of *apartheid* continues to stir the Christian conscience. These are but examples: it has yet to be seen whether a rising world conscience may not abate the worst abuses.

The *non-self-governing territories* are also an area of U.N. concern. Here the newer nationalisms suspect the older colonialism. Such pressures are a goad to quicker progress, but they also create political and psychological obstacles to its orderly pursuit. And here, ecumenical and church agencies because of their inclusive membership and long missionary experience can serve an important conciliatory function through informal contacts.

International technical assistance is one of the relatively bright spots on the horizon. It has been urgently stressed by Christian bodies both as a matter of social justice and positive peace strategy; and in some quarters, there are signs of greater appreciation of the experience of Christian and other nongovernmental bodies in such fields. Ecumenical representatives have mediated between the viewpoints of underdeveloped and of more developed countries, and National Commissions have been concerned in similar fashion with bilateral and regional programs. But present effort is far from commensurate with present need, and the wide public conviction necessary to sustain and expand so great and humane an enterprise is lacking.

Refugees continue to provide an acute international and political challenge, intensely human in its impact. Through programs in which Christian agencies have played a significant part, some succor has been given. In such regions as West Germany, India, and Pakistan, and in spite of immense difficulties, millions have found homes, jobs—and hope. But in the Near East, in Korea and elsewhere their plight remains unchanged or has even deteriorated. New arrivals from Eastern Europe, from China and from war-torn Indo-China swell their numbers. Resettlement has hardly been systematically approached, and the long-range issues have faded from view. The renewal of the life of UNICEF is a gleam of hope, but, for the rest, the need for immediate, imaginative and continuing action must be pressed on the conscience of the nations.

From all this, it is clear that one unmet need is a sober analysis of the *limitations and potentialities of the U.N.* as an instrument of international co-operation and order. Similar considerations apply to the Council of Europe and other regional groupings. Both inside and outside the churches many have held unwarranted illusions about the semiautomatic solution of international tensions through the U.N. Others have underestimated its present and potential significance. Charter revision is due for consideration in 1955 and this gives point to efforts to find a larger ecumenical consensus on the present and future significance of the U.N. for the defense of peace and justice, the progressive development of international law, and the building of a genuine world community.

D. Underlying Questions for the Churches

Beneath the immediate issues of international affairs which claim attention, there are certain fundamental questions which the churches must bear in mind. Among them are these:

1. What are the particular doctrines, or aspects, of the churches' faith which supply a basis for Christian approach and action?
2. In what ways is the churches' approach distinctive, and how much ground is shared with men of general good will?
3. What lessons can be drawn from the churches' attempts to deal with these questions?
4. What features in the life, witness and unity of the churches themselves render Christian action in the international field more difficult?
5. Do the churches possess the spiritual and material resources for such action, and can they be mobilized when needed?

6. Is there sufficient agreement on the principles of Christian action for any agency to act confidently in the name of the ecumenical fellowship?
7. What are the long-term international objectives for which the churches must strive, without prejudice to work in disputes and the causes of disputes as they arise?
8. What are the notes of warning that the churches must sound?

Here is a partial survey of the road the ecumenical movement has traveled in recent years in the struggle for world community. The road that has been traversed should provide some additional perspective of humility, courage and hope as the road ahead is undertaken.

PREPARATORY COMMISSION IV

on

INTERNATIONAL AFFAIRS—CHRISTIANS IN THE STRUGGLE
FOR WORLD COMMUNITY

Members

Sir Kenneth GRUBB, C.M.G., United Kingdom, Chairman
The Rev. Dr. Richard M. FAGLEY (Commission of the
Churches on International Affairs), Secretary
Dr. K. A. BUSIA, Gold Coast
Professor W. GREWE, Germany
*Dr. Gustav W. HEINEMANN, Germany
*The Rev. Professor J. L. HROMADKA, Czechoslovakia
Professor Werner KAGI, Switzerland
*Dr. J. LEMEINA, Indonesia
*Dr. Charles MALIK, Lebanon
Mr. Philippe MAURY, France
Mr. S. A. MORRISON, United Kingdom
The Rev. Professor O. Frederick NOLDE, U.S.A.
*Mr. Wesley F. RENNIE, U.S.A.
*Miss Marion ROYCE, Canada
*Mr. Soichi SAITO, Japan
*Professor Arnold J. TOYNBEE, United Kingdom
Professor Baron F. M. van ASBECK, Netherlands
Mr. Maurice WEBB, South Africa
*Mr. Erling WIKBORG, Norway

Central Committee Consultants

Sir Kenneth GRUBB, C.M.G., United Kingdom (member of
the Commission)
*The Rev. Professor J. L. HROMADKA, Czechoslovakia (mem-
ber of the Commission)
*The Rev. M. KOZAKI, Japan

Ad Hoc Consultants at August, 1953, Meeting

Dr. Alice ARNOLD, Switzerland
The Rev. E. Philip EASTMAN, United Kingdom

* Not present at August, 1953, meeting

The Rev. Dr. Whan Shin LEE, Korea
The Rev. Philip POTTER, Haiti
The Rev. W. MENN, Germany
The Rev. Professor R. B. Y. SCOTT, Canada

INTERGROUP RELATIONS—
THE CHURCH AMID RACIAL
AND ETHNIC TENSIONS

An Ecumenical Survey
prepared under the auspices of the
World Council of Churches

CONTENTS

iv   *Contents*

I

INTRODUCTION:
THE TERMS OF REFERENCE

One of the sections of the Second Assembly of the World Council of Churches will consider the topic "Intergroup Relations—The Church Amid Racial and Ethnic Tensions." The assignment has been defined by the Central Committee of the Council as follows:

The Section on Race at the Second Assembly should deal with the general question: How can the Church contribute to the correction of racial prejudice and injustice? To phrase the general question of the section in this fashion is to distinguish its task from the task simply of defining a Christian position on race, or of analyzing the race problem sociologically, although both of these will be involved. Moreover, this question directs the attention of the Assembly to what can concretely be done in reference to this problem.

Under this general head, at least the following areas should be dealt with:

1. How can the message of the Gospel be presented so as to affect the deep springs of race prejudice?
2. How should the Christian Church deal with race within its its own membership? What import should the Churches attach to questions affecting racial and ethnic homogeneity within the Churches? How can the Church—in the congregation, in the nation, and in the world—so exemplify Christian conviction concerning race as to contribute toward the alleviation of injustice?
3. How may the Christian community utilize and co-operate with government and other secular agencies in the alleviation of racial injustice?

It will be noted that each of these questions will involve both analysis and solution.

In taking this action, the Central Committee desired to exclude specific and explicit treatment of anti-Semitism, principally because this question involves other issues of such depth and scope as to place a full consideration of it outside the bounds of a discussion on race. It is to be noted, however, that anti-Semitism is in at least some aspects a problem of the relationships between ethnic groups, and that to this extent what is said here under this head is applicable. Moreover, as is noted (page 13), the anti-Semitism of Nazi Germany forced people and churches throughout the world to give attention to the ethnic problem involved, and thus both directly and indirectly posed a sharp challenge to Christian thought on the total problem.

The process by which this Survey was produced is described in general terms in the General Preface. The Commission listed on page 53 has carefully considered it both in group discussion and in subcommittees. In this discussion, emphasis was placed on the first two chapters, since their content required the most careful analysis. They represent a consensus of the group, with not all members in agreement with all points. Each expressed his conviction, but could not always bring the group to accept it.

II

THE PROBLEM OF TENSION

Very few peoples of the world, and very few Christian churches, escape involvement in one way or another in racial tensions, which have come to comprise one of the paramount problems of our day. The churches are divided deeply—perhaps more deeply than in any other way—by racial lines. The patterns of racial division are varied, but the central fact of such division is one of the salient features of our time. Racial differences destroy the unity of the churches within the bounds of many nations. They cut across the contemporary division of the world into two great blocs.

A few instances may illustrate both the importance and the variety of racial divisions within the Church. The missionary and evangelistic task of the Church is rendered more difficult by racial attitudes imported to non-white territories by missionaries and by commercial and political representatives of the Western community. The attitude of the Indian Christian toward the white missionary has gone through three stages of development. The first stage was one of patronage by the missionary, when the Indian Christian looked up to him in docile acquiescence, a stage aptly pilloried as the "mission bungalow mentality." Then came the second stage, with the final phases of the freedom movement when there was a violent and often unfounded criticism of anything the missionary did. The third stage has now arrived, with the achievement of political independence, clearing the atmosphere to a large extent. The Indian Christian and the missionary meet on a common platform and work for a common purpose. Yet hidden complexes lurk in the background which, if not conquered, would lead to harmful results. The Indian Christian has not yet completely purged his mind of racial prejudices. On the other hand, the charge is brought forward, with some justification, that the speed of the transfer of responsibility to Indian Christians is not rapid enough. The mission bungalows may appear as final outposts of imperialism in India unless Indian Christians are given fuller responsibility more quickly.

Ethnic cleavages exist within the Churches' own membership, as well as in the missionary endeavor. Examples may begin with India. Though the race problem has never been very intense in India it is much more diffused than in many other countries. A chromatic scale of many shades takes the place of a sharp antithesis between black and white. Caste adds a further complication to an already confused picture. The two main manifestations are tension between Indians and Europeans and between members of different castes. Both are found within the Church also. The Indian Christian, unlike any other Indian, had to face the British on two levels—on the political, as an opponent, and on the religious, as a fellow worker. During the turbulent pre-independence days he found himself asking: What is my duty as an Indian? and What is my duty as a Christian? Often there was a conflict.

The Church in India is an interesting sociological unit and has drawn converts from all castes. In spite of his conversion an orthodox Brahmin does not give up all his past prejudices in the twinkling of an eye the moment he enters the Church. Besides, the early missionaries recognized caste as a social institution and made no attempts to fight it within the Church. Hence each convert brought with him into the Church his cultural background. Subsects began to form themselves within the Church, as converts from the same caste tended to come together. The purity of race idea finds its expression both within and outside the Church in a purity of caste campaign, and this has had repercussions not only on the question of mixed marriages but has much intensified caste distinctions within the Church. The more objectionable aspects of caste, e.g., refusing to kneel by the side of a Harijan at the Communion Table and separate seats in Church for separate castes, have now almost entirely disappeared. They now exist mainly on the cultural level—social intercourse, marriage and church politics.

The situation in Malaya presents peculiar complexities, since there is one indigenous racial group, the Malays, and three distinct immigrant racial groups, the Chinese (who are almost as numerous as the Malays), the Indians, and the Europeans, of which the smallest is politically dominant. Self-government and independence have been promised to Malaya and within these complexities the attempt is being made to build up a single nationality. The churches in Malaya reflect this pattern with one significant difference. The Indian and Chinese churches follow the ecclesiastical and linguistic traditions of their original homelands, but there is no Malay church. The failure to evangelize the Malays is due to obscure reasons but it represents a very definite unfinished, unattempted task. The Malayan Christian Council strives to ease the tensions between churches and to bring them together in common tasks such as the training of the ministry, but it finds its task complicated further by theological division, by the need of clear Christian teaching as to the implications of the Gospel in a multi-racial society and by the need to distinguish between the essential Gospel and cultural accretions and institutions which hinder its presentation and acceptance.

Racial conflict within the Union of South Africa has received world-wide publicity in recent years, but the comparable divisions within the Christian churches there are less well known. The Dutch Reformed Churches of South Africa, which provide perhaps the strongest bond for the Afrikaans-speaking community, are themselves organized into European and non-European churches, as a matter of avowed principle and policy. Other Protestant communions have repudiated the principle of racial separation, but with a few exceptions their practice hardly differs from that of the Dutch Reformed Churches. Indeed, their division is fourfold in certain instances, with separate churches for Europeans, Indians, Colored and Africans.[1] Communication may occur at various levels between leaders of these disparate congregations, but this interchange hardly touches the general membership of the congregations.

In Kenya the trend within the churches is toward integration, though there is a long way yet to go. The very great majority of congregations are of one race, but this is the natural reflection of deep differences of language and culture, and is in no way dictated by deliberate policy. Where these differences have been overcome, an increasing number of Africans and Indians are worshiping in churches hitherto exclusively European. The fellowship does not stop at the church door; it is significantly, though very slowly, affecting the traditional pattern of social separation. This widening of fellowship and co-operation between Christians of different races has been greatly stimulated by the very real religious revival which has been experienced during the last ten years. The outbreak of Mau Mau has been a serious setback, embittering relationships far outside the limited area directly affected. It is not so much that the European outside the churches has lost faith

[1] The term "European" in South Africa designates the all-white group of Dutch, French, English and German extraction. This group is made up of two language groups—those who use English and those who use Afrikaans as their home language. The latter group is usually called Afrikaners.

The term "Bantu" covers that large group which constitutes the main native African element. They are original Africans, but are divided into many subgroups with different languages and a degree of ethnic differentiation.

The term "Indian" is used solely for a group of East Indians brought to South Africa in the first instance as indentured laborers. They are mainly confined to the province of Natal and are on the whole Hindu and Moslem.

The fourth group, the "Coloreds," is the most difficult to define. They consist of about one million people of very mixed ancestry. They are mainly descended from Malay and other slaves, with some admixture of original Hottentot, and lately of Bantu elements. Apart from this substratum of colored groups there has for 300 years been a liberal admixture of white elements from many nations especially in the old seaport city of Cape Town.

in the Kikuyu; on that side there is some compensation in the heightened regard he feels for the Kikuyu Christians who have stood fast for their faith to the point of martyrdom. But that very fact has intensified the attack on the churches by Mau Mau, which sees in Christianity the instrument of the hated European power. In a message to Christians of all races issued in October, 1952, the Christian Council of Kenya urges them to re-examine their attitudes toward all matters, small as well as great, which have contributed to the present evils, and to be ready to co-operate with all men of good will. The Council has in its Citizenship Committee an instrument of great potential value.

In the United States of America the Churches are divided by race almost completely at the level of the local congregations. Less than one-half of 1 percent of the American Negro Christians worship customarily with white Christians. Probably less than 10 per cent of the local Protestant congregations contain any mixture of racial groups. At the denominational level, approximately 95 per cent of the Negro Protestant Christians belong to Negro denominations. Fellowship between white and Negro Christians takes place significantly chiefly in national and ecumenical meetings. Much the same situation obtains with respect to Christians of other ethnic minorities in the United States: Mexicans, Japanese-Americans, Chinese-Americans, etc.

Divisions of race and color are less prominent in certain situations than in most of the instances already cited. In Brazil, for example, there is no marked racial tension. In all churches people of all racial backgrounds are welcomed. The divisions in society are rather along class lines which sometimes run parallel with color lines, as on the whole the colored groups—Negro, Mestizo or American Indian—are economically dependent and constitute the lower classes of Brazilian society. There seems, however, to be a tendency in certain coastal cities and among groups of immigrants in Southern Brazil to stress race and color.

As illustrated in the foregoing instances, racial and ethnic divisions in the churches, as in the communities which they serve, are very concrete on the one hand and extremely complex on the other. No problem appears more hopeless in certain respects than racial and ethnic divisions: none promises more hope in the light of Christian perspectives and of world developments.

Least hopeful of all are those situations where confidence in the motives of other Christians has been virtually destroyed. In such situations, in addition to the usual difficulties of communication between racial groups, there is a profound suspicion of any statements, and this mistrust penetrates within the most well-intended personal contacts. The instances also show the acute challenge to the Christian members of both races, where both thought and action are concerned, and their loyalties to a group or to the Christian Church are not clearly indicated, so that they have the onus of decision as to where these loyalties lie. This conflict of loyalties is one of the most exacting elements in situations where races live in close association with one another and where small groups of Christians are living in a non-Christian surrounding.

A. DEFINITION OF "RACE"

Though it is an immediate and concrete reality to vast numbers of people, the concept of race has so far defied exact definition. Reports from correspondents associated with this present Commission have revealed remarkable variations in definition among various countries and Christian communities, and this diversity is confirmed also by many other surveys. At several recent ecumenical conferences held in the Far East, Europe and the United States, pronouncements have been made on racial tensions, but without coming to any clear definitions of what the groups designated as races consist of. A recent series of publications by UNESCO (United Nations Educational, Scientific and Cultural Organization) has assisted in clarifying the meaning of some of the terms used when discussing race problems.[2] World authorities in science, history and other fields have written this series.

The problem of definition of "race" is complicated by the diversity of racial patterns in the world. The congeries of relationships in New Zealand between Europeans and Maoris is not the same as that in the Belgian Congo between Europeans and Congolese. The situation in South Africa is quite different from that in the southern part of the United States. The racial mixtures prevalent in Brazil and in Hawaii are not of the same order. In short, race is alleged as a central feature in all of these contexts; the way in which it is used to designate and separate people into various racial groups varies immensely from one situation to another.

The question of terminology is so ambiguous and confusing as to demand tentative definitions at this point. UNESCO, in its book *What is Race?* quotes a leading authority as saying that a race consists of "a group which shares in common a certain set of innate physical characters and a geographical origin within a certain area".[3] The UNESCO Statement on Race of July 18, 1950, further explicates the meaning of the term as follows:

The term "race" designates a group or population characterized by some concentrations, relative as to frequency and distribution, of hereditary particles (genes) or physical characters, which appear, fluctuate, and often disappear in the course of time by reason of geographic and/or cultural isolation. The varying manifestations of these traits in different populations are perceived in different ways by each group. What is perceived is largely preconceived, so that each group arbitrarily tends to misinterpret the variability

[2] "The Race Question in Modern Science" (series in eleven volumes). Published by UNESCO, 19 Avenue Kleber, Paris, 16e. Each volume: $0.25; 1s.6d; 75 Fr. francs.
What is Race? Evidence from Scientists. Price: $1.00; 5s.; 250 Fr. francs.
"Races and Society" (series). In process of publication.
"The Race Question in Modern Thought" (series). In process of publication.
[3] Page 36.

which occurs as a fundamental difference which separates that group from all others. . . .

National, religious, geographic, linguistic and cultural groups do not necessarily coincide with racial groups: and the cultural traits of such groups have no demonstrated genetic connection with racial traits. Because serious errors of this kind are habitually committed when the term "race" is used in popular parlance, it would be better when speaking of human races to drop the term "race" altogether and speak of *ethnic groups*.

As the reports from UNESCO indicate, scientific research has cast increasing doubt on the viability of the term "race." Scientists agree that there are no pure races in the world, nor are there any fixed racial groups, since from prehistoric times the peoples of the world have been migrating and mixing with one another.

All alleged "races" are of mixed ancestry and the mixture is still taking place in many parts of the world, despite stringent measures to the contrary in some of them.

Scientists neither assert that all men are equal in natural endowment, nor do they affirm that there are superior races. Most scientists today are agreed that there are no innate biological differences between races that justify an assumption of superior moral or intellectual capacity by any race over another. Such differences as exist are apparently the result of different physical environments, ways of living and social conditions. In fact, biologists, anthropologists and psychologists find it difficult to discover significant and clear-cut distinctions among the so-called races of mankind. Races are more or less distinguishable subgroups within a single species, *homo sapiens*. From this point of view there is only one race—the human race.

With respect to the effects of racial mixture, the UNESCO findings are:

There is no evidence that race mixture as such produces bad results from the biological point of view. The social results of race mixture whether for good or ill are to be traced to social factors.

Statements by individuals and groups about the purity of the races to which they belong have in most cases been made for two reasons: (1) in support of measures to maintain the alleged purity of that race by forbidding interbreeding; (2) to assert the superiority of that race as against other racial groups. Scientists have challenged the foundations on which these policies rest.

Pragmatically, barriers are set up among alleged racial groups by local theories, prejudices, custom or law. It is at this level that the problems of racial discrimination must be faced.

B. Definition of "Ethnic Group"

As indicated above in the UNESCO statement on race, efforts are being made at the present time to substitute the term "ethnic group" for the term "race." In assigning the tasks of this present Commission, the Central Committee of the WCC desired that tensions more extensive than those ordinarily denoted as racial should be considered.

The proposal that the term "ethnic group" be used has merit in that it may be employed loosely to cover several kinds of human groups. It may encompass the essential meanings of such other phrases as "nation," "Volk," "people," "color," etc. It must be recognized that such terms are differently understood by different sets of people, as the Oxford Conference of 1937 made clear. (See its Report, pp. 219 ff.) The flexibility and objectivity of the term "ethnic group" commend it as a useful common term to cover a multitude of diverse groups. Its primary reference, in most usage, is to a common tribal or national origin, but it has connotations of nearly all the other terms discussed above, and its use often leads to transfer of inapplicable concepts. For example, refugees in Europe or America are often of Caucasian origin, and are white in color, but their ethnic distinctness often leads to false designation of them as a racial problem.

In short, the diversity of racial and ethnic patterns among

men becomes more apparent as investigation of them becomes more universal and effective. The central fact seems to be that they are defined *culturally* rather than by nature or nature's God, and they are determined for the most part locally rather than on a world scale. Racial discriminations are none the less burdensome for those who bear their brunt; they are none the less dangerous for those who impose them.

C. The Rise of Racial Prejudice

It has been quite well established that race prejudice is not innate. It is learned. Strangeness induces responses varying from fear or suspicion to friendly interest or fascination. But in a society where tension exists, the child absorbs or learns otherwise the prevailing attitude of his racial group so early in life that he appears to have inherited it. Such inheritance is social, not biological.

The broad pattern of major racial group tensions which trouble the world today had its historical origins in the period of European overseas exploration and expansion into America, Asia and Africa. The resulting exploitation of one group by another, involving groups differing in race, varied in the three continents. But the same general relation of asserted superiority and inferiority developed between the white world and the colored world. Color became first the symbol, and then the accepted characteristic of the intergroup tension.

At the present time many peoples who have no conscious or recognized involvement in the "race problem" are nevertheless caught up in it to some extent. It has become a world problem through the development of international organizations, the break-up of former imperial systems, and the rapidity of modern communications, among other factors. The recent world war intensified racial tensions in certain situations, while opening possibilities for the improvement of race relations in other respects. A few examples may illustrate the accentuation of tension.

Correspondents from Africa report changes in the attitudes

of Africans who have fought beside whites in Europe, sharing
—in some instances—equal work, facing the same hazards,
fighting, risking their lives in a common enterprise. If they
were good enough for this, they ask, why are they not good
enough to share the same opportunities when they come back
home? Moreover, they remember that the war was fought
against a nation that insisted on maintaining a pattern of pre-
tended race superiority.

British reports speak of colored men from the colonies who
went to sea on merchant ships during the war and then
resented being displaced by whites when the war was over.
They are now waiting around port cities, unemployed.

In every country that has been occupied by foreign troops,
there have always been a considerable number of babies having parents of different races. Definition of the appropriate
social position to be given to mixed marriages and to the
children of interracial mating has been an intense social problem in a number of countries.

D. RECENT DEVELOPMENTS

At the time of the Oxford Conference in 1937, the question
of race was being posed sharply for the whole world by the
Nazi racial doctrines. This ideology, with its designation of
the Negro as subhuman and of other races as definitely inferior
to the "Nordic" one, provoked comment and resentment
around the world, and sometimes had unexpected repercussions on the relations between white and colored races.

At the present time the most widely discussed ideology on
the subject of racial problems is that of the communists, who
have used their doctrine of racial tolerance and absence of
discrimination in all their propaganda throughout the world,
with considerable effect. Actually the U.S.S.R. has met her
extensive ethnic problems in a variety of ways, and has by no
means succeeded in solving them. The official constitution of
the U.S.S.R. outlaws racial discrimination explicitly. But the
republics of the Soviet Union are organized so as to coincide
roughly with recognizable ethnic groups. The resulting pattern

is that of pluralism rather than of full integration. At the same time, impenetrable ethnic barriers are virtually non-existent, and members of all ethnic groups have opportunities to mix freely and to improve their status through education and economic advancement.

Whatever the internal situation may be, the U.S.S.R. and the group of communist-dominated countries have succeeded to a large degree in convincing the nonwhite world that communism offers, at least in theory, a better racial alternative than that achieved in the past by the Western world. No great imagination is required to surmise that the communist grand strategy aims at the alienation of Asia and Africa from the Western world, and the doctrine of racial equality is a prime instrument toward the fulfillment of that purpose.

During the last fifty years, the imperial system built up in the previous two centuries has been undergoing gradual liquidation; in the decade after the beginning of World War II, this process was greatly accelerated, and a large number of peoples achieved their independence. Ralph Bunche has pointed out that the number of subject peoples declined in this period from some 750 million to about 250 million. The achievement of independence by certain Asian countries stimulated the nationalist movements in all other dependent territories. Impatience with the rate at which emancipation from colonial rule has been achieved has led to a notable increase in racial tension. The communist movement has sought to capitalize on the various movements toward independence and has thereby often intensified and confused local issues and heightened racial tension. It has strengthened its position by identifying itself rather consistently with the aspirations of subject peoples for political independence. But the decline of the imperial system has been of a scope far transcending any communist influence.

Probably the United Nations has had more effect on race relations since World War II than any other agency. In this organization the delegates from member nations are together on a basis of equality and without segregation on grounds of race or cultural or ethnic origin. This experience provides a basis for comparison or contrast with the patterns which prevail in some countries.

The procedures of the United Nations provide a basis for comparing the racial policies of the various nations before a world-wide audience. For example, "the question of race conflict in South Africa resulting from the policies of apartheid of the Government of the Union of South Africa" was discussed in nine meetings of an Ad Hoc Political Committee in November, 1952, even though the representative of South Africa declined to participate in the discussion except to challenge the competence of the United Nations to deal with the matter. This discussion was of special interest to the constituency of the World Council of Churches because of the many references to the moral and religious sanctions of human rights. Representatives of Moslem countries spoke of the requirements of racial equality in their religion. Others referred to the teachings of Christianity.

Studies conducted by the United Nations bring the race practices of many nations under scrutiny. No nation can any longer define and explain its own behavior without being subject to challenge and criticism, even though its domestic policy and action are not under the jurisdiction of the United Nations. The United Nations has a direct responsibility for what happens in some dependent areas. Periodic surveys by the Secretariat of the U.N. of social conditions in non-self-governing territories include the factor of race relations. The varying practices are brought under review by world public opinion and made liable to examination by both friendly and hostile critics in the light of various traditions and moral standards.

E. Some Psychological Aspects of Tension

Tension and conflict arise in intergroup relations out of a wide variety of causes. The apparent cause may mask the real ones and several causes may be so mixed up that in many cases it is impossible to disentangle them. It is not our task to make a detailed analysis of the basic and remote causes of ethnic tensions but a brief reference to the major ones may not be out of place.

In racial contacts where tension occurs it shows itself in individual behavior reflecting group attitudes. This inter-relation between the individual and his group is basic in all human relations, but it is particularly evident in inter-racial situations where individuals appear to reflect a group attitude which they adopt or which is imposed on them by the social group to which they belong. This is no less true in inter-racial situations where the relations between ethnic groups appear harmonious. The potentiality of tension is always present as long as individuals identify themselves with the political, social and economic interests of the ethnic group to which they belong.

It has been pointed out in several recent studies that the causes of racial tension are as much sociological as psychological. This is a generalization which covers political and economic relations between ethnic groups as well as differences in cultural backgrounds and modes of living. When one country conquers or acquires political power in another country, the inevitable rise of freedom movements both underground and overt sets the stage for the intensification of all racial, ethnic and color tensions. If the conquering race is of a different color, and settles down in large numbers in the conquered territory, then the situation is replete with possibilities for tension. As far as the purely emotional reactions are concerned, a benevolent bureaucracy seems to be no better than an acknowledged autocracy. As a result two groups may live in close juxtaposition but with no attempt to understand each other. In many parts of the world where permanent white settlement has taken place, the non-white indigenous peoples have either had their land taken from them, or have agreed to part with it without realizing what it would mean to them as their population increased. In these same areas of white settlement, tension may be caused by providing educational and other cultural facilities for the immigrant ethnic group, and then using their educational attainments as an excuse for discrimination in the economic sphere.

In recent years psychologists have given much attention to the analysis of the causes of racial prejudice. Some of the UNESCO series of publications referred to on page 9 examine the roots of prejudice, the existence of racial myths and questions of mental development; personality and temperament.

In varying degrees of obviousness and subtlety the following factors operate in most tension situations in and out of the churches.

A complex combination of factors has contributed to the tensions. Once group tension among different races is established, race becomes an actual tension factor. Parents bequeath prejudices to children, and groups instill them into new members.

Inroads of one cultural group on another lead to *fear* of lowered living standards, and the unknown. The favored group, if small, fears being physically overpowered, and overtaken, or outnumbered if numerically inferior. Traditional color *symbolism* is effective when transferred to skins (ergo: black is evil), and *stereotypes* (the spiritual Indian, the inscrutable Chinese) have harmed the concept of universal brotherhood and the respect for the dignity of man. Such types have been emphasized through films and popular magazines. *Jealousy* prompted by a sense of inferiority exists in matters of scientific discovery, adventure, exploration, sports, sex, etc., though mainly unconscious in operation.

Contrariwise an exaggerated sense of *superiority* may result if the group claiming superiority is also dominant. Achievements in modern science and its consequent improvement of living standards foster feelings of white race superiority, creating a gap between the so-called inferior and superior races. The Oriental offsets this with feeling his is a superior spiritual culture. Differences in mores, despite seeming triviality, make *unfamiliarity* a social barrier, rendering the exchange of hospitality difficult. Not as prolific a source of prejudice as is commonly assumed, *ignorance* leads rather to indifference. Its consequence does not result from a lack of knowledge, but a lack of the right sort of knowledge.

It is sometimes suggested that the removal of the *internal tensions* of inner frustration is a necessary condition for the understanding of the significance of external conflict. These frustrations themselves may seek substitute satisfaction in making a group of people the scapegoat in their need for relief. There is a school of psychology which claims that the whole struggle between black and white races is nothing but an externalization of the inner struggle going on inside the individual between instinct and inhibition, repression and expression.

F. The Problem of Communication

Anthropologists are seeking to discover how people express themselves verbally about the relationships within their own society and how far verbal expression—as, for example, respect for age—and behavior correlate. They are attempting to understand, for example, how Africans behave toward "whites" (usually meaning Europeans and Americans) and how far this behavior expresses their attitudes toward, and ideas about, whites and how far behavior does not express attitude.

More fundamental but less easy to discern for the white anthropologist are the explanations which people give for their attitude to whites. In most areas of Africa, particularly where white settlement is on a permanent basis, Africans differentiate sharply between different categories of whites. Their attitudes, as are the attitudes of the whites, are built up out of a multitude of personal encounters with whites who are missionaries, government officials, settlers, white miners, commercial men, and others. They also differentiate between whites of different nationalities.

The spread of modern education has brought Africans into

relationships as colleagues in church and state, and to a less extent in business, with whites. Thus there are now something like three spheres within which inter-racial attitudes are developing. At one end are the Africans living more or less their own lives, geographically and in many other ways separated from whites. At the other end are the whites also separated and apart. In the middle is a wide sphere of relationships where Africans and whites meet and work together, as colleagues or as employers and employed. It is in this "middle belt," where personal encounters take place, that attitudes are formed and communicated by each racial group to its own separate group who live largely apart.

Herein lies the fallacy of the assumption by some whites that educated Africans cannot speak for the masses of their fellow countrymen in the villages. Whites may not realize the implications of the colleague relationship with Africans in the "middle belt" and may resent the fact that the educated Africans now stand between them and the masses in the villages, with whom they had always thought, with some justification, that their relationships were harmonious and founded on mutual understanding.

It is within this changing pattern that race relationships develop within the churches. It is virtually impossible for Africans to dissociate race relations within the churches from what they know and experience in inter-racial situations in politics, in social living and in economic enterprises of many kinds. It is perhaps almost equally difficult for whites in the churches to take a wholly detached view. In one important respect, however, whites and Africans are not in the same position in this relationship. Whites in the churches can readily express their attitudes and ideas on race relations and can show how those attitudes conform to or differ from those of other white groups in the community. On the other hand, Africans in the churches have much more serious obstacles to overcome in expressing verbally their attitudes and ideas on relations with whites. The nature of those obstacles and the ways in which they can be overcome constitute an important challenge to the churches in the problem of communication between groups in inter-racial situations.

This challenge applies not only in Africa but in every similar situation at the local and national levels, in the parish church and the Christian Council, and hence in the ecumenical movement. It cannot be fully met by getting more Africans—to continue the illustration—on the Christian Councils and at ecumenical gatherings, though that would help. They will still be numerically overpowered by whites, and many of them will hesitate, partly out of loyalty and partly out of courtesy, to question statements made about racial tensions and to put forward their own statements. The paternal relationship between whites and Africans in the churches is still operating, whether consciously or unconsciously, to make it difficult for Africans to be articulate on this vital concern of the Christian Churches.

G. Ethnic Groups, Cultures and Territories

Intergroup relations, being relations among people, are not easily classified and assessed. Attitudes are important, as well as community patterns. Customs and convictions are important, as well as laws. The administration of law may be as significant as the text of the law on the statute book.

Among the situations which are found in different parts of the world are three which are clearly defined. The first occurs in those territories where the inhabitants share a common culture, but are of different racial or ethnic stock; the most typical example of this situation is found in the case of the Negroes in the U.S.A. Another set of conditions is found in territories where the inhabitants are of different ethnic stock and retain their different cultural backgrounds, as in Malaya, Ceylon, Kenya, British Guiana. A rather different situation arises in those countries where the basic population is of one ethnic stock possessing one culture, but where immigrant groups, whether students or workers or refugees, come temporarily to live among them. (Many instances might be cited, but the examples of the United Kingdom, Holland, France and Germany are especially instructive.)

The difficulty of classifying race relations by patterns is illustrated also by the situation in Australia. Its major concern is with its "White Australia" immigration policy, which discriminates at present mainly against Asians and may be applied against other colored races. But factors other than race are involved: the fear of cheap labor lowering the standard of living; nationalism; and the fear of a "fifth column" in the event of war. Australia also has some 50,000 aborigines and 25,000 half-castes. American Negro servicemen experienced little discrimination as visitors during the war even though some of their own fellow countrymen sought to have them segregated in restaurants and theaters. Some Australian servicemen have brought home Japanese warbrides. Australia welcomes a considerable number of Oriental students to institutions of higher learning.

As these situations indicate, there is no direct proportional relation among race, culture and territory. Apparently any ethnic group can assimilate any culture, if given the opportunity to do so. It can at the same time retain certain specific elements of its own culture, while adopting a common culture of the territory in which it lives.

H. Alternatives in Ethnic Relationships

The complexity revealed by the foregoing paragraphs makes it very difficult to describe clearly the alternatives in the field of race relations. In general, three alternatives represent the broad range of possibilities, though various modifications and combinations of them are possible. These alternatives are by no means mutually exclusive, and particular situations might be described under more than one of them.

(1) *Integration.* For the groups encompassed within this policy and pattern it is the prevailing purpose and practice to recognize no lines of cleavage as separating them. For all these

groups, political rights, economic opportunity, social accepta-
bility, access to educational facilities, eligibility for marriage
are available without distinction. There are other lines of
cleavage and classifications that result in discrimination within
this pattern, but they are not determined by ethnic or racial
origin. Ethnic and racial tensions are at a minimum within this
pattern, though they may exist.

A number of nations and particular states have enacted
laws in the effort to prevent discrimination and to promote
integration of ethnic groups. In addition to general constitutional guarantees against discrimination, there are specific
statutes having to do with equal opportunity for employment,
freedom of worship, equal opportunity for unsegregated education, and the like.

(2) *Pluralism.* The social policy underlying this pattern
assumes that ethnic and racial differences should be recognized and accepted as desirable, at least for the present, and
that groups may maintain and cultivate their distinctive differences without disadvantage to themselves or to the community.
Whatever lines of cleavage there may be among groups are
vertical lines, rather than horizontal lines placing one group
above another in privilege. Whatever separation of groups
there may be is voluntarily chosen.

Illustrative of this pattern is the relation between the Scot-
ish and the English, the French and the British groups in
Canada, the various ethnic groups in Switzerland, and the
several ethnic strains in Indonesia.

It is difficult and hazardous to cite illustrations of this pattern, because it is much more commonly espoused in theory
than carried out in practice. It is difficult in practice to encourage group distinctiveness without establishing discrimination. This pattern is constantly under pressure from the policy
of integration on the one hand and segregation on the other.
It is difficult to maintain.

At one time, the alternative of pluralism was widely held
as the most appropriate solution of ethnic problems. The

resolution adopted by the Oxford Conference reflects the wide-spread acceptance of this view at that time. Many former exponents of it have now moved sharply in the direction of the first alternative described above.

(3) *Segregation.* The social policy underlying this pattern assumes that racial groups, and, in some cases at least, ethnic groups, should be kept separate, distinct and free from infiltration from other groups. Segregation must, therefore, be observed—imposed if necessary. Although there may be a measure of actual separation in the pluralistic pattern, it is strictly voluntary, a result of mutual consent; whereas in the pattern of segregation separation is imposed by the dominant group, upon itself and upon other groups. Segregation means involuntary or imposed separation.

There are wide variations of practice within this pattern. The segregation may apply at only a few points in the relation among groups—for example, in social organizations; or it may be comprehensive, as in Negro-White relations in some parts of the United States and in relations between Europeans and non-Europeans in South Africa.

It may be useful, in view of a great deal of confusion on the matter, to distinguish between segregation and discrimination, though any such effort must always be more or less arbitrary. In general, segregation is a carefully defined policy or social strategy, regulating most of the important relationships among the ethnic groups involved. Discrimination is more largely a matter of individual behavior, which may or may not have the support of social opinion and prevailing social sanctions. In practice, segregation, being by definition an imposed pattern of assumptions, almost always and inevitably involves discrimination in public services, economic opportunities and educational facilities. Separation without discrimination would be in the pluralistic pattern and therefore is not segregation as the term is used in this classification.

III

THE CHURCHES' APPROACH
IN PRINCIPLE

As race has become an increasingly pressing problem for the Christian Churches, general patterns of theological thinking concerning it have begun to emerge. In some particular churches, confronted in a special way with the race problem, and especially in the ecumenical movement, Christians have been forced to think about the bearing of their faith upon the problem of racial discrimination, and upon the meaning of the races in human history. The most extensive attention was given to the problem in the Jerusalem Conference of 1928, for which an extensive volume was prepared and which received a full report on the matter. But the subsequent ecumenical conferences—Oxford and Edinburgh in 1937, Madras in 1938, Amsterdam in 1948, Lund in 1952—have from their differing viewpoints dealt with the matter. In some instances the concern has been the life and work of the churches in society; in others the missionary outreach of the churches into the world; in still others the internal life of the churches. Moreover, the World Council of Churches, at its Toronto meeting in 1951 and its Lucknow meeting in 1952-53, gave concerted attention to the problem, particularly in South Africa. As a result of this considerable body of ecumenical thought, buttressed by the thinking of a number of the churches participating in the ecumenical movement, it is possible to trace certain broad outlines of agreements and disagreements of the churches concerning race.

A word of caution is, however, needed. Although the above is all true, the ecumenical conferences since Jerusalem have dealt with race in a somewhat fragmentary fashion, in connection with other subjects and not as a subject in itself. A comprehensive theological analysis has not been undertaken on these occasions. Moreover, it is frequently the case that theological thought concerning race may be current in a whole church or even groups of churches without having been explicitly formulated by the church officially. To summarize the theological positions of the churches on race is, therefore, somewhat of a tour de force.

A. The Bible and Race

It is clear that the central group in the Old Testament is Israel. The main theme and message of the Old Testament is that God chose a certain people with whom He made a covenant. He would be their God and they would be His people. When they turned away from this covenant and were faithless, or when they were dispersed into foreign countries, He preserved a remnant still faithful to Him. His injunction to Israel to preserve itself was in principle a religious one and referred to a people, and not a race. Racially, Israel was a mixed people. Groups of different languages and of different nations appear in the Old Testament, frequently in such a way as to make clear that they too are used by God and fall under His judgment. Yet it remains true that Israel is God's chosen servant.

In the New Testament, the old covenant is superseded by the new, the old Israel by those who believe in Christ. A struggle, recorded in Acts, as to whether "The Way" was to be confined to those adhering to the Jewish law, or whether it was meant for all men, was decided in favor of the universal view. Christ had died for all. Henceforth, the people of God in principle and in fact were drawn from different nations and races. Indeed, a new people had come into being "a chosen race, a royal priesthood, a holy nation, God's own people" (I Pet. 2.9, Revised Standard Version).

The central categories and main message of the Bible are inclusive of all people and the Bible is well aware of group tensions. It does not, however, deal with race in the modern sense of the word, nor explicitly with the problems of racial tension as the modern world knows them. Although, for instance, the Bible allows for varieties of peoples within the membership of the Church, there is no basis in the Bible for disunity or division in the Church based on race. Similarly, the Bible contains neither prohibition nor advocacy of intermarriage between persons of different races. The Bible is concerned with the development of a single people, limited at first, but then growing and transformed into a people to be drawn from all the nations (Matt. 28.18-20).

B. RACE AND CHURCH HISTORY

So vivid was this conviction that in the early days of the Church, Christians were known as the "third race," and the early Church in fact fully included in its fellowship people of varied color and race. Race or color evidently did not enter as a qualification for membership in churches or congregations. It was not, in fact, until the seventeenth century that the outlines of the modern race problem began to emerge. Whatever the contributing causes, the process whereby the white race spread with increasing rapidity over the globe, subjecting peoples of "color" to it, marked the beginning of our modern race problem. The Churches on the whole have not transcended the problem, but rather have conformed to the racial patterns which have evolved in the process, being themselves torn by the conflicts which have ensued. We deal, therefore, not with a problem of long standing within Church history, but with a modern one. Why has it appeared? The complex mixture of social, economic and political issues with racial antagonism is a subject for widespread study and research, to which reference is made elsewhere in this paper. It is important, however, to bear in mind that this is a problem of the modern Church, and not of the whole history of the Church.

What, then, can be reported concerning the position of the

churches within this modern situation? The following sections on Christian Positions are set forth in an attempt to describe the agreements and the variations of conviction within the churches, and are based upon reports from a representative number of churches and upon the statements of the ecumenical conferences since 1928.

C. Positions: Agreements and Differences

(1) *Creation.* The churches agree that since mankind, according to the plain teaching of both the Old Testament and the New Testament, is created and sustained by God, the human race is of one blood, possessing a fundamental unity in spite of secondary differences.

Within this common affirmation, however, there are two different interpretations. The great majority of the churches stress the unity of the human race as created by God. Racial and ethnic differences serve, not to keep groups of humanity isolated from one another, but rather to enrich one another and the total. Far from being fixed patterns, racial differences are in a constant process of change, but this does not affect the basic unity of mankind. Within the total racial complex, however, the pride and sin of man appear, causing conflict among the races and the domination of one by another.

The consequence of this view for race and for the churches is to challenge the churches to witness to the unity of the creation, which has been shattered by man's pride and aggression and restored in Christ. It is not, therefore, the duty of the churches to separate the races from one another, but rather to exhibit the unity of the races with one another in their own life and work in society at large toward the end that righteousness may be established and segregation abolished there among the races.

The other interpretation, advanced in a few quarters, would hold that the differences of races are fixed and, humanly speaking, permanent. They belong to a certain order of preservation, established by God for the purpose of restraining sin.

The consequence of this view for some who hold it is that the order established by God must be respected and therefore that the races must be kept separate. This imposes the duty upon Christians for action in society to keep the races apart, whether they all desire it or not, by custom, practice or statute, if necessary accepting the initiative of the state in doing so. Within such a situation, those churches adhere to the fixed pattern, and advocate the establishment of justice and harmony within it.

(2) *The Incarnation.* Among many New Testament texts, three stand out as a basis for the agreement of the churches concerning the Incarnation and its bearing upon the race problem.

And the Word was made flesh, and dwelt among us . . . [John 1.14]
God was in Christ, reconciling the world unto himself [II Cor. 5.19]
For God so loved the world, that he gave his only begotten Son. . . . [John 3.16]

The churches affirm that the Incarnation challenges us to effect a new relation between the peoples. Jesus Christ revealed God to be the Father of all. He was made "in human form," and he died for all men, rising from the dead that all might be born again. In him, men are therefore required to live in a new relation with one another. "By this all men will know that you are my disciples, if you have love for one another" [John 13.35]. His mission therefore confirms the equality and value of each person in the sight of God, in whose infinite love each sparrow (Luke 12.6) has its place, and who seeks and cares for each of those who are lost (Luke 15.1-10). His mission restores the unity of mankind—lost through human sin in the Fall of man—with God and within itself.

Within those affirmations, it would also be agreed that Christ revealed God to be the Father, and that we are therefore brothers. But a few would maintain that this Fatherhood and this brotherhood are, as it were, recognizable and applicable only to those who have been particularly called or elected

by God as His sons, or only to those who have found salvation
in Christ Jesus. This view has tended to promote identification
of a particular racial group as the chosen people. Most
churches, however, would stress that being created by God
we are His children, and would view the Father revealed by
Jesus Christ as the Father of all men. As children of God, the
"little ones" for whom Christ died, men of all sorts and conditions have equal value and status before God. Among them
there is a new sense of brotherhood, in which there is no
fundamental inequality and in which injustice, discrimination
and segregation have no place. The brotherhood inaugurated
by Christ is that which transforms our present sinful division
and injustice into the original brotherhood of the race. The
Fatherhood of God is thus a universal concept, and the
brotherhood of man is, if not fully realized now, potentially a
universal fellowship. Again, according to this view, the unity
of the races, rather than a special designation of a single one,
is fundamental.

(3) *The New Creation.*

Therefore, if any one is in Christ, he is a new creation; the old
is passed away, behold, the new has come.

[II Cor. 5.17, Revised Standard Version.]

The Kingdom of God is amongst us whenever His will is
done; it will come in its fullness when His will is done on
earth as it is in heaven. Thus it is, on the one hand, the hope
by which we live in the present; and on the other, it is the
goal toward which the Church is directed. The people of
God, drawn from all the races, thus possess a common hope
and a common goal, to which they must witness and which
they must demonstrate.

Human beings suffer and are degraded because of the conflict among the races. The indignity and the frustration and
the fear of those who are oppressed, and the warping of spirit
and the fear of those who oppress, call alike for salvation and
for hope. What hope does Christ hold out to them?

Christ gives us the hope for a new life now. He makes men

into new men, establishing dignity in the human spirit, replacing fear with trust, and freeing the human spirit from its twisted confines. This is our first hope in Christ. "Therefore, if any one is in Christ, he is a new creation; the old is passed away, behold, the new has come."

Christ gives us hope for the future. His Kingdom, in which there is love and mercy, and in which evil and cruelty disappear, will come in its fullness. Part of His work of making men into new men is to give them the assurance that His Kingdom will come. The future is not, therefore, endless injustice and frustration for those who are oppressed. The future is determined by Christ, who will bring about "a new heaven and a new earth" toward which men are called to move. Men do not know His new creation, and neither is it made visible, unless it now becomes real in men's lives. When assumptions of superiority are turned into the recognition of equality in Christ; when frustration is turned into the purposeful work in and toward the Kingdom of God; when cruelty has been turned into love and mercy, the Kingdom of God is apparent on the earth. And as the Kingdom of God does appear among us, we know that it shall come in its fullness. Therein is our hope.

(4) *The Church.*

For as the body is one, and hath many members, and all the members of that one body, being many, are one body: so also is Christ. For by one Spirit are we all baptized into one body, whether we be Jews or Gentiles, whether we be bond or free; and have been all made to drink into one Spirit. [I Cor. 12.12-13.]

Be like men who are waiting for their master to come home from the marriage feast. [Luke 12.36, Revised Standard Version.]

Reported agreements from the churches reveal that they recognize a two-fold task.

First, they must proclaim and exemplify in the world at large the unity in Christ. In this task, they serve the Kingdom of God, which they know in part, but which shall be fully understood in the future. They must proclaim this unity to all men. Yet they do not. Even granting that the churches do not understand fully the goal toward which they move, they fail to live up to what they do see. Reconciliation in Christ is confessed by many Christians and churches who do not give evidence that they know or practice a reconciliation with men. Deep-going repentance is therefore needed, and connected inevitably with the task of the churches. As Christians strive, in constant repentance, to exemplify the unity of Christ, they are supported by the continuous witness of Word, sacrament and fellowship known by the Church through the ages. Here repentance is brought about and renewal of life is given.

Second, as part of their witness in the world, the churches affirm that they must seek to establish justice and reconciliation among the races. At least three measures are appropriate. In the first place, the churches can give encouragement and assistance to every good movement outside the churches which is working to better relationships among the races. Frequently the churches are silent when outside organizations strive to improve racial conditions, whereas a word of approval or actual participation in the effort would make the work of such organizations more effective. In the second place, the churches can assist the individual church member to see what his Christian duty is in his vocation and in his daily contact with members of other races. The individual Christian can never escape his responsibility to witness for his Lord in every area of his life. The churches can assist him to see more clearly what his Christian duty is in the area of race. Third, oppressed racial and ethnic groups can never receive justice until discriminating laws are abolished. The churches can study these laws and when they are found to be unjust, they can take appropriate initiative to get such laws changed or abolished.

Within these affirmations, there is a wide and serious variation of conviction. Agreeing that the people of God move toward an ultimate goal and end in which there is no distinction of race, there is disagreement as to the manner in which the churches at present should exemplify and set forth that ultimate unity. How shall they wait for the Master? For some, unity in Christ is a spiritual unity, not to be embodied in existing churches and social structures; such embodiment is to be avoided in the interests of upholding the order which God has established among the separate races. For most, the final unity of the Kingdom of God is to be approximated now, made visible by the workings of the Holy Spirit in the churches and in society. Here again, the unity of Creation, re-established by Christ, is the dominant concern. Moreover, the concept of justice and reconciliation among the races in society differs according to which of the views is held. One view, holding that a spiritual unity in Christ among those of different races is sufficient, calls for just treatment and right relationships among races which are separated from one another. The other view requires that the unity of the races will be exemplified in society as well as in the churches, and stresses that neither justice nor reconciliation can be effected until this unity is achieved. They recognize that to deny justice to any man or to impose segregation upon him because of race or color is to deny to him that dignity to which he is entitled as a child of God. It penalizes him for being what God has made him and for a condition which he cannot change. A person may change his church membership, his theology, his nationality; or he may improve his mind if ignorant, his economic status if poverty stricken; or his body if unclean; but he cannot change his color or physical characteristics. The growth of a unity, therefore, which recognizes and accepts the physical differences of various races and ethnic groups, is a prerequisite to the establishment of justice among them.

The churches affirm that a heavy responsibility in Christian discipleship rests with the individual. As the object of God's love, the lost sinner for whom Christ died, he cannot postpone or evade the requirements of obedience. These requirements call for rigid self-examination, which, in regard to race, necessitate honest scrutiny as to the extent and depth of prejudice within himself. No solution to race tension can be achieved unless this beam is first cast out. Every relationship which an individual has with other races will also come under review in the light of Christian principles. Some of these relationships will be direct and personal: social manners, language, friendships, indeed any expression of attitude will be screened for traces of prejudice in any of its subtle forms. Other relationships will be less direct and more impersonal. The support of organizations working for racial justice; the advocacy and support of governmental policy at all levels directed toward the same end; the seeking of full education and employment opportunities for all racial groups—these and a dozen other social duties rest upon the Christian individual. The Christian is, in fact, the "ambassador of Christ" to every realm of life. "No one who puts his hand to the plow and looks back is fit for the kingdom of God" (Luke 9.62).

D. The Problem of the "Interim"

All Christians are involved in the problem of how we shall behave in the great interim between now and the final coming of the Kingdom of God. Set in historical situations in which they can choose only lesser goods or lesser evils, Christians must take heed lest their intended obedience become in fact disobedience. In regard to Christian behavior concerning race relations at least four problems appear.

The first of these applies equally to both general positions on race which we have described. The majority of churches acknowledge that the Gospel requires equality among the races, and an end to discrimination, injustice and segregation. Yet they all too frequently, in official policy as well as in practice, put forward a policy of the gradual attainment of these goals, turning deliberately away from the absolute requirements of the Gospel at this point. Is it correct to do so as a matter of deliberate policy? Is it not required that they ask themselves afresh whether the Kingdom of God demands a different behavior in the interim; whether, that is, the admitted and explicit demands of the Gospel do not condemn a deliberate policy of gradualism? On the other hand, the minority of Christians face the problem in a different way. They hold that the unity of the Kingdom of God can be realized only when the Kingdom has come in its fullness and that it is not to be embodied in the present scene. But is this a correct conclusion for this interim period? Does this take seriously enough the full position of the Gospel that the Word was made flesh, that men here and now are to enter into the unity of the Body of Christ? Can there be a true unity, here and now, which is not visible? Both positions contain serious dangers of attitude and action, and for both serious questions concerning behavior in this interim period are raised by virtue of their respective conceptions of the Gospel.

Another problem cuts across this one. There are those who, so confident in the coming of the Kingdom of God, and so impressed with the depth of human sin, either neglect their present duty or acquiesce in the inevitability of wars and rumors of wars, of injustice and of poverty. Such a position clearly avoids the fundamental conception of the Gospel that discipleship, to the full extent of personal commitment, begins now. "Take up thy cross, and follow me." Others, however, take virtually the opposite position. So mindful of the responsibility of man to perform his duty, they view the establishment of the Kingdom of God as a work of man in co-operation with God, and do not fully face the fact that it is "God which worketh in you both to will and to do his good pleasure." This position is inclined to overlook the depth of the revolution wrought by Christ in the human heart as well as in the history of mankind. The problem for both of these extreme positions, as for every Christian, is to find the proper balance between the need to act under God in the battle against evil, and the need to understand, in that action, the depth of human sin which can be redeemed only by God's grace.

A third interim problem also embraces all positions on the Gospel and race. This is the problem stated by Troeltsch in terms of Church and sect, and by Richard Niebuhr in terms of Christ and culture. Realizing that there is inevitably inter-action between Christianity and the society in which it is set, how should the Church find its way through the intricacies of that interaction? In terms of race, it will be made clear later in our treatment that the patterns of segregation, no less than the patterns of integration, which have prevailed in the surrounding societies have had their decisive effect upon church life. In turn, the churches have affected these racial habits of the communities. Yet no Christian is content, or should be content, to leave this to mere chance. If, however, it is to be a matter of conscious strategy, how may the Church conceive and plan that strategy? Whatever plan may be devel-oped, it is always true that Christians must strive to find their way mindful of the ultimate demands of the Kingdom of God.

All of these problems may perhaps be summed up in a fourth. This is the constant problem, from which Christians are never free, of maintaining the proper sense of inner urgency and tension. In part, this is the tension caused by the conflict between Christ and the evil of the world. So the love of Christ constraineth us to action now. In part, this is a ten-sion between the new which has come to us, and the comple-tion of it in the future. Thus we look forward with eager awaiting. We cannot escape the fact that the full Gospel requires us to witness in present day-to-day living, and in every aspect of our life, to a Kingdom which is amongst us now, but which is also still to come. If our view starts with life in Christ now, we shall perforce press on toward the goal of full stature in him. If our hope is centered upon the King-dom to come, we cannot but feel the pressure of its coming upon our everyday living. The deepest problem of living in the interim between now and then is to live at the same time in a Kingdom which has come and in the expectancy of its final coming.

IV

THE CHURCHES' WITNESS IN WORD AND DEED[1]

In Chapter II the tensions which the churches confront were described. In Chapter III the churches' understanding of the Word given in the Bible with regard to relations among the races was reviewed. The question as to what is required of the churches in the application of that Word in the sinful world now, during the interim before the final coming of the Kingdom, was analyzed.

This chapter attempts to describe in broad outline the various ways by which the churches attempt in word and deed to bring the influence of the Gospel to bear upon the situations of tension in which they find themselves.

There is no country and no church that is not involved, directly or indirectly, in the world problem of racial and ethnic tensions. Some churches report that they are confronted by tensions among groups within their own communities. Others mention interest in foreign students or refugees. Still others report their concern for matters of national policy with regard to assistance to "underdeveloped territories," or investments in commercial enterprises among people of other races, or their involvement in the world tension resulting from the "rising tide of color." The missionary movement has directed the attention of many Christians to the problem. Whatever aspect

---

[1] A statement of the attitude of the Roman Catholic Church toward the racial question would lie outside the scope of this paper. It may conveniently be studied in a booklet by Father Yves Congar: *The Catholic Church and the Race Question* (UNESCO).

Readers will also wish to study "Churches and the Racial Problem" by W. A. Visser 't Hooft (UNESCO, 1953).

of the problem may be reported from each situation, it is agreed that every church faces a responsibility to exert its influence on behalf of justice and good will in relations among the races.

The policies of the churches constituent to the World Council of Churches vary greatly. There are some churches which, so far as their official records are concerned, report no policy with regard to the relation of the church to intergroup tensions either because no tensions are recognized or because the church assumes that they constitute no problem for it. In some instances where the tensions are recognized the church has formulated no policy because it has assumed that the fact of tension is inherent in society and therefore inevitable, so that there is nothing for the church to do. In some instances the church recognizes the fact of tension, but assumes that it constitutes no problem distinguishable from any problem of human relationships which is to be resolved by a change in the attitudes of individuals. Believing that right attitudes follow inevitably from conversion, its policy is simply to convert more individuals.

Where positive policies are stated, they range from segregation to integration, though often the edges of the policies are blurred in inconsistencies of practice. Some churches which practice segregation deny that they have a policy of segregation; they defend or explain their practice on grounds of social expediency or necessity. Others practice integration less as a matter of deliberate policy than as an uncritical reflection of the general community pattern.

The distinction between the avowed policy of the churches and their practice is important. Where policy and practice are different and the policy involves a recognition of principle or a commitment to principle which is not reflected in practice, there is a tension between principle and practice which tends to draw practice in the direction of principle, and acknowledgment of principle in the direction of practice. It is one thing for a church to repudiate segregation in principle while it continues to practice it apologetically and with uneasy conscience as a matter of supposed expediency. It is quite another thing for a church to adopt segregation as a deliberate policy and not only practice it but defend it as right in principle. In the first instance the church inevitably moves away from the practice of segregation; in the second instance it is confirmed in its practice of segregation and intends to continue in it indefinitely.

Since space does not permit a comprehensive review of the ways in which the churches meet the whole range of various situations, attention is directed primarily to the most difficult and urgent ones. In Chapter II it was seen that tension is generally most dangerous where segregation prevails. In Chapter III it became apparent that the community pattern of segregation and the practice of discrimination constituted the greatest difficulties and the greatest challenge to the churches. Therefore, the reports of the churches with regard to the problem of segregation are selected for special emphasis in analysis.

It is significant to note that few churches define their policy as that of pluralism. Those that report a practice of pluralism indicate that it has its tensions, which in turn give rise to problems of policy; for pluralism is in unstable equilibrium between the pulls toward segregation on the one hand and toward integration on the other, the first tending to discrimination and the second to homogeneity with the loss of the contribution of distinctiveness.

A. The Positions of the Churches on Segregation in Principle

No member Church of the World Council reported supporting segregation in theological principle, though there are doubtless individuals who do so. Such support has been stated by a Church *not* a member of the World Council thus: "The Almighty God saw fit, in His infinite wisdom, to segregate the races in the beginning, and we earnestly believe that the will of God (will) be best served by continuation of the total segregation of the black and white races."

The churches generally, by separate action and in their councils, have in their official statements repudiated segregation in principle. Several instances are here cited:

(1) The National Council of the Churches of Christ in the U.S.A. (1952):

The principle of segregation is a denial of the Christian faith and ethic which stems from the basic premise taught by our Lord, that all men are created the children of God. The pattern of segregation is diametrically opposed to what Christians believe about the worth of persons, and if we are to be true to the Christian faith, we must take our stand against it. . . . The National Council of the Churches of Christ in the U.S.A. in its organizational structure and operation, renounces and earnestly recommends to its member-churches that they renounce the pattern of segregation based on race, colour or national origin as unnecessary and undesirable and a violation of the Gospel of love and human brotherhood. While recognizing that historical and social factors make it more difficult for some churches than for others to realize the Christian ideal of non-segregation, the Council urges all of its constituent members to work steadily and progressively towards a non-segregated church as the goal which is set forth in the faith and practice of the early Christian community and inherent in the New Testament idea of the Church of Christ. As proof of our sincerity in this renunciation, the National Council of Churches will work for a non-segregated church and a non-segregated community.

(2) This same position has been taken by numerous national bodies of Churches in the United States, as, for example, the Congregational Christian, Evangelical and Reformed, the Presbyterian Church in the U.S.A., and the American Baptist Convention.

(3) The Lambeth Conference of 1948: "Every churchman should be assured of a cordial welcome in any Church of our Communion and no one should be ineligible for any position in the Church by reason of colour." The Anglican Bishops of the Church of the Province of South Africa associated them-

selves "fully and completely" with the findings of the Lambeth Conference.

B. Church Policies and Practices with Regard to Segregation

Despite the fact that they either do not support segregation in theological principle or that they specifically disavow it, some churches take the position that it is justifiable in practice, while others repudiate it in practice.

Since the position of the Dutch Reformed Churches in South Africa has been a matter of widespread discussion, and since it is a position held in general principle in a few other churches, it is reported at length.

The Bloemfontein Conference of the Missions Council of the Dutch Reformed Churches in South Africa in 1950 said:

In spite of separation, the unity of the faith must, however imperfectly, be practiced. This is the nucleus of the matter. We may accept that there is scriptural evidence not only for the birth and continuation of separate nations but also for separate churches. We may acknowledge that especially for practical reasons it is without doubt more useful to organize whites and non-whites separately. But that does not mean that we have finished our task. We are members of the same body and need each other. It is imperatively necessary that our churches do not merely confess spiritual unity in Christ as an article of our faith, but that they also apply it in practice, for instance, in family-devotion.

* * *

The fact that two non-white congregations still belong to the mother-Church, that here and there non-whites share in the privilege of membership in the mother-Church, and that our missionaries and other whites worship in mission-churches and go to communion, shows that *no principle is at stake in this matter* ("apartheid"). [*Italics supplied.*]

The exegesis of the Bible often put forward (e.g., in the Report submitted to the Synod of the Dutch Reformed

Church of the Transvaal, 1951) is that the nation is a "divine order," the existence and maintenance of which is willed by God. The breaking up of the original unity of the human race is the result of sin, but in the providence of God the creation of separate nations and races also contains a blessing. The original unity can only be restored by the victory over sin; but this can only be realized in the eschatological future. The Gospel bridges the gulf between nations and races, but does not wipe out national or racial distinctions. True spiritual unity between the faithful of different races or nations does not require the sacrifice of racial or national identity. The unity of the Church does not mean the equality of its members. The more advanced have the calling of trusteeship toward the less advanced.

While these views are held by many, there is a wide divergence of opinion within the Church, especially as to the biblical basis for separate churches. While some hold that separate churches on a national or racial basis is a matter of principle, many others believe it is a question of practical consideration only.

At variance with this policy which supports segregation in the community there are many examples of support for a prevailing pattern of integration in the community in such countries as Brazil, the United Kingdom, and those states in the U.S.A. in which the law demands integration in such matters as employment, public education, transport, and health and recreational facilities. This is the simplest pattern for the Christian conscience.

Even so, it is admitted that there are places where the churches, even though in policy they support the community pattern of integration, continue to practice a measure of segregation not enforced by the community. In some parts of the U.S.A., for example, segregation is prevalent in the churches even though it is not observed in the public schools, in transportation, and in other public facilities, including playgrounds and bathing beaches. Practices in church-controlled hospitals and colleges are similar to those in the same types of public institutions. Some theological seminaries are segregated. Less than 1 per cent of the Negro Protestant Christians worship regularly in churches with fellow Christians of another race. It was recently stated by a popular magazine that eleven o'clock on Sunday morning is the most segregated hour of the week.

Official profession of policy undoubtedly has some effect upon the community as well as the Church, but the profession of policy is probably not as effective in influence on the community as is actual practice. In fact, inconsistency between policy and practice is likely to create an unfavorable impression upon the community, which interprets professed policy as insincere or hypocritical when it is not demonstrated in practice. This applies in the first place to practice within the fellowship of the Church; but that cannot be satisfactorily detached from practice within the community as a whole.

What constitutes an appropriate witness to the Gospel and an effective challenge to the behavior of the community depends upon the situation in the community. It would not be fitting for the Preparatory Commission or this Background Paper to evaluate the practices of particular churches. However, the reports from the churches indicate that many of them realize that they are under the judgment of God in this matter and on trial before the world.

The practices of the several churches fall somewhere on a scale between avowed support of a community pattern of segregation at one extreme and open defiance at the other. Gradations on the scale are somewhat as follows:

> avowed support of that pattern;
> silent acceptance;
> apologetic compliance;
> strategic tension;
> repudiation of, but compliance with, the laws of the
> community; and

rejection of the community pattern with open challenge to the laws enforcing it.

Avowed support of segregation in the community is found in churches which approve it as a matter of policy and which practice it in their own organization and fellowship.

Silent acceptance of the community pattern is found in the practice of some churches which, recognizing tension, assume that they have no responsibility to deal with the problems it raises otherwise than through conversion.

The practice of *apologetic compliance* is found among those churches which have adopted a policy which challenges the community pattern, but accommodate themselves to that pattern, waiting for a gradual process of education and social change to modify it and the practice of the church.

Strategic tension characterizes the practice of those churches which challenge the community pattern in such a way as to arouse the conscience of the community and to demonstrate practical and appropriate ways of modifying the community pattern, not only by education but by criticism of prevailing policies and activities which are not normal in the community pattern. The church which has no color bar in a community where the bar is recognized may establish a strategic tension.

Repudiation of, but compliance with, law is found among those churches which, while committing themselves to a policy at variance with the community pattern and practicing their policy, do so only so far as is permitted by the laws of the community. For example, churches may practice no segregation in their own membership, life and worship, but if they are in communities where law requires segregation in public accommodations they will comply with the law if they have a meeting in a public auditorium. It is to be noted that the World Council of Churches refuses to compromise in this way. Since it is not pinned down to one area, it is, of course, better able to take this stand than a church which cannot evade an issue by moving into a more favorable environment. Yet the fact that it has taken an absolutely firm stand, often in the face of very real difficulty, has been an encouragement to its constituent Churches. Its refusal to send any but a multi-racial delegation to South Africa is a case in point.

The extreme of practice at variance with the community pattern is found in the *rejection of the community pattern and open challenge to law.* No examples of such practice by a church body have been reported. However, certain church leaders have advocated this position or have put it into practice. One church leader recently criticized a theological seminary which practiced segregation for the alleged reason that it was required by law. He wrote:

The Church has often been healthiest when it was illegal. . . . We got our start that way, as a matter of fact. . . . The picture of the theological faculty behind bars, instructing students gathered on the lawn around the country jail, is one which could inspire us to realize that the Church is not meant to "conform to this world," and could attract many now indifferent people to a church which often, all too easily, blends with its surroundings.

Among various factors mentioned as having an influence, worthy or unworthy, on the policy and practice of the churches are the following:

(1) The transfer of responsibility from missionaries to indigenous leaders should not be more rapid than the competence of the latter justifies.

(2) Class discrimination may be in effect race discrimination even on the part of those who have no admitted race prejudice.

(3) Some churches fail to abandon a policy of segregation because they fear the withdrawal of a minority of their members who oppose such a step.

(4) Some correspondents state that the activities of their churches are inconsistent with their principles because

they are not willing to pay the price of doing what they know they ought to do.

(5) Some church leaders report—"Our people are not yet ready."

C. Specific Activities of the Churches

A selective and partial list of specific activities by churches or church councils will be suggestive of what is being done in some places to meet the challenge of tension:

(1) Publication of a study and action program to be considered by groups organized for that specific purpose in local churches.

(2) Organizing hospitality and assistance for foreign students.

(3) Providing a speakers list for study groups.

(4) Conducting a conference on the needs of workers from minority groups, drawing in welfare workers, leaders of labor organizations and representatives of government.

(5) Admitting children regardless of color into a church-controlled day school.

(6) Overturing the national government to abandon race discrimination in immigration policy.

(7) Organizing a department of race and ethnic relations in a denomination or council of churches.

(8) Conducting leadership training institutes.

(9) Publishing a news bulletin on race problems.

(10) Integrating the church's teaching on race into the curriculum material for religious education.

(11) Producing and distributing motion pictures.

(12) Co-operating with government and United Nations agencies in work for better race relations.

(13) Initiating joint inquiries into the causes of racial tensions in the community by educators, welfare workers, recreational leaders, the courts, the police, industrial leaders and representatives of other civic groups.

(14) Supporting legislative measures in the interest of justice and civil rights for all, regardless of race.

(15) Designating specified Sundays or periods each year for special attention to race relations.

(16) Producing radio programs to set forth the churches' message and program.

(17) Setting up permanent communities or temporary camps in which people of various races do work together which is normally done only by members of one race.

(18) Providing orientation courses for newcomers to a country.

(19) Organizing interracial clubs.

D. CO-OPERATION WITH NON-CHURCH AGENCIES

Few correspondents provided specific information with regard to the co-operation of the churches with other agencies in matters of race relations. However, various papers and reports indicate extensive collaboration, in a few instances officially as between agencies, more frequently unofficially by participation of leaders who serve on commissions or join in meetings and conferences.

In no instance did any report intimate that the churches relied entirely upon governmental or other secular agencies to deal with problems of race relations, leaving the churches without an essential role. No report protested against a usurpation of the churches' function by others. On the other hand, no report complained that the churches were alone in their concern or efforts with regard to the problem.

Government agencies and university experts are cited and accepted frequently as sources of information, not only for facts such as census statistics, but also for descriptions of conditions and analyses of problems. Thus, a Danish correspondent relies largely upon a Danish government report for a description of the situation in Greenland.

Collaborating in a Conference on Non-European Overseas Personnel under the British Council of Churches were not only church leaders but also individuals from the Y.M.C.A., Y.W.C.A, the East and West Friendship Council, the Ministry of Labour, the Colonial Office, the Victoria League, Toc. H. and the National Council of Social Service.

A report from New Zealand states that "the vigilance and efforts of the Aborigines' Protection Society in England undoubtedly was a great factor in creating" an attitude of responsibility toward the Maori people. Australian reports indicate close co-operation between church groups and anthropologists in the universities.

The U.S.A. report lists eighteen agencies—none of them governmental—with which church groups co-operate in efforts to improve race relations. Some of them rely largely on church people for support in their programs. In addition, the churches co-operate with numerous government agencies.

There appears to be no warranted generalization with regard to collaboration between church groups and other groups. In some instances scientific or humanitarian interests independent of the churches have created agencies working for better race relations. In others, church members stimulated in their concern by the influence of the churches have taken the initiative in organizing more inclusive agencies. In nations where race relations are tense there appears to be extensive co-operation—usually unofficial—between the interested groups in the churches and other specialized groups in common objectives of education and social action.

Co-operation is thus achieved with a wide variety of organizations, including the United Nations (with its associated agencies, such as UNESCO, WHO, FAO); Government and University Departments in metropolitan and colonial territories; and a great diversity of private societies (such as the East and West Friendship Council, the Royal Africa Society, various Institutes and Bureaus of Race Relations).

In the Preparatory Commission discussions it was pointed out that there is a danger in co-operation with government departments that the churches may identify, or seem to identify, themselves with the political policies of the government; and this is especially to be watched where government grants are involved. It would be better for the churches to decline financial assistance than to accept any limitation on their freedom to criticize. In the main, however, it was thought that no undesirable conditions appear to have been attached to the grants that were discussed.

The Commission also observed that it is a mistake to think, still more to speak, of all non-church organizations as "secular." The intimation is often resented, and with justice. In purpose and in personnel many of them are markedly Christian; they do not duplicate the functions of the churches which they alone can perform, but they play most important complementary roles.

Another kind of problem, it was noted in the Preparatory Commission, is sometimes posed by the "pressure" type of private organization. Its members commonly hold particular political, sociological and often religious views that not all Christians can accept. There is a danger that members of such societies may regard all those who do not agree with them and enthusiastically assist in their campaigns, particularly if they are church members, as culpably feeble and lukewarm and that the churches may respond by classing them as "cranky" and irresponsible. For their part, the churches ought to examine themselves to see if the charge of lukewarmness may not be well founded; they must also find means to sustain in their fellowship those whose actions they may indeed regard as seriously mistaken but whose Christian concern they cannot well doubt.

V

OUTLINE OF MAIN ISSUES

The main issues, implicit or explicit in the topic, as revealed by reports from the churches or suggested by the analysis of this Background Paper, are herewith summarized. It is suggested that they be considered by the Section of the Assembly and that some of them at least will require continuing study by the World Council of Churches.[1]

CHAPTER II

(1) Is it inevitable that churches accommodate their policies and practices to the racial patterns of the societies in which they exist?

(2) Is involuntary and compulsory segregation compatible with Christianity?

(3) How can the churches teach more effectively their principles with regard to race?

(4) What counsel should the churches develop with regard to inter-racial marriage?

(5) What is the proper response of the churches to the challenge on race presented by the communists?

CHAPTER III

(1) How is race to be defined in terms consonant with Biblical conceptions and with the facts of history and science?

(2) What is the significance of the existence of distinguishable races at any given point in history?

[1] If field inquiries or extensive questionnaires are involved, it should be borne in mind that the churches and Christian councils in East and Central Africa are already engaged in an urgent study of problems of common citizenship in a multi-racial society and that in those areas prior consideration should be given to the study already begun.

(3) How do differing racial theories and practices affect relations between the churches?

(4) What, if any, responsibility have the churches in their ecumenical councils to state or to imply judgment with regard to

(a) the teachings of the churches with regard to the races or

(b) the policies and practices of the churches?

(5) What is the significance of differences in attitudes toward history and Christian hope found among races and ethnic groups whose own histories vary in terms of the time spans of their respective civilizations—e.g., Bantu, French, Chinese?

(6) Does the responsibility of the churches in their ecumenical councils with regard to the problem of race differ from their responsibility with regard to economic and political problems? If so, how?

Chapter IV

(1) What is the bearing of the racial practices of the churches upon their progress of missions and evangelism?

(2) What has been the experience of the churches with regard to segregation, pluralism and integration in their own organization and fellowship?

(3) How should the churches contribute to the improvement of communication between racial and ethnic groups that are in tension?

(4) How can people who are inarticulate be helped to be articulate so that issues may be adequately defined from all points of view?

(5) What are the churches doing to improve relations by (a) their own example, and by (b) their work in the community? What is the relation between such action and the churches' professions?

(6) What has been the experience of the churches with regard to mixed marriages?

(7) What is the nature and value of efforts of the churches and mission agencies to teach the bearing of Christian principles on problems of race relations?

(8) How can the churches anticipate developments that may give rise to tension?

(9) How can the World Council co-operate more effectively with the United Nations on matters of race?

PREPARATORY COMMISSION V

on

INTERGROUP RELATIONS—THE CHURCH AMID RACIAL AND ETHNIC TENSIONS

Members

The Rev. Dr. Roswell P. BARNES, U.S.A., Chairman
*Professor G. BAEZ-CAMARGO, Mexico, Vice-chairman
Rev. Robert S. BILHEIMER (W.C.C.), Secretary

Professor S. P. ADINARAYAN, India
*The Rev. Professor J. H. BAVINCK, Netherlands
*The Rev. Charles BONZON, France
The Rev. Gerhard BRENNECKE, Germany
Mr. L. B. GREAVES, United Kingdom
*Professor UHLA BU, Burma
The Rev. Dr. B. J. MARAIS, South Africa
*Professor Z. K. MATTHEWS, South Africa
President Benjamin E. MAYS, U.S.A.
*The Rev. Allan T. McNAUGHTON, New Zealand
Mr. Alan PATON, South Africa
Dean Liston POPE, U.S.A.
Professor Margaret H. READ, United Kingdom
*The Rev. Dr. John KAREFA-SMART, Liberia
*Dr. Channing TOBIAS, U.S.A.
*The Rt. Rev. Bishop M. H. YASHIRO, Japan

Consultant

*The Rev. Dr. Norman GOODALL (International Missionary Council)

Central Committee Consultants

*The Rev. Dr. L. E. COOKE, United Kingdom
*The Rt. Rev. Bishop L. DIA, Philippine Islands
President Benjamin E. MAYS, U.S.A. (member of the Commission)

* Not present at August, 1953, meeting.

Substitutes and ad hoc Consultants attending the August 1953
meeting

Mr. E. J. BINGLE, (International Missionary Council)
Mr. Richard G. KATONGOLE, Uganda
Dr. Tracy STRONG, U.S.A.

THE LAITY—THE CHRISTIAN
IN HIS VOCATION

An Ecumenical Survey
prepared under the auspices of the
World Council of Churches

CONTENTS

iii

Contents

I

INTRODUCTION

This is the first time in the history of the ecumenical movement that the subject "The Christian in his Vocation" or "The Laity" has been put before an ecumenical gathering with such great emphasis. This in itself is indicative of the fact that in many churches all over the world in recent years some fresh movement has arisen, not organized from above but born of a widely and deeply felt need on the part of the Church to meet man in the modern world where he really lives and of a new joyousness on the part of its members in witnessing to Jesus Christ as Saviour and Lord of all realms of life. It is through its lay membership that the Church enters into real and daily contact with the workaday world and shares in its problems and aspirations. It is in the life and work of the lay membership that the Church must manifest in the world its regenerative and redemptive power. One of the greatest tasks of the Church today is to grasp clearly the significance of the lay ministry *in* the world.

By "laity" we mean, for the purposes of this Survey, the vast body of church members who spend their lives in what is called a *secular* occupation, which absorbs the major part of their time. It is a self-deception not to admit that theirs is a particular situation distinct from that of the clergy and others occupied full time in the service of the organized church. It may, however, be regretted that there is no other term to describe the situation of most church members but "laymen" which is tainted with all sorts of hereditary class distinction or discrimination within the Church. In this study we wish to exclude from the word "laity" any other meaning but that which has been indicated.

1

Within the ecumenical movement, the man who first raised the point of the crucial significance of the lay ministry in the world for the life and witness of the Church was Dr. J. H. Oldham, in the preparatory volume for Oxford (1937) *The Church and Its Function in Society*. In one of the main papers for Amsterdam he made a further plea on this matter, this time by demanding for a theology of the common life. Meanwhile, particularly after the experiences many Christians have had with the totalitarian state and during World War II, the paramount importance of the laity for the Church's witness and impact upon the world has been widely realized. Alongside the older lay organizations such as the Y.M.C.A., the Y.W.C.A., W.S.C.F., Men's Movements and Women's Movements of the Churches, the Sunday School Association and others, new movements have sprung up, first in Europe, and now also in America, India and other parts of the world, concentrating very much on developing the implications of the Christian faith in social, occupational and political life. They found expression in groups such as the Associations Professionnelles Protestantes in France and Belgium, and the Christian Frontier Council in Britain, in centers like the Sigtuna Foundation in Sweden, the Evangelical Academies in Germany and the Kerk en Wereld Institute in Holland, in special communities in America, in conferences in India and Australia, in the big German Church Rally assembling hundreds and thousands of laymen and women once a year, in movements such as Zoe and Aktines in Greece, and in the vast and active Actio Catholica with its manifold ramifications all over the Roman Catholic World.

It was only logical that "The Significance of the Laity in the Church" became one of the four concerns which formed part of the Amsterdam Assembly. The Committee for this concern put before the Assembly a recommendation that the Central Committee of the World Council of Churches discuss the question of how to enable the laity of the Church to make their Christian witness in their secular and professional lives.

This resulted in the European Laymen's Conference held at Bad Boll, Germany (1951), and the conference on "The Christian in His Daily Work" held for the U.S.A. and Canada at Buffalo (1952). Within the World Council of Churches, the Ecumenical Institute seeks to support and strengthen these attempts by a great number of various courses and conferences for laymen, while the Secretariat for Laymen's Work has been established in order to keep the necessary contacts with the ongoing work of those groups in the churches.

It is on the basis of the work and experience of these pioneering groups that this Survey was drafted. In addition to the current material collected by the Secretariat for Laymen's Work, quite a number of national surveys have been received, notably from Britain, Egypt, Germany, Japan, Sweden and the U.S.A. Finally, many books and articles have been consulted, a selected list of which is attached at the end of this Survey.

II

HOW THE PROBLEM ARISES

It is an almost universal conviction revealed in many reports that there exists at present a gulf between Christian preaching and teaching and man's actual experience of life. To a large extent the experience of modern man is made up of what is experienced in work. Work very often demanding the majority of waking hours and of resources of energy dictates, as it were, the rhythm of the rest of life. It may well be that it is the task of Christianity to reverse the order of work and leisure. But it is a fact, at least in the West, that the modern world is a workaday world, and it seems likely that in this respect the today of the West will be the tomorrow of Asia and Africa. That is why in this Survey we are concentrating so much on work. We keep in mind, however, that from a Christian point of view work has not necessarily priority over other features of life, and also that work does not find its sole expression in a man's job or occupation. In all domestic, social, political, cultural and ecclesiastical life, there is an element of work which must not be obscured by the way in which we treat our subject here. It is for reasons of convenient brevity that we concentrate on work as done in an occupation from which men gain their living. It will, however, be seen that a study of this limited field reveals realities of the modern man's life which go far beyond his experiences in working hours.

The estrangement between the present world and the Christian message arises largely from two areas: work in modern society and the actual life of the organized church.

4

A. REASONS ARISING FROM WORK IN MODERN SOCIETY

Almost any generalization about "what modern work is like" will be untrue of conditions in some work or in some parts of the world. There is, however, one obvious fact: the coming of modern techniques, sometimes called "industrialization," which influences not only what millions of workers do during their working day but also the social and family life of the increasing majority of the world's population though in widely varying degrees and in different ways. In general, it may be said that there is a tendency toward mechanization, high organization and corporate decision-making inherent in many forms of work today.

The classic case for what is meant by industrialization with all its implications on the structure of work and society is manufacture, mining and transport. For our purpose we mention only a few characteristics:

(1) Modern transport and large-scale production has separated many producers from those who use the things they produce. Thus a village shoemaker of the pre-industrial age was making shoes for people he knew and saw, while the worker in modern shoe factories makes shoes, or more likely a part of a shoe, for a person possibly at the other end of the world. One result of this is for some people a lack of consciousness of purpose. Logically the purpose of the work may be the same, but it is difficult to realize this vividly.

(2) Mechanization itself has had a very varied effect on the consciousness of the individual workers and their relations to their jobs. In some instances it has changed jobs which required highly developed traditional skill into mere machine minding. On the other hand, it has made new and difficult demands on individual skill, and given rise to new forms of pride in craft. While machine production has at times a deadening effect on the worker, it has also awakened new interests and abilities—interests and abilities which it cannot always satisfy. Many traditional skills required little

intellectual activity outside the skill itself; but modern technical production requires a great increase in literacy—if only so
that factory workers can understand notices in the factory
and instructions on machines. This extension of literacy cannot stop at this point and has widespread human repercussions. Similarly, many routine workers develop an elementary
interest in scientific and technical studies from their work,
and so come into touch with the world of scientific thought.

(3) Mechanical production makes many workers dependent on the machine and on the organized structure of production. Thus an individual craftsman of a pre-industrial
society with a few tools could practice his craft almost any-
where. In contrast, an engine driver or machine tool worker,
in order to practice his craft requires not only an engine or
a lathe, but also the whole organized structure of the railway
system or of the factory. If this elaborate structure (both
technical and organizational) becomes broken the modern
worker is peculiarly helpless.

(4) Along with these changes in technology and partly
related to them, have gone important changes in the organization of economic life and indeed of society as a whole. As Peter Drucker has indicated, the big business corporation has
become a new and very important social institution. An increasing proportion of professional workers (e.g., architects,
draftsmen, engineers and even physicians and lawyers) exercise their profession as officials within an organized hierarchical
structure. The large-scale productive unit has become increasingly important, although the extent of very large-scale production should not be exaggerated—the greater part of manufacture is still done in small and medium-sized units. Along
with these developments, but distinct, has gone the increasing
importance of corporate policy-making bodies. Many industrial decisions are now made not within the individual firm,
but within organizations of employers and workers. Technical
standards are often set within technical and trade societies.
The technique of collective activity (committee work, ap-

pointment of representatives, etc.) therefore plays an increasing part in the lives of workers, managers and technicians alike.

Beside industry agriculture must not be overlooked. Still two thirds of the people of the world are employed in agriculture, more people are engaged in farming, as owner-operators, absentee owners, tenants and farm laborers. There are still many parts of the world where agriculture is associated with drudgery and grinding poverty, and where illiteracy creates special problems for those working in agriculture.

Within recent years, the use of machinery on farms in many areas has profoundly altered the conditions of agricultural work and the outlook of farm workers. It has often resulted in the consolidation of small farms into large-scale farms or "factories in the fields." In some circumstances it has caused unemployment and the displacement of small holders and small tenant farmers. A result has been the disintegration of the traditional social and economic pattern of life in the family farm. An even more radical development in some countries has been that of the collective or state farm.

One of the most clamant questions of work in almost all states of society is the relation of work to reward. Differences between rates of payment for different kinds of work is one factor, though not the only factor, in causing differences in wealth and standards of living. More than the standard of living is involved, however, vital though that is; there is a strong tendency in society to measure the prestige of work and the worker by wage and salary rates. Jobs come almost unconsciously to carry a social prestige depending on their earning power.

Closely allied with this is the question of the "dignity of work." Many essential jobs have been arduous, unpleasant, ill-paid and consequently held in low repute in society. The increased freedom of transference between jobs, especially when allied with full employment, has made it very difficult to recruit into these occupations. These facts, quite apart from moral considerations, have in many countries brought about radical departures from traditional "wage differentials." In some countries there is wide government control of the whole wage system. There is, however, little sign of a principle, whether theoretical or practical, for deciding how wage rates should be related between different jobs.

The question of "incentives" relates to this subject. There are, in the consciousness of the individual, two distinct elements whose relative importance varies for different people and different jobs. First, there is the long-period, more logical or reflective element, which is mainly concerned with the purpose of the work. This comes in when the worker sits back and asks the question, "What is it all for anyhow?" Yet the answer to this question is only rarely in the worker's conscious mind when he has "his hand to the plough"; it is inadequate in itself to maintain effort. So, in the second place, there are a whole complex of incentives which operate in the short run— e.g., the pay packet, emulation, hope of promotion, pride in the job, the drive of good leadership, loyalty to one's workmates and so on.

The events of the last thirty years make it impossible to avoid the question of unemployment, and by this is meant not merely occasional periods of transference between jobs, but large-scale, permanent involuntary unemployment. It is clear that all governments and political groups wish to avoid unemployment of this type and it is almost universally recognized as an evil, to be avoided if possible. Different parties and groups, however, differ in the price they would be willing to pay to avoid unemployment.

The evil of unemployment is not confined to the unemployed. Large-scale unemployment in a country leaves employed persons far more completely at the mercy of employers and very much more helpless in the face of exploitation and injustice. Moreover, it is mainly potential unemployment which forces people to remain in jobs which are deeply repugnant to them.

We must now look into some conclusions which often are drawn from the situation as it has been described:

(1) Many people speak of the "depersonalization of labor relations." Karl Jaspers states that almost everybody in modern society is but a functionary of the anonymous machinery for securing life. In fact many decisions arise from remote or apparently anonymous officials or organizations. But it is important to realize that this tendency is neither universal nor simple. For example, some decisions which were formerly the result of the impersonal play of market conditions are now made by persons who can be identified. It is perhaps truer to describe the process as one of increasing complexity rather than one of mere depersonalization. In this process the individual worker, manager and employer, the farmer, the doctor and the unemployed often feel lost or confused.

(2) Technocracy having subjected the human being and having made him a slave of the machine is also one of the pictures most widely spread. Obviously for some workers in some jobs it is the tempo of the machine on which the rhythm of their lives depends. On the other hand, the machine has liberated the manual worker from a good deal of drudgery and even in mass-producing factories most of the workers are not usually employed at the assembly line itself but in ancillary jobs, such as maintenance, yard laboring, etc. There is a substratum in work, as it bears on the worker, which is less changed by technical developments than is generally expected. This is even more true of small-scale production, a great deal of retailing, personal service and a large range of jobs in distribution and transport where fully mechanized methods are still inapplicable or at least little used.

(3) Frequently the feeling has been expressed that as a result of technological refinement people have been forced into a rigid hierarchical system with no choice of their own. Because of the highly developed specialization of work, it has indeed become increasingly difficult to exercise an occupation, for which originally one was not trained. It is also true that

higher education and training still involves financial resources which are beyond the means of many people, though in some countries in more recent years several ways have been tried in order that all walks of life might be open to everybody. On the other hand, modern production and transport have allowed a novel individual freedom in the choice of occupation. In traditional societies occupation was normally strictly limited by the opportunities of birth and environment, sometimes reinforced by a caste system or rigid social stratification. Most people were fixed in an occupation before adolescence. Modern education and transport (particularly local buses) have given to many people the opportunity of deliberate choice of occupation which did not exist before, and this opportunity is much increased where there is substantial full employment. This increased freedom is not necessarily a blessing, since it can lead to serious unsettlement in work and may give people the opportunity of choosing between jobs without knowing how to choose. In some countries (e.g., Britain) military service in early adult life has aggravated this sense of unsettlement by breaking the habits of an accustomed job. In some authoritarian countries deliberate legal limitations have been put on freedom of transference between jobs, perhaps to counteract the social cost of undue mobility.

(4) There is much talk about the "sense of purposelessness" in work. It is important to distinguish between two senses in which this term may be used: a worker may have consciously thought out the purpose of the work he is doing and decided that it is useless, wasteful or unacceptable; or a worker may have an emotional sense of futility in his work (which may be quite valuable in itself) because the conditions do not bring its purpose home to him vividly. It is often hard for a man to trace the cause of his malaise which may arise from the general social situation, from the conditions under which he works or from the result of his work.

Everything that has been said above is suggestive of a three-dimensional aspect to work, namely, the job, the occupation and the larger social context, none of which can be separated from the others. The job is the work a person actually does. In the limits of his job the individual is responsible; he can do the job badly or well. But these limits are narrowing down in increasing measure. The effect of the work a man does in his job depends largely on the structure of the occupation in which a job is done. Even a good engine driver produces mediocre or bad results if the transport system is bad; even a good lecture delivered by a university professor does not do much good if the university as an institution is outmoded or without real purpose. In its turn what we have called the occupation is in many ways dependent on the society of which it is a function. The transportation system can only work if society as a whole produces people who are morally and intellectually gifted enough to perform the various jobs in that occupation. The university makes sense only if unrestricted spiritual freedom involving a certain amount of political freedom is guaranteed by the society in which the university does its work. The complex nature of modern work depends largely on the interplay of these three factors at nearly every point. Taking one's job seriously almost immediately leads to questions of social structure and to political considerations.

Perhaps the most important point for the Church in the whole development of work in modern society is its community character. For many people the sociability and friendship arising out of work are quite as important as the inherent interest of the job itself. It has been noted that some of the more lively-minded workers prefer a large unit because it offers a greater scope of personal relationships. This is one of the reasons why occupational associations have been created and are playing an increasingly prominent role in the life of many who work.

The other reason is, of course, the interrelation of job, occupation and society. As a rule, no individual can hope to change the structure of his occupation. Labor unions, farmers' groups, medical associations are organs of the "community of work" through which the individual members of this community try to carry the social and political responsibilities inherent in the work they do. The danger that these associations may be made instruments in the hands of a small clique exercising power, or may become pressure groups doing more harm than good to society as a whole, has not always been avoided. But excesses of this kind must not obscure the fact that "work in modern society" cannot possibly be conceived without the organizations expressing the new sense of community to which work in a technological age has given birth and at the same time the responsibility for the structure of the whole society, counteracting the tendency of departmentalization in modern life.

B. REASONS ARISING FROM THE CHURCH

It is not the task here to expound the question as to whether the gulf between Church and workaday life is a relatively new fact. Most people assume that it has opened only in our age largely in consequence of the effects of industrialization, while others maintain that a certain defect in this respect has dogged the life of the Church for a long time, and is not a direct result of the conditions in modern work. At any rate, this estrangement is the component of various factors, the roots of which are very deep-seated in the Church. It would seem that at least five different attitudes can be distinguished which cut across national and denominational barriers, but which are typical of certain groups within the churches, though not always explicit.

A great number of Christians show an almost complete indifference toward the problems of "secular" work. They are not interested in man as a worker; they are interested in man only in so far as he has a presumably immortal soul which must be saved. The human contacts which work in a community offers may be used for the purpose of saving souls; otherwise work in human society is regarded as a training ground, where the Christian virtue of "remaining unspotted from the world" may be exercised. It should not be overlooked that very often strong and sincere evangelistic zeal is combined with this attitude of indifference toward work, and that those who hold such an attitude have some good reason to point to certain passages in the New Testament, and to a similar attitude in some circles of the early Church. Underlying this attitude, however, is often a certain spiritualization of the Christian faith as it originated in some trends of thought at the end of the eighteenth century and during the nineteenth century, with the result that religion was considered a matter purely of relationship between the individual and God. On the other hand, there are also some less noble reasons for indifference, such as carelessness or thoughtlessness on the part of the clergy or those who represent the congregations. Sometimes this indifference may be due to a vague sense of helplessness in the face of the problems of modern occupational life.

A church which has no explicit concern for the questions of work and occupation is likely unconsciously to adapt itself to its environment and membership, thus practically reinforcing the social grading in a given society through its preaching and teaching, and more often through the conduct of its members. The view that a white-collar worker does a more dignified, or as is sometimes heard a more "human" job than a garbage collector is more widespread in church circles than one would suppose. A Christian civil servant who condescends to attend church and to take a mild interest in church affairs is considered a veritable pillar of the church, we are told in a report from India. By losing its distance to society and the social grading prevalent there, the Church ceases to convey a message to the working world.

A peculiar ecclesiastical gradation of occupations is introduced wherever the concept of vocation is used to distinguish certain jobs from others. At the top of the grading scale is the ministry and perhaps some other occupations in the wider framework of the Church. A deaconess has a vocation, a doctor, a teacher or an artist may also have one, but a worker or a

businessman or a farmer is certainly excluded from the province of genuine vocation. This attitude too is often based on
the assumption that Christianity has to deal with the spiritual,
the spiritual being identified with the non-material. It should
be stressed that in most cases this attitude is not backed by
official doctrine, nor even by explicit conviction. It is, however,
peculiarly slow to die even when condemned time and again
by the explicit teaching of a church.

A fourth attitude toward work has been described as "a
country church put down in a city." What is meant by this is
a certain conservatism in a Church's teaching on work. It is
just as if the thinking of the Church in this regard had stopped
at a certain moment in its history and become ossified. Much
of the Christian teaching on work relates to a patriarchally
organized agricultural society, where craftsmen and princes
also have a place but where neither modern industry nor
modern farming, neither government as it is today nor salesmanship fit in.

Though in decreasing frequency, a "Christian version of the
secular gospel of work" is still found here and there. In this,
work is virtually identified with Christian obedience and discipline. The vocation of the Christian is considered to be work
and still more work, and work in its turn is easily identified
with being busy at some place which modern society provides
for work. Here a man's occupation and his Christian calling
are nearly congruent, and the old Benedictine saying "*laborare
est orare*" is taken out of its wider context and frequently
quoted with emphasis. The results of this attitude in practice
may be different: on the one hand, a certain social activism
on the part of a church and its members can be traced back
to this source; on the other, a social conservatism has been a
result of this attitude in some places, since overemphasis on
industriousness in one's occupation may easily blind to the
fact that a change in the structure of society is imperative.

Leaving aside in this section doctrinal considerations we
wish to draw attention to some of the more sociological reasons
which are contributing to the present state of affairs:

(1) Though in many churches the actual teaching in Sunday School, Bible Classes, etc. is largely in the hands of devoted laymen and laywomen, in most churches the standards of what to teach, and even to a certain extent of how to teach in the church are set by the clergy, or by professors of theology. Now the clergy, including theological scholars, are very often, practically speaking, a class of their own, with their special social problems, which are not the same as the problems other people have to face in occupational life.

(2) This class of the clergy is often more closely related to certain classes in society, e.g., the *bourgeoisie* or lower middle class, rather than to others, e.g., the working class, the intellectuals and the artists. Sometimes this results in particular blindness and ignorance on the part of the clergy concerning problems arising in large portions of the working population.

(3) In addition to that, quite a number of people feel today that future ministers are not given an adequate training with regard to conditions under which work in modern society is done. It is often felt that more practical experience of working life and more theoretical study of modern sociology, psychology and related subjects would enable the ministers to meet these needs better than hitherto. In this context, it should be noted that several reports from the Near and Far East stress the fact that it is not in their churches and through their ministers that people find help and guidance in occupational questions, but in groups like the Y.M.C.A. and the Y.W.C.A.

(4) Still in respect of the clergy, some people remark that ministers today are frequently overburdened with what is called routine work, such as administration, teaching, etc., and also with holding services and supplementary duties such as marriages, burials, visits to old and sick people, etc. By this kind of work they do not come much into contact with the active part of the working population, and they are not left with time to converse with those church members who are not ill or aged, about their problems in work, let alone study those problems seriously. It should not be overlooked, however, that quite a number not only of clergymen but also of

laymen regard this as the right order of things and the proper task of a minister.

(5) If we now look at the congregations, it has often been pointed out that in some parts of the world they are, as it were, imprisoned in a sociological ghetto, which separates them from the life of the rest of men. Often the prevailing atmosphere in a church is *bourgeois* or middle class, and it is extremely hard for, let us say, a worker or a modern newspaperman to feel at home in a community which is so obviously based on a different social stratum.

(6) Another factor which prevents the Church from coming into real contact with the working world is its institutionalism. Church members, and in particular the most active church members, are often interested in other men only in so far as they are potential new members of the organization of the church. For the rest, this institution has its own life, and is busy to expand and enrich it, leaving little room for a real concern with the problems of modern society, including problems of work and occupation.

The reports received do not try to evaluate these reasons in the light of the fundamental question as to whether such a gulf between the Church and everyday life is something which by no means ought to exist, or whether and in how far a separation and even a certain dissimilarity between the life of the Church and the life of society is inherent in the nature of the case. Everybody agrees that the Church and the secular world are two different things, the difference of which must come out at many points. But it is this essential difference by which the Church is set aside from the world which enables it really to speak to the world and to help and assist men in their troubles in the world. The essential distinction between Church and world must not be blurred by the introduction of wrong social, class and institutional differences which after all reflect only too penetrant a conformity of the Church with the world.

III

BIBLICAL AND THEOLOGICAL
CONSIDERATIONS

The question of "work and vocation" has given rise to many theological studies in recent years, which influence in various ways what the churches are thinking and doing in respect of their laity. It is often in groups where theologians and laymen meet together that these problems are discussed and clarified. In this and the following chapter a survey is given summing up a few highlights of these discussions. An amazing degree of agreement seems to be emerging while a number of questions are still open or very much debated. Without going into detail, we seek to follow the line of agreement, indicating at the same time some essential disagreements. While in the following chapter the Christian understanding of some of the most burning questions of work in modern society will be discussed, this chapter tries to give a survey of the discussion of fundamental theological problems. This will be done in three sections, the first dealing with the biblical teaching, the second with some typical or even classical attitudes which have emerged in the course of the history of the Church, and the third with the prospect of a new consensus in this field.

A. Vocation and Daily Work in the Bible

The Bible does not speak of "vocation" in the sense of a profession, occupation or avocation. The term "vocation" is always meant in the strict sense of calling or summons. Three questions must be asked in order to get the terminology straight: Who is calling? Who is called? Called to what?

(1) The subject of vocation in the biblical sense is God. He calls the stars into being and He calls men into his service. To

17

be sure, God calls men through various media, such as visions, dreams, experiences with nature and, particularly, through their fellow men. But He remains the author of the call, and the call is always a particular one. Vocation in this sense, therefore, must not be identified with some sort of inherent gift, natural inclination, inner experience of the individual or with the demands of society and the so-called necessities of the moment. All this may become a medium of God's call but in itself it has no vocatory quality.

(2) In the Old Testament we are told that Abraham was called. The Fathers were called. In them and through them God's people is called. With Deutero-Isaiah the suffering servant and Kyros are called as the instruments who bring about the final restoration of God's people. In general the Old Testament is very sparing in the use of the term "vocation" and its derivatives. It does not even apply it to individuals such as Moses, the great prophets, kings or priests. In the New Testament, on the other hand, not only has Jesus "called" his disciples, not only was Paul "called" to be an apostle, not only is the Church as the prolongation and restoration of Israel "called" by her Lord, but every believer is "called."

(3) The individual is called to repentance and faith into the membership of the Church which is the people of God, the "*laos theou.*" In our day the word "laity" is frequently traced back to this New Testament expression. In this sense it can only mean "belonging to the people of God." From this point of view laity includes both clergy and non-clerical members of the Church. The Old Testament background as well as the larger context of the New Testament itself remind, however, that individuals are not "called" just for their own sake. Individuals are called into the people of God, the Church, and the Church as a whole, its individual members, are called to be signs and instruments of salvation. Salvation is universal in character not only including "the people" and its members, but aiming at the whole world. The most emphatic biblical term for it is the Kingdom of God.

God calls His people, His Church, the sign and messenger
of His coming Kingdom to priesthood, to prophetic teaching
and to kingship, in other words to share with Christ in His
threefold ministry of prophet, priest and king. He is *the* Called
One. The whole history of Israel's calling culminates in Him,
and all that is to be said about the Church's and its members'
having a vocation in the biblical sense is rooted in Him. Therefore, God's calling is based on something which has happened
in the life, death and resurrection of Christ; it has its present
effect on the Church and her members by Christ's working
through the Holy Spirit and yet there is still something to wait
for. Vocation in the biblical sense includes a strong element
which points to some future event, namely, the open manifestation of Christ as the Lord of Lords. The content or substance of vocation can thus be described in New Testament
language as hope, though it must be kept in mind that this is
only one way of speaking of God's calling. Everything the
Church and the individual Christian do in virtue of their vocation bears the hallmark of having its value not only in itself,
but in something beyond its immediate appearance.

What now is the relation of this vocation to the work men
and women do in human society? Some have assumed and
some still assume, that at least in one passage of the New
Testament a direct relation between the two is established,
namely in I Cor. 7.20. Modern scholars doubt this very much,
feeling that the term "calling" here is used in exactly the same
way as elsewhere in the New Testament and that it has nothing
to do with the occupation or station in life. However this may
be, it would be misleading to build a whole theory of work
and vocation on a single passage in the New Testament.

On the other hand, not only is the Old Testament full of
instances where people are shown doing their work, and where
some teaching about work is given, but also in the New Testament quite a number of references are made to work and
workers, notably in the Epistles. The teaching there is simple

and acts as a sobering influence on all sorts of romantic and
sentimental conceptions of work.

It is God's will and mandate that work must be done, and
done in order to gain a living, which will make man independent in his material existence, so that he can live decently and
soberly and not spend his time in idleness and all kinds of
illusive fantasies, and in order to enable man to help his neighbor who is in need. It is obvious that St. Paul himself worked
with his hands for such reasons, to which was added in his
case care for the independence of the Gospel preaching, while,
on the other hand, he allowed for the practice of other preachers of the Gospel who had given up manual work and lived
on the gifts of the Christian congregations. The famous rule of
II Thess. 3.10 ("if any will not work, neither let him eat"
A.S.V.) is directed against mistaken eschatological notions of
the Kingdom of God being already a plain reality. It includes
an ironical element in so far as these enthusiasts who for "holy"
reasons refuse to do ordinary work do not think to refuse ordinary food. Feeding and working belong to the same order of
things, which though passing away is still existing.

According to the Gospels, Jesus Himself makes reference to
many occupations from those of kings to those of shepherds
and housewives. But He makes no comment on either the value
of such "secular" work in general or the comparative worth of
any of these employments. This is all the more striking since
He Himself—to all our knowledge—was brought up in an
artisan's house and presumably shared in the craft of His
earthly father before He began to preach (Mark 6.3 but cf.
Matt. 13.55). The New Testament writers, however, do not
seem to realize that this fact is worth meditation and theological expounding. Modern interpreters draw different conclusions from this fact.

On the whole, it is clear and always has been clear to the
Church that a Christian understanding of work in relation
to God's call must be derived not from isolated passages in the
Bible, however frequent they may be, but from the essence

of the biblical teaching on God and man, the Creation and the Fall, redemption and consummation as a whole. Our subject, thus, is closely related to the entire network of Christian doctrine. To demonstrate this in detail is obviously a task that cannot be carried out within the limits of such a survey. We can only in passing mention some of the more particular conceptions of work and vocation as they have largely influenced Christian thought and action in the course of history and point to some questions within the limited field of our subject itself as they are discussed today.

B. Various Concepts of Work and Vocation in Christian Thinking

In regard to the relation of vocation in the biblical sense and to "secular" work, at least six types of Christian teaching can be distinguished. This is of course a very rough-and-ready breakdown which must not be pressed. Space does not even permit the description of various types, let alone adding necessary qualifications:

(1) Indifferentism: Men, even Christians, must do some kind of work, but what they do does not matter in terms of heavenly vocation. An attitude mainly found in the early Church but also frequently since.

(2) Antagonism: Work is an evil in itself, because it contributes to maintain this ungodly world; therefore, it is opposed to the heavenly calling, and should be reduced to the minimum. A doctrine rarely developed in full, but prevailing in the practical attitude of hermits and extremists of various kinds.

(3) Asceticism: Work is good if used as a means to develop higher virtues or abilities making Christians worthy of their high vocation. Often combined with monastic and mystical theology; but also intraworldly asceticism in, e.g., Puritan thought and practice.

(4) Hierarchism: Work is the common lot of mankind, sanctified by the fact that it serves in providing a basis for the Church which is called to foreshadow and to represent God's

Kingdom; although any decent kind of work is good and necessary the value of what men are doing is graded (sometimes
seven grades), the top of the "pyramid" being the religious or
spiritual professions. An attitude most elaborate in scholastic
teaching yet implicitly underlying the feeling of many Christians in various churches.

(5) Vocationalism: Work is not good in itself, but by God's
continuous creation the "station" and its duty are objectively
good, and provide subjectively the vantage ground for a Christian's gratitude, obedience and service to his neighbor, whereby
all earthly work can and should be related to the heavenly
calling at any point. Mainly the doctrine of the Reformers; in
Lutheranism later corrupted by pious quietism and social
conservatism.

(6) Missionarism: Work is man's mission; even the Christian's vocation to the Kingdom expresses itself more or less
exclusively in terms of work or effort. Mainly the doctrine
of some neo-Calvinists and in a more social version of social
gospel theologians; secularized to the "gospel of work" or a
"l'art pour l'art" philosophy.

We have been dealing so far with the questions of the value
of work in relation to vocation. We can approach the problem
of a Christian doctrine of work also with the question, What
is the motivation to be considered as the proper Christian in-
centive for work beyond its immediate necessity? With this
question in mind at least three fields of motivation can be
distinguished which are not necessarily mutually exclusive
but which put the emphasis on different points.

(a) Work is an offering to God, bringing back through the
work of our hands the fallen Creation to its original destination
in God's plan and at the same time offering our own bodies
and minds through the discipline of work as a living sacrifice
to God. This is a predominantly Orthodox and Catholic view
in the broadest sense of these words. It relates man's work
with the Church's worship of God, particularly the worship of
God in what is then explicitly called the Eucharist. Here is the

sanctification of all earthly work whether done by Christians or non-Christians. Through the bread and wine, as the fruits of God's gift and man's labor, all human work is offered up to God and is accepted by Him as the elements of His presence in grace.

(b) Work is the fruit of the faith, accomplished in obedience to God and His Commandments. This is a predominantly Reformed view, which has exercised great influence even in the making of modern society. This kind of Christian teaching is largely responsible for those ethical standards still found in trade and business today. A clear distinction between good and bad, and a strong appeal to discipline, self-commitment and sacrifice in work are the characteristics of this view. Notable dangers are the possibility of legalism and moralism.

(c) Work is a service of love to one's neighbor springing from the gratitude for God's gift of forgiveness—a predominantly Lutheran viewpoint. From there results an open-mindedness toward new situations and a freedom of service which is not bound to any rule or commandment. This freedom of service, however, becomes dangerous when it turns into arbitrariness, or when it accepts without question the conditions under which work is done in a given occupation or society.

Another point of much theological debate is whether work belongs to the order of Creation or the order of Salvation. The new emphasis on eschatology supersedes this controversy, in so far as the consummation of the world for which Christians hope will be the fulfillment of Creation and the manifestation of Salvation at the same time. It has been said that by definition laymen are people whose primary concern is with things and tasks which are by their nature transitory and which will pass away together with the transitory world in which we live. God wills that these things should be recognized as transitory, and at the same time that they should be taken seriously. It is in this transitory world that God has placed men in the community of mankind and in the smaller communities in which we live and work; it is in this world that Christian charity and stewardship must be exercised; finally, it is for this world that Christ died. The Christian hope to which we are called must not be understood as an attitude entailing neglect of earthly matters. The Christian knows that a final point is set to all earthly activities. This final point makes the history of mankind and the life of the individual irreversible, thus rendering every moment in time eternally significant. It is in the light of the coming Kingdom that all what men do here and now receives its decisive value. No higher criterion can be applied to work than that.

C. Toward a Common Understanding of Work in Modern Society

In this section we would summarize some of the main points made in recent publications, such as Professor Calhoun's, Dr. Oldham's and other books. Though varying in emphasis and theological background they open up perspectives which are fairly common to all of them and which provide a basis for further inquiry and study of the matter.

No work, as such, no job and no occupation must be identified with God's vocation. But every job and every occupation must be subjected to the criterion whether God's call to men may come through them and whether men may respond to this call within them. The dignity of work consists not in its being an end in itself, but in its being a medium of both God's summons and man's response. It is by no means the only medium. In fact, from a Christian point of view work definitely occupies a secondary place. In a much more direct way God's call comes to men through the Bible, through Word and Sacrament as preached and administered in the Church, through the testimony of the witnesses of His Kingdom throughout the ages. Man's primary and indispensable answer is Christian faith expressing itself in worship and prayer, in devotion and meditation and in many other forms. But even so God's call does come through persons with whom the individual stands in responsible relationships in a given situation. The persons with whom he has to do in his job are not excluded from that possibility, neither can it be said that the situation in which the worker finds himself in modern society is not something through which God may seek to speak to individuals or to whole groups in that society. Equally, it is true that faith and devotion have an inner urge to show themselves in action. Again, all sorts of action are the potential field of that urge, but work cannot be excluded from it. Work as a medium of God's call and man's response must be seen from at least four angles:

(1) Work is a human necessity. The Christian knows that this simple statement reflects only the more basic fact that work is a divine mandate, one of those fundamental rules which God has given in order to maintain life on earth. As such, the necessity of work contains a commandment and a promise extended to all mankind whether they recognize God or not— the commandment that man should make an effort, and the promise that the fruits of his labor will contribute to maintaining life. This mandate to mankind comes to every individual who is capable of doing some work as God's appointment, sometimes felt as a blessing, sometimes as a curse. In the world outside Paradise, in which we live, it is indeed both. It is a blessing because through work man is invited to draw nearer to God as being made in His image, to serve and to co-operate with Him in the work of preservation, replenishment and subjection of the earth. It is a curse because through work man is tempted to put himself in God's place, to counteract His purpose, to exploit the earth and to subdue other human beings to his domination. Hence the many evils and the grave problems which work presents.

These evils must at the same time be accepted and counteracted in work. They must be accepted because if men were to wait to start working until all evils were abolished they would never work at all. They must be accepted as a means of self-discipline and even of self-abandonment. Men do not work just for their pleasure and entire satisfaction; they work because God has ruled that in the long run life cannot be sustained without work. The evils of work, from drudgery to monotony, from feeling frustrated to being overworked, must also be accepted because they are signs of God's judgment on sin, in which all men are involved and because they point to the fact that real life is something more and better than man can accomplish through the work of his hands or his brains. However, these evils are also the result of human selfishness and social injustice. As such they must be combated. Work is meant to serve the betterment of life and not its debasement. The promise of work inherent in God's appointment can only be reflected in the human response if the work a man does contributes in some way to the preservation and enrichment of his life. Work which has no such effect on the worker either is not worth doing at all and should be abolished or corresponds so little to the disposition and abilities of the individual worker that he should think of giving it up.

(2) Work is a social necessity. This means in a Christian perspective that it is God's call to serve your fellow men and to accept and realize the service fellow men are doing to you. Both sides are equally important, especially in the highly organized society of our day. The old Christian concept of the neighbor must be translated into the customer or the client whom the worker perhaps sees once in his life, into the consumer of the goods he produces whom he will never know, into the fellow workers with whom he forms a team, into the enterprise or occupation in which he works, into the whole fabric of society of which his work is a function. These are very different aspects of "neighborliness" each with far-reaching consequences.

One of them which Dr. Oldham has underlined is that the primary aim of industry must be the production of goods for the benefit of the community, and that work must always be the satisfaction of real needs. Even if it is difficult to draw an exact line between relatively needful and relatively needless jobs this is a valuable criterion of work which the Christian should always bear in mind. Dr. Calhoun has stressed the demand that the actions of any man in the work process must be so co-ordinated with the actions of fellow workers, of employers and consumers, of dependents and friends that what he does as workman may become a fitting part of an undivided pattern of human relationships. This seems to be the categorical imperative for the ethics of work in modern society. One of the further conclusions to be drawn from the basically social character of work is directed against unemployment. If daily work is a duty resting upon the individual, then there is an obligation resting upon society to provide for the opportunity to work. In our interdependent society daily work is denied largely due to circumstances beyond the control of the individual worker or employer himself. The Christian understanding of the meaning of work lays upon the laity the sense of importance for uniting with others as workers and citizens in these social measures that undergird the right and the duty of the individual to work.

(3) Work is an indispensable part of the self-expression of man. That does, of course, not mean that all men were naturally inclined to work forty or forty-five hours a week in a workshop, office or laboratory. But it means that there is an inner urge in man to express himself outwardly by word of mouth, by gestures or tunes and by the work of his hands. Men like to create something, be it sand castles on the beach, drawings on a rock, or motor cars. Again, the Christian knows that in this God's call to creativity and man's response to it are reflected. Creativity on man's part must not mean what it often is, a diabolic imitation of God's creatorhood but joyful response to God's invitation to share in His work by imagination, invention and achievement. There is no doubt that also in this respect, as in every other, work may become a curse guiding men further away from God. This is very obvious from the way in which often particularly creative minds are intoxicated and even obsessed by their ideas and inventions, and finally lose

all sense of reality. It is manifest also in the idolatrous venera-
tion which is sometimes offered to heroes of the screen and of
sports, or to artists and scholars. On the other hand, it is God's
will that even the humblest work not only must be done, but
demands that the worker think how to do it best. Every
worker gives something of his individuality to the work he
does; if he does his job well, he even loses himself, as we say,
in the work at least from time to time. If a man is so built and
if the conditions are such that a good piece of work can be
done, the worker is transcending himself in his present task,
thus sharing in the process of transformation in which the
world is continually transcending itself in order to be re-
established with new dimensions.

It would be wrong to make the inner satisfaction which such
activity is likely to produce the sole criterion of work. The
larger part of work in this world must be done just because
it is a human and a social necessity. But without at least
some measure of distinctive individuality and creative daring
expressed in one's job, work turns to be inhuman and as a
consequence unchristian. All efforts to stir the resourceful
imagination of even the merest routine worker at the assembly
line or in an administrative office must be supported from a
Christian point of view. Loving self-identification of a worker
with his task cannot be expected if the worker is not given
independent responsibility for a certain piece of work in a
limited field adapted to his abilities. The same effect can be
achieved in certain places by a team of a small number of
people endowed with the necessary freedom to perform a task.

(4) The natural rhythm of life is made up of activity and
rest. The Christian knows that "life is more than food," that
man does not live in order to work, but works in order to
live. As Karl Barth has said, "It is not work which gives meaning to life, but it is life which gives meaning to work." As we
are entirely dependent on God, the primary end of man is not
to produce but to receive. Since men in modern society have so
little ability to cultivate their receptive organs in meditation on

God's Word, in resourceful observation of nature, in quietly listening to other people, their work has become distorted in that each time-saving invention produces more nervous break-downs. The Old Testament Sabbath commandment, traced back to God's work of Creation itself, is an indication that work must be seen in the perspective of eternal rest and thus reduced to its true proportions. It is not a legalistic Sabbath observance which is most badly needed but an inner aloofness from work and purposeful activity which leisure and quietness and play may promote but which has its deepest roots in true Christian worship. Here, in meaningful anticipation of the Kingdom, the God is worshiped in Whom through Jesus Christ everything is accomplished. There is no place for hurry, hectic activity and hard labor, only for repentance and gratitude in joyousness.

This is an anticipation. It does not mean that for Christians all problems are solved. The survey prepared by a Swedish group stresses the fact that the deepest meaning of life, including the meaning of work, is revealed only in the mystery of the Cross, which to human eyes seems to be the abyss of meaninglessness. The man Jesus Christ who died on this Cross will return as the living Lord in glory to be manifested to the whole earth. It is at that time beyond our time that through judgment and grace our life and work will receive its ultimate meaning. That is what Christians hope for with certainty, and it is for that hope that Christians work with perseverance.

IV

OCCUPATIONAL LIFE IN CHRISTIAN UNDERSTANDING

A. The Church, the Laity and the Occupations

It is the common conviction of those who have contributed to the preparation of this Survey that the "secular" occupations are a part of the life of the Church in that they are a part of the daily experience and involvement of the laity. The Church can be effective in this field, although it cannot and must not give easy formulas or precise solutions. What a Christian bank clerk, teacher or farmer should do in his job or occupation must depend upon his understanding of the relation of his Christian responsibility to each particular situation. But the Church can and by its laity should be expected to provide directive guidance by which the laity will gain their own answers when at work. It has been stressed most vigorously that this directive guidance should come largely from the laity themselves. Out of their own Christian experience on the one hand, and their involvement in the world of work on the other hand, they can help the Church to help them. They must insist that the Church recognize the high priority of this need and provide means and occasions for its being met.

Daily work involves making decisions. This is inherent and constant in every job, in every occupation and at the many points where work, life and society meet. Much of this decision-making has its technical aspects, but also much of it has its ethical aspects. Among these latter, some are limited, while others are far-reaching in their consequences; but to them both the laity must be aware, sensitive and responsible. In these decisions with ethical contents the Church in its laity meets and struggles with the world on behalf of God. In respect to some ethical issues in work there will be easy recognition and acceptance as to where the Christian will stand, e.g., the decision against an occupation of gross anti-social results and, in the occupation chosen, against the violation of generally accepted standards of honesty. But the struggle of the Church with the world lies far beyond issues such as these. The Church must continue to be especially vigilant in helping its laity identify and come to grips with those tough ethical dilemmas that lie beneath the surface and beyond the prevailing standards in one's job and occupation and their interrelatedness with the larger social context.

In many groups who have worked on that, the knowledge is growing that the Christian approach to work is not characterized by a rigid ethical code or by the picture of a perfect society. Christians have the ultimate hope that God will finally triumph over evil. This hope makes them free to do in every moment what is possible under present circumstances—without resignation or despair. They must never betray their loyalty to their Lord, but they must be ready to co-operate with those who do not recognize the Lord. They do not give up work if the ideal cannot be achieved, but they work with perseverance for the state of things achievable which is next to the ideal. For that Christians may not be ashamed, although they will be alert to the fact that the time may come when they will have to take a stand which may well be decisive to their employment, or even to their career.

B. Some Major Ethical Areas in Decision-making

(1) *Relativities in the Rewards of Work.* As has been shown, work as a human necessity is always done for the sake of its results. To the majority of workers in the modern world, the fruit of their work comes home in the form of rewards. The question of the relation of rewards to needs is ever present in the question, "Who (or what groups) should get how much?" But in decisions on this matter there is always implicit the

qualifying phrase, "Who (or what groups) should get how much in relation to what others get and need?" For beyond the minimum needs for survival the needs of no group are absolute; the needs or claims of one group are subject to adjustment with the needs or claims of other groups. Following are a few examples of the relations of rewards which are especially acute in today's decision-making; they are only described to the extent needed to identify them.

(a) To what extent should Christians support inequality in remuneration as a means to an increased and more efficient productivity in work? On the one hand is the fact that, given adequate incentives, some persons will work better to the benefit of both present and future generations; on the other hand is the Christian sensitiveness to the effect of serious inequality upon the reality of community.

(b) Certain types of work by their nature involve greater drudgery and hardship, yet because these are unskilled in most cases they are among the lowest in rewards. In the Christian perspective, should such jobs receive special forms of reward because of the measure of their drudgery?

(c) What is to be done about the deterioration of a group's purchasing power through the successful effort by another group to increase its income? For instance, in some countries the greater organized strength of industrial workers seems to lift wages to a point which impoverishes agricultural workers who must buy what industrial workers make; in other countries this problem is felt at times in reverse.

(d) Is it better policy to provide pensions or to pay much higher rewards to the workers in governments or private services respectively, in order to save for the future?

(e) For many reasons a large number of people seek an opportunity for promotion and advancement in their work. Problems are clearly involved here, if justice is to be done both to those who seek greater scope and responsibility and those who will be affected by their promotion. No general positive solutions are possible, but it is clear that Christians cannot approve of discrimination against any person otherwise suitable for promotion, merely on grounds of race, class, creed or sex. This implies also that the whole question of opportunities for education and vocational training must be considered, as must the problem of rewards for special groups of workers. There can, for example, be no grounds for paying men and women different wages for the same work, provided family needs are met by an adequate system of family allowances.

(2) *Human Relations.* Work, as has been said, is essentially a social experience. The human-relations sphere of daily work raises many decisions of pressing importance and considerable difficulty.

(a) NEIGHBORLINESS. Do I see my fellow workers as indeed my neighbors, and do I act toward them in accordance with that truth? The Christian worker will not only be a maker of goods or a provider of services, but at the same time he will seek to be a maker of a work neighborhood.

(b) STEREOTYPES. Do I see each other worker possessing worth or dignity, as a person, or do I think and act toward him in terms of some label or abstraction (i.e., he is a "Mere Worker" or he is one of "Those Heartless Managers" or he is "Another Intellectual")? Equal distortions of the worker as an individual lie in labels related to cultural, national or racial differences.

(c) COMPETITION. Modern work life tends to be strongly competitive. Among the issues at stake is often the urge not merely to increase but even to hold on to what one now has in monetary advantage, together with status, prestige and power. This leads to the tendency to "use" others in the service of one's own competitive position. For instance, a foreman or supervisor uses those under him as an instrument to win an ahead-of-schedule reputation for himself.

(3) *Power: Personal and Social.* In a significantly large number of occupations a job carries powers over the working life of others. This fact in itself affects the environment and the nature of decisions with ethical content. The way this

power is both derived and exercised has consequences for others in the work process and the larger social context far beyond the knowledge and, in many cases, the adequate sense of responsibility of those who exercise it. Here we simply suggest some indications of what is involved.

(a) THE SOURCE OF POWER. Questions like these lead into what is ethically involved. To what extent does power rest upon special privilege? Upon taking advantage of or manipulating circumstances? Upon outmoded patterns of relationships and authority?

(b) THE EXERCISE OF POWER.

(i) PERSONAL POWER. The manner in which authority is exercised can often distinguish between being "a man with authority" and being "authoritarian." The importance of "communication" cannot be overstressed. Of ethical importance too is the possibility of deceiving oneself about the obnoxious character of one's use of power by a form of paternalism in some areas where it is in one's power to give or to withhold. Basic to the Christian is the recognition that differences in the level of power are only differences in the work situation and not differences in the work of the worker and the dignity of his work.

(ii) SOCIAL POWER. Through their own organizations, employers, employees, farmers and professionals acquire power, the use of which may vitally affect for good or ill both those in the occupations and those in society as a whole. The Christian will be especially sensitive to the overruling regard for the public welfare, as he participates in the use of power by his own particular group.

C. OCCUPATIONAL PROBLEMS

As has been shown in our first chapter, the mass-production principle is a principle of human organization which results in two main conditions under which an increasing number of men are working: the hierarchical structure and the corporate decision-making character of work in modern society. Farmers, artisans, owners and workers in small enterprises have become part of a hierarchical unit working under those who themselves are under others. The expansion of organization has not left untouched the professions, although the persons thus affected are indeed small in number compared to those above. For instance, a doctor on a hospital staff is in an entirely different position from the traditional "private practitioner." His medical skill now takes its place alongside of his institutional relationships. Again, a worker's place in the structure of today's organized economic activities carries characteristics quite apart from those of the particular occupation. For instance, the character of the decision-making process met by those on the administrative level in any occupation has a common quality, whether the administrator is in a store, a factory, or a government office. Similarly, a filing clerk in a railway office may have problems more in common with a filing clerk in an insurance office than with a supervisor in the railway administration.

Thus an occupation is no longer an area relatively closed in itself, where work is based on specific training and skill and is characterized by the same features everywhere; it is a certain combination of circumstances, skills and other abilities tied up at many points with other occupations and with the whole fabric of society. Nevertheless, there are a few problems characteristic at least of the work of the majority of those who work within a certain occupation. These problems are now seen and studied by Christians in order to understand better the world in which the Church lives through its laymen and to give guidance to those who are in need of it.

Much work in this direction has been done in recent years by groups, organizations and institutions of the churches entirely devoted to such a task and much more needs to be done. Space only allows us to mention two illustrations, from areas as different as industry and government. Other fields worked on by numerous groups are the large areas of agriculture and the important job of housewives, the smaller area of education and salesmanship and the numerically quite small but socially important professions such as doctors, lawyers, social workers, office employees, politicians, engineers, newspaper and radio men, actors, etc. Material about all these may be found in the bulletin *Laymen's Work*. The reports of the Buffalo Conference and of similar meetings are particularly instructive. (For all this see Bibliography.)

(1) *Industry*. The section of economic life we describe as "industrial"—i.e., manufacture, mining, transport and communications—embraces a large section of the employed population in many countries, and contains within it a vast range of very varied occupations, each one of which is as distinctive and as fraught with its own peculiar problems as is a profession like teaching or medicine. Further, the more generalized problems of conduct arising in industry are shared with many other forms of employment (e.g., large-scale retailing or office work). Yet the world of industrial production is of vital importance: it is the place where many social changes originate, it dominates the life of a large part of the human race and it is in many ways less in touch with Christian thought and Christian influence than the intellectual and "liberal" professions. Very many ordinary churchgoers are involved in industry, yet they often feel more abandoned by the Church in their occupational life than are professional workers.

There have been many useful short-period conferences of groups within industry with a clear-cut common interest:

(a) mid-level managers in large-scale industry,
(b) managers in small units,
(c) trade-unionists (including professional union organizers and active "lay" trade unionists),
(d) accountants (especially cost accountants),
(e) personnel managers,
(f) scientific and professional men employed by large concerns.

Another method of working is the small "working group" considering a problem, having appropriate and varied experience within the group, and aiming at producing a monograph. A British group on "Responsibility in Industry" was an example. This method can be valuable, but is difficult and should be attempted only when the subject is clear-cut and pressing.

Discussions under Christian auspices between employers and workers can have first of all personal value, and many single conferences of this type have been of great value to individuals in helping them to understand the perspective of others. In countries like Germany, Holland and others they have visibly contributed in creating an atmosphere in which social tensions have been settled and legal measures such as co-management and joint consultation have been possible. It is also by this kind of meeting that the organized Church and trade unionism as well as the Church and the organization of management have come into closer co-operation and as a consequence to a better understanding.

"Bridge discussions" on specific human problems between persons involved in industry and those in other walks of life (such as agriculturalists, teachers, doctors, government officials) have been valuable—usually in an *ad hoc* form.

A major problem in all such conferences is time and cost. It is vitally important to ensure that the practical arrangements, such as times of day and of week, traveling expenses, etc., are carefully arranged to suit the *main* group which it is desired to touch. Otherwise they will become merely the haunts of hardened conference-goers and not of people truly involved in the subject. Besides short-period conferences, some churches have tried to establish long-term training courses for young people who have been, and after the course will again be, employed in industry as workers, foremen, trade union leaders, social workers, etc.

(2) *Government Officials.* Christian thought has always given attention to the position of "the Christian ruler" or "governor." Recent social changes, and especially the coming of the "welfare state," have transformed the work of govern-

ment as radically as the industrial revolution has transformed production.

The work of the civil service involves a large, diverse and variously qualified group of "lay" politicians, professional politicians and permanent officials, employed in the service of national and local government and other public authorities.

A surprising proportion of the active laity in most churches, in most countries, are engaged in government. It is thus easier for the Church to draw on the experience in this field than in some other fields, but there seems not to have been a great deal of discussion (perhaps as a result of the need for discretion on the part of public servants, and also the fact that in some countries public officials, rightly or wrongly, feel more simple conviction and fewer moral difficulties about their work than do workers in other occupations). Subjects needing attention are:

(a) The position of the official as "one under authority" who must, as a matter of duty, curb the expression of his *personal* opinions.

(b) The place of fairness and objectivity in a religiously or ideologically mixed society (the U.S.A., Britain, India, Western Europe).

(c) The public servant in an authoritarian or clericalized society (e.g., in a Communist or a Moslem State).

(d) The conditions of purity and prevention of corruption in public service (which is a social rather than an individual problem).

(e) The expression of "collective charity" through state-sponsored social services.

(f) Relations between officials and the public.

V

WHAT DOES ALL THIS MEAN FOR THE CHURCH AS AN ORGANIZED BODY?

Through its lay people the Church is virtually omnipresent and it is certainly not restricted to the limits of its organization. The surveys received from India as well as from other places draw the conclusion that consequently the organized Church does not exist for its own glorification or even for its own edification. Its *raison d'être* is God's Kingdom—and its concern is the world. The organization of the Church and the inner life of the organized Church must be such that they do not obscure its *raison d'être* nor impede the pursuit of its concern. This does not mean despising the organized Church and the various ministries which are necessary therein. They carry an enormous responsibility. But their task is not just to run a church but to help both its members and those outside the Church to realize that there is a Lord and Saviour of the world.

The all-decisive question which is now raised by many people, church leaders and simple Christians, therefore, is: Does the message of the Kingdom of God, as proclaimed by the Church, reach the people in the world for whom it is meant? It cannot reach the people if the Church either does not live where the people are or does not speak and understand their language. The structure of work in modern society has impregnated the whole life of the people. It has changed their outlook on life, their expectations and their fears, their feelings and their reasonings. It has also changed the place where people live, or where they feel that the center of their life is. In many cases it is no longer the home, the family, the neighborhood. It is now the workshop, the laboratory, the city twenty

miles away from home with the cinema, it is their sport association, their trade union, it is the barracks of camps for workers or the lonely room in a strange house into which the
necessity of work in modern society has forced a girl or an old
man separating them from their parents, their husbands and
wives. Does the Church live where these people live and does
the Church understand the language these people speak and
make itself understood? There are, in particular, some recent
attempts made by various churches to which we must look for
an answer to this question. We classify them roughly into
four categories, though in actual fact they are more differenti-
ated, and more combined. The four types are not mutually
exclusive but in fact call for one another.

A. MEETING PLACES

One thing that has been happening in some countries and
in various churches in recent years is frequently called a new
encounter between Church and world. Somebody has described the situation in his country as follows: the Church was
practically finished, because with its traditional methods it no
longer reached men and women in their active life of work,
except for a steadily decreasing group of traditional church
adherents; the working world was no less finished, because the
old ideals such as self-development and self-expression and the
old ideologies such as progress and orthodox Marxism no
longer worked. Both sides had reached an impasse. The majority within both groups tried to conceal this fact in various
ways. But there were a few courageous men in both groups
who admitted it to themselves and to others. They have found
contact with one another on the basis of some sort of scarcely
definable human solidarity and new confidence. This is, of
course, typical only of a very particular Continental post-war
situation, but something of the sort is happening here and
there all over the world. Church and working world are less
sure of themselves than they used to be twenty-five years ago,
and this has given rise to new opportunities of meeting each

other. In several countries discussion on questions of the Christian faith in its bearing on the issues of modern life is going on in the press, radio, forum and other meetings, followed with deeper interest by more people than used to be the case.

In some countries such as Sweden, Germany, Holland, France, Britain, the U.S.A., Canada and India, centers have been founded which can best be described as meeting places. In occasional five-day or weekend conferences, Christians and non-Christians, trained theologians and experts in, let us say, industry or education discuss freely some of the most burning issues of modern life. Sometimes it is questions of politics and citizenship, or structural problems of society and of economics of a more general nature, which are discussed there. More often it is more detailed aspects of occupational life on which the program of such conferences is built. Nearly always such discussions lead to the ultimate questions of human life, and to the question of renewal of faith. It is becoming clear thereby that the Christian message not only concerns the inner life of man, but calls to definite responsibilities in occupational, social and political life. Non-Christians who used sometimes to be in the majority of these meetings have been becoming more aware of the fact that virtually all so-called secular matters and relationships have a spiritual dimension without which they are not recognized fully, even in their more technical aspects. Christians, on the other hand, are beginning afresh to take worldly things seriously as the concern of Christianity, and to take their fellow men seriously, not only as potential converts but as human beings.

B. Study Groups

It is quite clear, however, that a number of issues concerning the implications of the Christian faith on daily life require serious and long-term study which cannot be done at occasional meetings. There are not only many fields on which theology as such is not competent at all, but even issues of a genuinely theological nature which badly require further study, especially in the field of social and political ethics. In both cases, the Church as an organized community needs the special efforts of competent laymen in order to understand the present world as it is, and consequently to make an intelligent impact on the life of modern society. These "frontier problems," as they are sometimes termed, call for a new type of teaching in the Church, which is substantiated not only by the lonely work of a theological professor in his study or by the ecclesiastical pronouncements of an assembly of church leaders, lay or clerical. The new teaching must be undergirded by the daily experiences made by men and women in secular life, and elaborated in a sort of team work whereby the shrewdest minds of the theological and the scientific world work together permanently, or at any rate for a considerable period.

Interesting experiments in this direction have been made in a number of cases, of which we mention only a few for illustration. In Great Britain such team work has been done under Christian auspices in a study of the role of the modern university, in a comprehensive review on the medical profession and in an analysis of responsibility in industry. The National Council of Churches of Christ in America is sponsoring a publication series on the ethics and economics of society, achieved by a similar procedure. The Dutch Reformed Church has established a Sociological Institute from which experts penetrate the life of the Church and the society in which the Church works from a sociological point of view. In Germany a larger association of scholars interested in these frontier problems, and a permanent center for such studies with a theologian, a physicist, a historian and a lawyer as full-time staff, have been created. Many, perhaps most, churches nowadays have standing committees or *ad hoc* commissions in which laymen together with clergy study certain aspects of modern social life. The Study Department of the W.C.C. has engaged in a world-wide inquiry on "The Responsible Society," to which individual laymen and national groups of experts contribute.

C. TRAINING CENTERS

Partly as a consequence of this, partly alongside it, there is a strong awareness on the part of many Christian laymen that Sunday and the work from Monday to Saturday belong together. But how are they to manifest this essential interdependence of worship and work? How are they to live up to the Christian faith under the conditions and often the pressure of the working world and, on the other hand, how are they to understand this world in the light of the Christian message of salvation? It is clear that neither occasional meetings nor serious study work done by groups of experts is in itself sufficient. These tensions are lived through day by day by millions of Christians dispersed in workshops and offices all over the world. It is these Christians who must get more help from the Church in their struggle than can be given by the Sunday services and the Bible evening of the congregation. In most cases, this additional help in respect of their place and function in the working society of our day can be given only by those who live and work under the same conditions. Therefore, with the exception of certain very striking special cases such as that of the worker-priests, the helpers needed cannot be clergymen. They must be fellow workers and colleagues. Are there enough of those in the workshops and offices who are convinced and devoted Christians, able to give intelligent "response to the faith which is in them" and in addition good workers in their jobs, knowing something of the structure of their occupation and possessing a certain gift of leadership? It is this kind of helper which is most badly needed, and it is one of the most important tasks of the organized Church to find and to train these people in the most appropriate way. It goes without saying that of necessity to a large extent training courses must be given by lay members of the Church.

Again, something is already being tried in that direction.

Under church auspices or on a private basis Christian Training Centers have been created. For some considerable time the famous Scandinavian People's Colleges have been doing something of this kind. The Adult Education Movement has established boarding schools, day schools and evening courses at many places in quite a number of countries, notably in Britain. It cannot be said, however, that the strategical importance and purpose of this training has always been clearly realized by the churches concerned. The students of these schools too have often regarded this special training in a purely individualistic way, so as to profit from it for their occupational career, for their personal education or for their religious life. The idea of service through leadership in their particular community of work concerned was basic to the foundation of some newer types of training centers. Here and there special training courses are being held for workers, farmers, housewives, social workers, teachers and journalists. In Germany a training center for young workers was established a few years ago, where, after a careful process of selection, able boys of the working class are gathered for some three full-time courses of about six weeks in consecutive years. The boys are there free of cost at the expense of their Churches, by agreement with both their trade union and their firm. The subjects taught are Bible study and Christian doctrine, social and economic subjects, trade unionism, political science and some group psychology. A considerably fuller training in these and other fields is given in a four-year course, including one practical year, to people from various walks of life, by a large institute of the Dutch Reformed Church. Most of the pupils from this school, boys and girls, later go in for social work among both industrial and farm laborers. It is noteworthy that this school also works in close contact with the respective occupational associations and labor unions. An experiment similar in substance, yet on a somewhat different basis, is being made with university students in the U.S.A. The method applied there is for the students, while living for two years in a special community, and following the ordinary university courses in their various fields, to undergo a certain discipline of life, including extra-curricular courses in Bible, Christian doctrine, social ethics and the like.

D. CELLS

If there are in a factory, in an enterprise, at a university or in an occupation such "helpers" as we have called them, they will soon become the crystallization points around which other Christians and those interested in these questions gather. Where this happens, it means that the Church has taken the decisive sociological step of entering the structure of the modern world of work as such. For at least two hundred years, traditionally Christian community life has been almost exclusively based on the parish, which in its turn is composed on the principle of the family home and the local neighbor-hood. There is no reason to abolish that, but there are good reasons for complementing it by some other pattern of Chris-tian community life today. What the members of a local parish have in common is the general human problems, beginning with birth, going on to marriage and ending with death. In-cluded in that frame are the problems of family life, the specific developments of the various ages and stages (child, adolescent, adult and old), problems of child education and troubles such as illness, loneliness and similar human situa-tions. On the whole, it is this sort of thing the organized Church is concerned with, and rightly so. But that is not the whole of life. The estrangement between the working class and the Church, and also between the intellectuals and the Church, is largely due to the fact that the Church was not present where *they* have been spending most of their waking hours and energies. To meet the demands of the hour the organized Church must adapt itself to forms of life hitherto unknown to it, through which the concern of the worker and of the administrator are brought into the light of the Gospel as much as the concern of the mother or the sick.

It is amazing to see how new Christian units, often called cells, are springing up in different parts of the world quite independently from one another, under the auspices of the Church of Scotland, of Men's and Women's Work, the Evangelical Academies and the "Kirchentag" in Germany, of the Institute Kerk en Wereld in Holland, etc. These units are built on the sociological stratum of the working community. Different from any former pattern, they are not professional or occupational associations of Christians who happen to be employed in one particular job. As the Church as a whole is responsible for the world, these cells feel responsible for the working community in which they live. Therefore they are never closed organizations with a program of their own; their concern is the life of the working community itself. They do not apply the principle of membership, clearly distinguishing between members and non-members. Rather there is a nucleus of a few determined Christians, sometimes in the form of a sort of religious order, around whom others gather, some regularly, some frequently, some rarely and many not at all. But everybody belonging to this working community is on principle admitted. Consequently, they do not develop a social style of their own but live in the forms of life which are natural to that working community to which they belong: if workers strike, they strike, if journalists have a party they are of the party. As a report from Germany states, these cells have an evangelistic effect, but they have no evangelizing purpose, set apart from their concern for the working community and detached from what they do in their work and their occupational activities. To use the terminology of today, their primary aim is not the conversion of individuals—which has sometimes had the effect of saving them out of the community—but the Christianizing of the atmosphere in which people live and work, in factories or elsewhere.

The four types of work we have glanced at are all beginnings, particularly the last one. But they are of the greatest importance for the structure and life of the Church as an organized body. However, the reports do not only stress their experimental character; they point also to certain implications which must be faced with courage and circumspection. In the space remaining, we can mention only a few of them.

(1) The organized Christian community, as represented by pastors, elders or council, must stop measuring the faithfulness toward the Church, and indeed the Christian faith of laymen, by the hours they spend on church premises or in religious organizations. In most cases, the vocation of the layman as a living member of the Church does not lie in the church building, the parish hall or the vestry, but rather in his office or workshop, in the working community or occupational organization, in his family and in his participation in the life of the nation and its smaller communities. What has been said in the last four paragraphs must not have the effect of overburdening Christian laymen with new work in church organizations. Some laymen, of course, will have to serve in a new way as speakers, teachers and instructors for other lay people, but even for them it will often be in line with what they are already doing in their jobs. The majority, however, will profit in terms of time if the churches are willing to scrutinize the worth-whileness of many of their programs and activities from the point of view indicated, and some laymen need to be pushed out from the sheltering umbrella of the organized Church in order to serve Christ where they earn and spend their money.

(2) All that has been described has its roots in the Church as the Christian community. In the end it will also serve the local parishes in their common life, but it cannot be confined to their limits. In most cases, meeting places, study groups, training centers, cannot and should not be carried by one local community. They must operate on a larger scale, for reasons of material support, and even more for reasons of personnel as regards both able instructors and the necessary variety of students. Non-Christians touched by this kind of work have not always found it easy to join one of the existing more tradi-

tional parishes. Some of the new institutions have decided to help these people by creating special circles where those newly reached can meet and discuss their problems together with mature Christians. The cells finally are built on a different principle from the parish. All this calls for the recognition of paraparochial forms of church life. Immediately the question of the relation of parochial and paraparochial work of the Church arises. It is an open question today, and no answer to the problems involved is certainly better than too easy an answer. It can be asserted, however, that a real solution is not impossible. We shall revert to this point at the end of this survey.

(3) This whole approach has also ecumenical implications. While the work of the churches on the local level has largely been done in an entirely isolated way by one denomination after the other, modern problems cannot be served denominationwise only. In the meeting places not only Christians and non-Christians but Lutherans and Reformed, Methodists and Anglicans will meet. In the study teams the best brains on the subject in question are needed. Cells in a factory will not be Baptist or Congregationalist but Christian cells. This only reflects the simple fact that seen from the world and the divisive issues at stake in modern society, Christians are already much more at one than they themselves realize. This does not mean that the deep differences immediately disappear, but it does mean that they must be fought through in common, and together with issues such as a Christian understanding of work in modern society, occupational and professional ethics and the like.

CONCLUSION

If there is some truth in what has just been described, it is obvious that many of our congregations, both pastors and laymen, need to be re-educated. Nobody from the outside and no special group from the inside can educate them. They must re-educate themselves in the light of the Bible under the guidance of the Holy Spirit, with a keen awareness of the opportunities God gives to His Church through the rapidly changing social conditions under which we live. In the long run this will affect the way in which future ministers are selected and trained, the way in which religious instruction is given both to young people and to adults, the way in which pastoral care is offered in the Church, not only by pastors but also by laymen. It will affect the organizational set-up of the Church, its community life and its corporate action in society. It will affect the various services in the organized Church properly done by laymen, ranging from lay preaching to administration. Perhaps most of all it will affect the evangelism and mission work of the Church. If once it is recognized that laymen are the most natural and genuine representatives of the Church in the world, evangelism will not be a particular activity of the Church exercised by some specialists, but will be regarded as the normal result of the fact that everywhere in the world Christians live and work alongside other people. The trained theologian, the pastor and missionary, instead of being regarded as *the* evangelist of the Church—a job for which he is in a particularly bad position—will then be the biblical and theological instructor of the evangelists, a job for which he is in a particularly good position. The Church as a whole will not speak too frequently in much debated pronouncements; it will speak no less officially but in a less static and more dynamic way by the decisions Christians take daily in their life in society.

Christian community life will always express itself in congregations. Here the proclamation of the Word of God as concerning everybody under whatever conditions they live and work, and the Sacraments as incorporating every believer into the Body of Christ, have their proper place. In worship the world—for the most part so opaque—becomes transparent. Here life and work in the world is received from God in adoration and thanksgiving, offered up to God in repentance and prayer and intercession and illuminated and transformed by God's Word becoming flesh once for all in Jesus Christ and time and again in the sermon of a preacher, in the bread and wine in Holy Communion, and in any action inspired by the Holy Spirit. Even the parish (it has been said in an Orthodox paper) has a symbolic significance; assembled for worship it symbolizes the world united around the messianic table. On leaving the church after a service every believer is "sent" (*missa est ecclesia*) into the world with the Peace of God.

But in order not to lose contact with those to whom it is sent, the Church needs special groups or movements or communities outside the parishes, related to them but not dependent on them. Based on a common way of life or a common preoccupation, they offer a choice that corresponds to people's interests and to the task of the Church to penetrate the world. People feel at home in the Church through finding there the same human environment to which they are accustomed. At the same time spheres of work and life in modern society are symbolically restored to their proper nature when in such special communities they are brought under the light of the Gospel. These living communities will replace ethical codes on work and occupation which for Christians can never be written in a definite form. They do not exist for their own sake; they exist for the sake of the Church because they help her to represent her Lord in every realm of life, and they exist for the sake of the world, because their concern is job, occupation and society. These communities can and must take different forms, but they must always be open to everybody concerned, and be undogmatic and flexible in their methods. A Church with such communities, but without some sort of local congregations, could no longer endure. But a Church with parishes and without some sort of such communities could no longer move.

BIBLIOGRAPHY

The books and articles mentioned below are a selection of those which together with national reports and other papers have served as background material for this Survey. Fuller bibliographies on the various topics are to be found in the Bulletin "Laymen's Work" which may be obtained from the World Council of Churches' Secretariat for Laymen's Work.

A. General

JOHN BAILLIE. "The Theology of the Frontier." *The Frontier,* June, 1952, Vol. III, No. 6.

YVES M.-J. CONGAR. *Jalons pour une théologie du laïcat.* Editions du Cerf, Paris, 1953.

JACQUES ELLUL. *Présence au monde moderne.* Geneva, 1948.

G. D. HENDERSON. "The Witness of the Laity." *Scottish Journal of Theology,* Vol. II, 1949/50, p. 175.

H. A. JONES. *Evangelism and the Laity.* London, 1937.

JOHN R. MOTT. *Liberating the Lay Forces of Christianity.* New York, 1932.

GUSTAVE THIELS. *Mission du clergé et du laïcat.* Paris, 1945.

ELTON TRUEBLOOD. *Your Other Vocation.* New York, 1952.

H. H. WALZ. "Die Rolle des Laien im Zeugnis der Kirche." *Zeitwende,* August, 1952.

In English:

"The Role of the Layman in the Witness of the Church." *National Christian Council Review,* Vol. LXXIII, No. 3, March, 1953 (India).

Documents of the European Laymen's Conference (Bad Boll) 1951. Pub. by the Secretariat for Laymen's Work, WCC, Geneva, 1951.

Report of the North American Lay Conference (Buffalo) 1952 on "The Christian and his Daily Work," pub. by the Department of the Church and Economic Life, NCCC, New York, 1952.

B. *Work and Vocation*

ROBERT L. CALHOUN. *God and the Common Life*. New York and London, 1935.

"Christians at Work." Reports of the Industrial Research Group of the Youth Department of the British Council of Churches.

W. R. FORRESTER. *Christian Vocation*. London, 1951.

CAMERON P. HALL. *The Christian and his Daily Work*. New York, 1951.

KARL HOLL. *Die Geschichte des Wortes Beruf (1924)*. Tübingen, 1928.

"A Holy Calling." *The Student World*. 2nd Quarter, 1950.

ELMER G. HOMRIGHAUSEN. *The Vocation of the Christian Today*. New York, 1946.

JOHN HUTCHISON. "The Biblical Idea of Vocation." *Christianity and Society*, XIII/2, Spring, 1948.

FRANZ-L. LEENHARDT AND ALFRED PITTET. *Le Chrétien devant le travail. Genève*, 1941.

"Man's Work and the Christian Faith." Reports of a conference, pub. by the Industrial Christian Fellowship, 1948.

ALEXANDER MILLER. *Christian Vocation in the Contemporary World*. SCM Press, London, 1947.

J. H. OLDHAM. *Work in Modern Society*. SCM Press, London, 1950.

G. BROMLEY OXNAM. *The Christian's Vocation*. Women's Division of Christian Service, The Methodist Church, New York, 1953.

"People at Work." Published for the Present Question Conference. London, Vol. 3, No. 1, Autumn, 1950.

JOSEF PIEPER. *Musse und Kult*. Hegner Bücherei, München, 1949. in English: *Leisure, the Basis of Culture*. SCM Press, London, 1952.

ALAN RICHARDSON. *The Biblical Doctrine of Work*. SCM Press, London, 1952.

DOROTHY SAYERS. *Why Work?* London, 1942.

N. H. SØE. "Die christliche Liebe und das Leben im Beruf." *Luthertum*, 1932.

W. G. Symons. *Work and Vocation.* SCM Press, London, 1946.

"Vom Sinn der Arbeit." Heft 8 der Schriftenreihe *"Kirche im Volk,"* 1953.

Gustaf Wingren. *Luthers Lehre vom Beruf.* München, 1952.

Work and Vocation. A Christian Discussion, edited and with an introduction by John Oliver Nelson. Harper & Brothers, New York, 1954.

C. The Working World and the Church

J. A. Bakker, W. Banning, *et al.* "Gemeente-Opbouw." *Wending* No. 5/6, 1950.

"The Church and the Secular World." A Report of the Commission on Culture of the United Church of Canada. Toronto, 1950.

Rudolf Graber. *Die dogmatischen Grundlagen der katholischen Aktion,* 1932.

Walter Horton. *Centers of New Life in European Christendom.* New York, 1948.

Hendrik Kraemer. "Gemeente Opbouw," chapter of book *De Kerk en Beweging.* Boekencentrum, s' Gravenhage, 1947.

Eberhard Müller. *Die Welt ist anders geworden.* Furche Bücherei, Hamburg, 1953.

Rajaiah Paul. "How Can the Church help the Layman?" *The Lamp,* July, 1952.

Professional Life as Christian Vocation. Cahiers de Bossey No. III, 1948.

Hans J. Rinderknecht. *Die Laienfrage: Ein Nein und ein Ja.* Zürich, 1950.

Colin A. Roberts. *These Christian Commando Campaigns.* London, 1945.

Towards a Christian Civilisation. Athens, 1950.

H. H. Walz. "New Light on Laymen's Work in Congregation-building." *World Christian Education,* 4th Quarter, 1951.

E. P. Westphal. *The Church's Opportunity in Adult Education.* Philadelphia, 1941.

Ad. Wischmann. *Die Evangelische Akademie: Ein neuer Weg missionarischen Wirkens.*

PREPARATORY COMMISSION VI

on

THE LAITY—THE CHRISTIAN IN HIS VOCATION

Members

Professor Hendrik KRAEMER (W.C.C.), Chairman
The Rev. Dr. H. H. WALZ (W.C.C.), Secretary

*Mr. David W. K. AU, Hong-Kong
*Professor Jacques ELLUL, France
Mr. Joseph W. FICHTER, U.S.A.
Dr. O. H. von der GABLENTZ, Germany
The Rev. Dr. Cameron P. HALL, U.S.A.
The Rev. Olov HARTMAN, Sweden
*Mrs. Douglas HORTON, U.S.A.
Dr. A. W. KIST, Netherlands
Mr. Rajaiah D. PAUL, India
Miss B. Nancy SEEAR, United Kingdom
Dr. E. SOMASEKHAR, India
*Professor Douglas V. STEERE, U.S.A.
*President Clarence C. STOUGHTON, U.S.A.
Mr. W. G. SYMONS, United Kingdom
*Professor A. N. TSIRINTANES, Greece
*Dr. Reinold von THADDEN, Germany
*Mrs. J. A. TUMANKEN-GERUNGAN, Indonesia

Consultant

The Rev. Dr. Paul LIMBERT (YMCA)

Central Committee Consultants

*Principal Sarah CHAKKO, India (deceased)
*Dr. Reinold von THADDEN, Germany (member of the Commission)
*Principal T. M. TAYLOR, United Kingdom

Substitutes and ad hoc Consultants attending the August, 1953, meeting

Miss Madeleine BAROT, Geneva (W.C.C.)
The Rev. Professor Walter M. HORTON, U.S.A.

* Not present at August, 1953, meeting.

Professor Basil IOANNIDIS, Greece
Dr. Dorothea KARSTEN, Germany
The Rev. Canon Alan RICHARDSON, United Kingdom

REPORT OF THE ADVISORY COMMISSION ON THE MAIN THEME OF THE SECOND ASSEMBLY

Christ—The Hope of the World

CONTENTS

iii

FOREWORD

The Central Committee of the World Council of Churches meeting in Toronto in 1950 resolved that the second Assembly should deal with the theme of the Christian Hope. This theme was later formulated as: Christ, the Hope of the World.

The Central Committee also decided to set up an Advisory Commission of about 25 men and women, theologians and laymen, to do preliminary work on this theme and to prepare a document which would be the basis for the consideration of the theme at the Assembly.

This Advisory Commission held three meetings. At the first and second meetings provisional reports were prepared which were sent to the churches and which led to widespread discussion in the churches. At its final meeting in 1953 the commission drew up the present Report to the Assembly. In doing so it made full use of the comments and reactions received from the churches.

In preparing the Report, the Advisory Committee considered it a document to be disposed of by the Assembly as it saw fit. In writing it, however, the members of the commission had in mind the possibility that the Assembly might choose to adopt the Report in some way as its own. For that reason certain passages in it are worded as though this were such a report from the Assembly to the Churches. It must be made clear, then, that in its present form the Report is that of a commission preparing for the Second Assembly of the World Council of Churches. It is for the Assembly to decide when it meets in August what status it desires to give to the Report. It may decide to adopt the Report in its present or in a modified form, or to pass it on to the churches with the recommendation that they study it and comment on it, or it may choose to consider the report simply as a preparatory document for the Assembly itself.

At its February, 1954, meeting in Königstein im Taunus, Germany, the Executive Committee of the World Council decided to make this document available to the public prior to the Assembly. This decision was taken because of the widespread demand and interest on the part of church people in many parts of the world.

At the Assembly the Report will be dealt with in the following way. First there is to be a presentation of it in two major addresses at a public plenary meeting on Sunday afternoon, August 15. Secondly, fifteen separate groups, including all delegates and consultants, will meet for four sessions to discuss the Report, its contents and disposition. A Committee representing these groups will make appropriate recommendations to the Assembly growing out of the discussion. Thirdly, these recommendations and the Report will be considered at two plenary meetings.

Whatever action the Assembly may take, the Report is important in that it represents the corporate work of a distinguished group of theologians and lay leaders. It is the result of a coming together of men and women whose backgrounds and church traditions are indeed varied, but who have found a common word to say on the Christian Hope as the result of genuinely ecumenical encounter.

The Advisory Commission was chaired at its first meeting by Dr. Henry P. Van Dusen, and at its second and third meetings by Bishop Lesslie Newbigin. Its members are the following:

Professor H. S. Alivisatos	*Professor John Baillie
Miss Leila Anderson	*Professor Karl Barth
*Professor C. G. Baeta	*Dr. Kathleen Bliss

The names marked with an asterisk are those of members present at the third and final meeting which produced the present Report.

Professor Emil Brunner
*Professor Robert L. Calhoun
*President Edgar M. Carlson
*Reverend Owen Chadwick
*Professor V. E. Devadutt
Professor Paul Devanandan
*Professor C. H. Dodd
Mr. T. S. Eliot
*Professor G. Florovsky
Professor J. L. Hromadka
*Professor H. Kraemer
President John A. Mackay
Professor Donald Mackinnon

Dr. Charles Malik
*Professor Roger Mehl
Mr. Francis P. Miller
*Professor Paul Minear
*Dean Walter Muelder
*Bishop J. E. L. Newbigin
Professor Reinhold Niebuhr
*Reverend D. T. Niles
*Professor Edmund Schlink
Professor C. F. Thomas
*President H. P. Van Dusen
*Professor H. Vogel
*Professor Gustav Wingren

I. CHRIST OUR HOPE

A. A HOPE BOTH SURE AND STEADFAST

God summons the Church of Jesus Christ today to speak plainly about hope. Jesus Christ is our hope. In all humility and boldness we are bound to tell the good news of the hope given to us in Him.

The hope of which we speak is something different from what men usually mean when they speak of hope. In common speech "hope" means a strong desire for something which may be possible but is not certain. What is spoken of here is something that we wait for expectantly and yet patiently, because we know that it can never disappoint us.

We have this confidence because our hope is based upon what we know of God, and because we know of Him through what He has done. Our hope is not the projection of our desires upon an unknown future, but the product in us of God's acts in history, and above all of His act in raising Jesus Christ from the dead. That mighty event is faith's assurance that Christ has overcome the world and all the powers of evil, sin, and death; it is the beginning of a new life in the power of the Spirit; it is the guarantee of God's promise that in His good time His victory will be manifest to all, His Kingdom come in glory, and He Himself be known everywhere as King. It therefore begets a living hope, an ardent longing for that glorious consummation, and an eager expectation of its coming.

Our hope comes to us from God and rests in God. The Lord of heaven and earth is the Righteous One who has said, "Ye shall be holy for I am holy," the Judge who will by no means leave evil unchecked and unpunished. Therefore we

1

dare not speak of hope in God except we speak at the same time of judgment and repentance. He who was raised from the dead is He who died for our sins. Therefore what we say is said under the sign of the Cross. The Cross is that place at the centre of the world's history where the Lord of history has finally exposed the sin of the world and taken that sin upon Himself, the place where all men and all nations without exception stand revealed as enemies of God, lovers not of truth but of the lie, children not of light but of darkness, and yet where all men stand revealed as beloved of God, precious in God's sight, children for whom the Son of God was content to die. It is the crucified Lord who is the hope of the world.

Therefore the hope of which we speak, so far from being a mere extension or reaffirmation of our desires, begins at the place where we and all our desires are brought to naught. When we stand at that place where the Son of God died for our sins, all our human desires are judged by Him. We are stripped naked of all our claims and pretensions and clothed afresh with His mercy. We are dead and made alive again. In the words of the Apostle, we are begotten again to a living hope. This, the act of God Himself, is the beginning of our hope. The Creator and Lord of all has come forth in wrath and loving-kindness to shut up every false way, and to bring us face to face with Himself, the living Lord. He, by His own act, has put us in the place where we must hope and can hope only in Him.

We live at a time when very many are without hope. Many have lost the hopes they had for earthly progress. Many cling with the strength of fanaticism to hopes which their own sober reason cannot justify. Multitudes ask themselves, "What is coming to the world? What is in front of us? What may we look forward to?" The answer to those questions has been given to us in the Gospel. To those who ask "What is coming to the world?" we answer "His Kingdom is coming." To those who ask "What is in front of us?" we answer "It is He, the King, who confronts us." To those who ask "What may we look forward to?" we answer that we face not a trackless waste of unfilled time with an end that none can dare to predict; we face our living Lord, our Judge and Saviour, He who was dead and is alive for evermore, He who has come and is coming and will reign for ever and ever. It may be that we face tribulation; indeed we must certainly face it if we would be partakers with Him. But we know His word, His kingly word: "Be of good cheer; *I have overcome the world.*"

B. THE PROMISES OF GOD

The good news of hope which we proclaim comes to us through the Holy Scriptures. It is the gift of God Himself and rests upon His deeds in the world and His promises for mankind. In the Old Testament God reveals Himself as the Creator and Lord of all men and all things, who places His creation under the obligation of obedience and gives to it the hope of fulfilment. He promises seed time and harvest as long as the earth remains, and gives men visions of a day when the disorders of life shall be done away, and righteousness, truth, and peace shall prevail.

God's revelation of His faithfulness to His promises was given in His dealings with Israel. Throughout her long history this people learned to know the mighty hand of God in acts of deliverance and of judgment, and to cherish the hope for a Kingdom in which God's will should be done. This indestructible and life-giving hope is what gives unity to the whole history of Israel and makes it the story of a single pilgrimage. Though that people continually exchanged her God-given hopes for others that depended upon her own strength and wisdom, in every generation God's faithfulness produced men of faith, who in hope believed against hope, and recalled a wayward people to their appointed way. God's promise in the Old Testament is that He will Himself establish His Kingdom and that men shall come to know Him as God.

The story is told by many men gripped by God's promise

and possessed by His Spirit. They declare the doings and promises of God as concretely as possible, although these exceed the capacities of human language, whether historical prose or poetic imagery. God has used and uses their testimony to recall His people to the promise of the reign of righteousness, truth, and peace. Their testimony has often been distorted, both by those literalists who have mistaken symbol for fact, and by those philosophers who tried to treat facts as mere symbols of timeless truth. Yet through His servants in the Old Testament, as in the New, God continues to address His word of promise to all men.

The promise that God would Himself establish His Kingdom focused the hope of Israel upon the coming of the Messiah. As God refined Israel's hope in the crucible of failure and disappointment, it became hope for a Deliverer who should release them not only from their external foes but also from their bondage to sin and death. He who was to come would bear their iniquities and carry their sorrows. By His stripes they would be healed.

The New Testament announces that the promised Deliverer has come. The powers of the coming Kingdom are already at work in the world in Jesus Christ, and in the Holy Spirit poured out upon His people. God in Jesus Christ has entered into the tangled web of earthly history and met and mastered evil in all its forms. By His life, death, and resurrection He became for us both sin's Victim and at the same time sin's Victor. We cannot fathom all that He there did for us, but we know that He bore the judgment that was against us all, freed us from sin and death, and reconciled the world to Himself. His coming fulfilled the hope of earlier times—and transformed it. He brought to men a new birth into a new life, a new community, and a new hope. The new life is born in forgiveness; it finds both its pattern and its power in Jesus Christ, whose obedient love has freed men from the guilt and power of sin and from the fear of death, to serve their fellow-men. The new community is the Church, of which He is the

source, the head and the vitalizing power. The new hope
is still hope in God, the maker and ruler of all things, but it
is hope at once fulfilled and expectant. What we possess in
Christ is the most glorious life of which we know anything,
for it is fellowship with Him who is our Saviour and our
Lord. And yet this fellowship in the Spirit is but the foretaste,
the earnest, of the inheritance laid up for us. Christ is not
only our righteousness and our peace; He is also present in
us as the hope of glory.

C. The Kingdom That Now Is

We must now speak both of what we have in Christ and
of what we hope for, of what is given and of what is promised.
And first of what is given. In the ministry of Jesus Christ we
see the gracious power of the Kingdom already at work
among men, and in His teaching, especially in the parables,
we read His own interpretation of that working. The same
Spirit who was in Jesus Christ was, after His exaltation and
ascension, poured out upon His people. In Him a new humanity begins. As we die daily with Christ, we are exalted with
Him to receive His life-giving Spirit and to participate in
the glory of His Kingdom. To us as new men all things become
new. We see individual and social experience in a new
perspective. The whole course of history is transfigured. We
see the victorious Lord continuing His ministry of intercession and carrying on His warfare against every ruler of darkness. As we walk by the Spirit, we participate in His warfare, and participate also in His victory. In Christ and His
community we are already sons of God and heirs of glory.

Although even now we live in the New Age, its reality and
power are not yet fully revealed. "The earth," indeed, "is
the Lord's, and the fulness thereof." It is His creation, and
His work is good. Moreover, God so loves His world that He
gave His only Son for man's salvation. His providence governs
it, and His Spirit lives and works in the midst of it, overcoming evil with good in countless ways, and bringing to fruit

beyond human expectation or contrivance the deeds of devoted men and women. But neither the world of nature nor the world of men is as yet what God would have it be. Both are still enmeshed in the disorder of the unredeemed age and await their liberation. The ignorant and the wilful wrongdoing of many generations of men has distorted God's work and subjected human life itself to grievous corruption. Every man is born into a social order deeply pervaded by the accumulated results of individual and corporate aggression, deceit, and irresponsible self-seeking. And every man so born and reared adds his own share of distortions and corrupting falsehoods and starts new trains of suspicion, cruelty, and hatred. Evil, deeply ingrained and powerfully operating in all creation, often quite beyond our understanding or control, bedevils the whole course of earthly history.

Because this is so, neither the Church nor individual Christians can expect to escape suffering and at times even catastrophe. For the Church must live now in the world that crucified her Lord. Sometimes the suffering of Christian believers or congregations results from their own ignorance or unfaithfulness. Christians are not exempt from divine judgment; indeed they are more directly exposed to it than others. It is only as believers know themselves to stand under the judgment of God that they can know His mercy and yield themselves as instruments to His gracious purposes. Sometimes, on the other hand, their suffering results from their faithfulness in facing the powers of evil, in bearing the assault of slanderers, oppressors or persecutors, or in identifying themselves with Christ by carrying upon their hearts the burden of the world's sin and sorrow. But those who accept such judgment and such suffering without bitterness or despair are made sharers in the sufferings of their Lord, and sharers also in the power of His resurrection. They therefore receive strength to endure in faith towards God, in love towards all men, and in hope of Christ's final victory.

The trials which again and again come upon the Church

are reminders that in this present age the Church dare not try to settle down in earthly peace and prosperity. They are "signs of the times" that should keep every Christian and every congregation alert, knowing that the Church on earth is, even when danger seems remote, a pilgrim people forbidden by its divine calling to be at peace with the powers of evil, or to forget that in the living Body of Christ, when one member suffers, all the members suffer together. Moreover such trials, when they lead the Church to lay fresh hold on the hope set before it, provide a special witness whereby the world may see the power of the living Lord who in weakness makes us strong and in the midst of darkness enables us to hold fast our hope in Him. Not only so, they also disclose unmistakably the tangled, precarious nature of earthly existence itself—not least when its technical achievements and political powers have reached imposing heights. If the Church is to find complete fulfilment, and if earthly existence is to be saved from meaninglessness, we must look not only to the course of earthly history itself, but beyond it. Our hope must be anchored in God who comes to us in Jesus Christ; it must look at once to what He has done, and to what He is doing now, and to what He will do for His people and His world, in completion of His saving work.

D. Having and Hoping

The fact that our hope is thus anchored in a Kingdom that both has come and is coming gives to the life of every believer a double orientation. He both has eternal life and hopes for it. He has the first fruits, and therefore he longs for the full harvest. The Messiah, who though rich became poor, has given him surpassing riches. Yet he has this treasure in an earthen vessel. The flesh wars against the Spirit and the Spirit against the flesh. He remains part of this fallen world, involved in its corruption and mortality. His life is therefore a warfare, even though he is guarded by Christ's peace.

In this situation the believer faces a double temptation. On the one hand he is tempted to despair of this world and to fix his whole attention on that which is to come. He may forget that God keeps him in this world precisely as a minister of its reconciliation to Himself. He may be so daunted by the apparently unconquered power of evil that he loses all faith in the possibility that God who created and sustains the world can also make His power known in it. In his longing for the heavenly city with all its blessedness he may pass by his fellow-man, fallen among thieves, and leave him by the roadside.

On the other hand the believer is tempted in the opposite way. Because he has been brought out of darkness into light and made a sharer here and now in Christ's risen power, he may forget that what is given here is still only a foretaste. He may so confine his attention to the possibilities of this present world as to forget that the whole world lies under judgment. He may confuse man's achievements with God's Kingdom and so lose the only true standard of judgment upon human deeds. He may forget the true dimensions of man's existence as a child of God created and redeemed for eternal life, and by seeking the end of human life within earthly history make man the mere instrument of an earthly plan, and so dehumanise him.

We are guarded from these temptations not only by the logic of faith but also by our common fellowship in the Lord. Listening to His Word we are brought again and again to the point of decision, whether to accept both His No and His Yes. Sharing the Church's mission to the world, we experience both the distance and the nearness of the Kingdom. Week after week the routines and emergencies of the common life remind us of our wealth and our poverty. A true index of our having and hoping is given to us in the sacrament which under various names—Lord's Supper, Holy Communion, Eucharist, Mass—is common to the whole Church. Here Christ's people, united in an act of faith and adoration, call to mind at once His coming of old in great humility and His coming at the end in power and glory, and both are made present to them in communion with their living Lord, who comes to them in the breaking of the bread.

E. The Kingdom That Is to Come

The Kingdom that is now real moves with God's power and faithfulness towards its full realisation in the manifestation of God's glory throughout all creation. The King reigns; therefore He will reign until He has put all enemies under His feet. What we hope for is the fullness of what we already possess in Him; what we possess has its meaning only in the hope for His coming.

What Is Its Character? In the new age that now is, God has disclosed to eyes of faith what is the character of the age that is to come. We must here speak of matters which, in the nature of things, defy direct expression in explicit speech, matters for which the language of inspired imagination employed in the Scriptures is alone adequate, for these are things that can be discerned and communicated only by the Spirit. The pure in heart shall see God as He is and know Him as they are known by Him. Those who are now sons of God will receive the fullness of their inheritance as joint heirs with Christ. There will be a new heaven and a new earth. We shall all be changed. The dead will be raised incorruptible, receiving a body of heavenly glory. The agony of the created world will be recognised as the travail of childbirth. Blind eyes will see, deaf ears will hear, the lame will leap for joy, the captive will be freed. The knowledge of God will cover the earth. The Holy City will appear, made ready as a bride adorned for her husband. The choir which no man can number will sing Hallelujahs to the praise of the Eternal. God's people will enter into the sabbath rest, and all created things will be reconciled in the perfect communion of God with His people. It is in such visions as these that the Spirit enables us to point to the splendour of the salvation that is ready to be revealed in the last days. It is towards this salvation that God guides us in hope. This hope is not seen, or it would not be hope; but it is promised to us as suffering, sinning, dying, and believing men. Therefore we wait for it with patience.

What Is Its Range? In His Kingdom that has already come God has unveiled the unlimited range of His love. In Christ He has already broken down the barriers between races, nations, cultures, classes, and sexes: how much more will the coming Kingdom demonstrate the breadth of His redemption! Christ came not to the righteous but to sinners, to the lost, the least, the last; how much more will His return demonstrate the triumph of His descent into the abyss. In His death He suffered for His enemies in loving forgiveness and thus overcame every enmity; how much more at His coming will His sovereignty be disclosed even to all who crucify Him. "As in Adam all die, so in Christ shall all be made alive." Because our hope is *in* Christ, He commands us to hope *for* all those whom He loves. Because His love is shed abroad in our hearts, we are empowered to hope all things for all His brothers. And we hope also for our own participation in the endless life of His Kingdom. Of that participation we possess a sure token in His power to make our bodies the temple of His Spirit and to raise us from our daily dying. This power, however, prevents us from hoping for our own glorification apart from the fullness of glory that shall come to the whole body of Christ; for all who participate in the dying and rising of Christ are being knit together into a single body "until we all attain . . . to mature manhood, to the measure of the stature of the fullness of Christ." We long, therefore, for this perfecting of the Body of Christ. But not only so, the love of Christ prevents us from being content with any hope for a glorified Church which leaves the destiny of the world to the powers of evil. Solidarity with Him requires and produces solidarity through Him with the world in its transiency, futility, sin, and death. For God has promised the reconciliation of the whole creation, and we therefore hope for nothing less than the renewal of all things. This hope, however, never allows us to think of cosmic transformation apart from God's care for the falling sparrow and the hundredth sheep. Christ our hope thus embodies in Himself the destiny of individuals, of the Church, of earthly communities, and of all creation. So great is this hope in Christ that we are impelled both to press forward eagerly to its fulfilment and also to listen with full soberness to His command: "Strive to enter by the narrow door, for many I tell you, will seek to enter and will not be able."

What Is the Time of Its Coming? What has God revealed to His Church concerning the time of consummation? He has bidden the Church to live with loins girt and lamps burning, like servants waiting for their master's return, and to serve faithfully day after day, like a steward undismayed by his lord's delay. Our hope therefore bears the marks of patience and eagerness, of confidence and urgency, of waiting and hurrying. God has not disclosed to us just when His Kingdom will come in glory. In fact when we attempt to calculate the nearness or the distance of His Kingdom we confuse that hope of which Jesus Himself provides the clear pattern. His whole concern was the fulfilment of God's purpose rather than the satisfaction of man's curiosity. He met his impatient disciples with the command, "Take heed, watch; for you do not know when the time will come." Our obedience is one measure of our hope. It is for the Church to stand vigilantly with its Lord, discerning the signs of the time and proclaiming that now is the time of judgment, now is the day of salvation.

He who is both the beginning and the end, in whom all is to be consummated, is the One who meets us now and every day and invites us to commit everything to Him. We do not know what are the limits of human achievement, of our own personal history, or of the history of the race. We do not know what possibilities are in store for us or what time is before us. We do know, however, that there is a limit, for we must all die. If we do not know Christ, death is the only limit we know. And in that situation men try to find grounds for hope either in merely individual survival or in social progress. The one offers to individuals the promise of fulfilment but denies it to history as a whole; the other offers meaning to human history but denies the significance of the human person. Those who take death seriously but have not met Christ are shut up to these two alternative ways by which human wishing seeks to cross the chasm of death. But in Christ something utterly different is offered. He who has died for us and is alive for us confronts us with a totally new reality, a new limit, a new boundary to our existence. It is He who meets us; it is He with whom we have to do in every situation. It is He who is our life, He who is life for every man. We can commit ourselves and all our deeds into His hands with complete confidence, knowing that death and destruction have been robbed of their power; that even if our works fail and are buried in the rubble of human history, and though our bodies fall into the ground and die, nothing is lost, because He is able to keep that which we commit to Him against the Day.

What Is Its Relation to This World? On Calvary God's Kingdom and the kingdoms of this world met. Whoever has lived through Good Friday and Easter Day has the key to final judgment and eternal life. To him has been demonstrated the fragility of this world in comparison with the immense stability of that world which Christ brought within human reach. At the Cross God condemned the world which turns from Him and hates Him. In the coming Day this condemnation will be revealed in all its terrible finality. At the same Cross God accepted the world and disclosed how much He loves it. In the coming Day this loving acceptance will be revealed in all its unsearchable riches. Confidence in this terrible and glorious consummation of all things in Christ means neither that the history of this world will be swept aside as irrelevant, nor that our efforts will be finally crowned with success. The long history of this world which God created and sustains from day to day, and for the sake of which He sent His Son, is not rendered meaningless by the coming of His Kingdom. Nor, on the other hand, is His Kingdom simply the final outcome of this world's history. There is no straight line from the labours of men to the Kingdom of God. He rejects that history of which man fancies himself to be the centre, creator, and lord; He accepts that history whose beginning, middle, and end He Himself fixes and determines.

Thus at the boundary of all life stands One who is both Judge and Saviour. Because we know Him as Judge, we shall beware of confusing any achievement of ours with His holy and blessed Kingdom; because we know Him as Saviour, who died for the world, we shall beware of that selfish concern for our own salvation which would cause us to neglect our worldly tasks and leave the world to perdition. The operation of God's judgment and mercy in the Crucified is far from self-evident. But we know that in the age that is to come, what is now hidden from our senses will be openly revealed. The Church sees now through a glass darkly; she will then see face to face. But what she sees now she is bound to proclaim.

II. CHRIST AND HIS PEOPLE

A. THE PILGRIM PEOPLE OF GOD

We have spoken of Christ our hope. We must now go on to speak of that People which He has called into being to be the bearer of hope, the sign and witness of God's mighty acts, the means of His working, and the field wherein His glory is to be revealed. Our hope is grounded in one great Event, comprising the incarnation, ministry, death, and resurrection of Jesus Christ. In this Event the purpose of God for mankind, foreshadowed in His dealings with Israel and declared by the prophets, found fulfilment, and His Kingdom was inaugurated on earth, to be consummated hereafter.

This tremendous Event occurred within a brief epoch which soon passed, leaving the broad scenery of history ostensibly unchanged. One concrete result alone was to be discerned: the Christian Church. It appeared as a small, obscure community, unwelcomed and almost unnoticed by the great world. It knew itself to be a colony of the heavenly fatherland planted in an alien territory, and looked forward to an end lying beyond this earth and a day when the fullness of what God had done in Christ would be finally disclosed. It also knew itself to bear responsibility for the world for which Christ died, a responsibility that drove it to action and to suffering.

This Church still exists. It is a historical society living among other societies in the world, and yet not of the world. It is constantly tempted to settle down among secular societies, content with the achievement, influence, and reputation which a well-ordered and enlightened secular society might enjoy. But to do so is to deny both its origin and its end, and in fact

14

it is seldom permitted to do so for long. It is of its very nature that its members should know themselves to be strangers and pilgrims on the earth, pressing on towards the moment at which the Lord who died and rose again will confront them in His power and glory.

The Church lives in this world by the proclamation of the Gospel, by worship and sacraments, and by its fellowship in the Holy Spirit. In proclaiming the Gospel it is permitted to engage in God's own work of bringing His purpose to fulfilment. In worship and sacraments it participates in the life of the heavenly fatherland. In the fellowship of the Spirit it receives divine powers of growth, renewal, and enlightenment to which we cannot place a limit.

The Church thus becomes, in the first place, witness and evidence of that which God has done, and the sign of that which He is doing and will yet do. By this alone the world is apprised of the historical Event and its more-than-historical significance and issues.

Second, the Church is also the means through which God is carrying His purpose to effect. It is the Body whose members are members of Christ, united with Him and at His disposal. Its life therefore is both the extension of His earthly ministry and also a participation in His present and continuing work as risen Lord and Saviour.

Third, the Church is designed to be the field where the glory of God, once manifested in Jesus Christ to those who had eyes to see, will be revealed to the whole created universe, which meanwhile waits for the manifestation of the sons of God. The glory of God is already reflected in the Church's proclamation of the Gospel, in its worship and in its fellowship in the Holy Spirit, but the reflection is partial and imperfect, and the Church waits upon Him through whom alone it is changed from glory to glory.

This Church, as a historical body, is made up of frail, ignorant, and sinful men. Its foundation members were discredited deserters from their Master's cause. They became pillars in the temple of God only because, having stood under the judgment of God when the sun was darkened, they found forgiveness in the light of Easter Day. They could proclaim God's judgment and forgiveness to the world because they knew themselves the objects of both. The Church is still able to declare judgment and forgiveness to the world only because, and in so far as, its members have stood and stand under the judgment of God in penitence and have accepted His forgiveness. In doing so, they are exposed to the full impact of His grace, which has won its victories in the world, and is still winning them, through human beings who in themselves have neither strength nor merit.

The Church fails of its calling when its members suppose themselves to have already attained that which awaits them only at the end of the way; when, blind to their faults and proud of their virtue and insight as Christians, they despise their fellow-men and speak self-righteously to the world; when they seek glory of men and refuse the reproach of the Cross.

And yet, even when the Church fails to be itself, when its members fall short of their calling, nevertheless God is God, and He cannot deny Himself. In spite of assaults from without and flaws within, the Church stands upon the Rock and the gates of hell do not prevail against it. By God's ordinance and through His power it remains witness, instrument, and field of action for Him while history lasts, and will stand before Him at the end to be made perfect through His final judgment and final forgiveness.

B. The Mission of the Church

It is thus of the very nature of the Church that it has a mission to the whole world. That mission is our participation in the work of God which takes place between the coming of Jesus Christ to inaugurate God's Kingdom on earth, and His coming again in glory to bring that Kingdom to its consummation. "I have other sheep that are not of this fold; I must bring them also, and they will heed my voice." This is His word to us; this is the work in which He is engaged and in which we are engaged with Him. For He whose coming we expect is also He who is already present. Our work until His coming again is but the result of our share in the work which He is doing all the time and everywhere. The Church's mission is thus the most important thing that is happening in history.

And yet because the mission of the Church points beyond history to the close of the age, it has this significance too, that it is itself among the signs that the end of history has begun. The hope of our calling is set towards the hope of His coming. It is written, "This Gospel of the Kingdom will be preached throughout the whole world as a testimony to all nations; and then the end will come." In giving His commission to the Church, Christ has given also this promise: "Lo, I am with you always, to the close of the age."

Thus, moreover, are the true nature and dimensions of the Church's missionary work determined, for they are determined by Him whose work it is. It is a work which embraces the whole world, limited by no racial, social, national, historical, or political considerations. Jesus Christ is King over all the world. He died for all; and the world-wide proclamation of the Gospel is the direct consequence of His world-wide sway and all-embracing love. We evangelise, but it is He who is the Evangelist, the Messiah who is come and who is gathering the nations.

It is for this reason that we, who now have the earnest of our inheritance and the foretaste of salvation, yet have to wait for it. The same Lord is Lord of all—believer and unbeliever alike. He is rich in mercy towards all who call upon Him. "But how are men to call upon Him in whom they have not believed? And how are they to believe in Him of whom they have never heard? And how are they to hear without a preacher? And how can men preach unless they are sent?" The consummation awaits our obedience to His word "Go ye." In very truth we cannot know the fulness of God's salvation until all for whom it is intended share it with us. We without them cannot be made whole.

When the Lord's Apostles asked Him whether the Kingdom would not come at once, He answered, "Ye shall be My witnesses to the ends of the earth." To our cry "Lord, how long?" He answers, "Go ye and preach the Gospel to all nations." That is our summons to share Christ's compassion for all mankind; only as we obey it can we live as those who share His hope for all men. Indeed, when we contemplate the millions who have not yet known His love or heard His name, do we not stand rebuked for our slackness and callousness? We are among those who call Him "Lord" and do not the things which He commands. Not only does Christ say to the Church "Go," but through the non-believer He is also saying to the Church "Come." And the Church that fails to obey this doubly voiced command does not merely fail in one function; it denies its own *nature*.

How necessary it is, then, that the Church's obedience to the Gospel should also involve a determination on the part of the Church in every country to take this Gospel to other lands. There are frontiers which the Gospel must cross within each land, areas of life which must be brought into subjection to the mind of Christ. But it is of special significance when the Gospel crosses geographical frontiers, for it is when a Church takes the Gospel to another people and another land that it bears its witness to the fact that the new age has dawned for all the world.

The urgency of the Church's mission derives from the fact that its mission is the result of participation in the work of God. We can avoid the task of preaching the Gospel only by refusing to allow the Gospel to take possession of our lives. When we do allow it so to take possession, we are swept into the current of God's redemptive activity, and find it hard to keep pace with Him. It is because we have failed so largely to let the Gospel take possession of us that we have failed also so greatly to fulfil our evangelistic task. There is no other way of believing in the Gospel than by witnessing to it. If we really took our stand upon it we should be compelled by that very situation to be urgent in staking Christ's claim for all men and for all of life. If we but truly believed that Christ had already claimed the Hindus, the Buddhists, the Muslims, the Jews, the Communists, and the great pagan masses of our time for Himself, we should no longer skirt around these groups as hesitantly as we often do. Our evangelism is not to be determined by the likelihood of immediate response. It is to be determined by the nature of the Gospel itself.

And yet in spite of our every failure we must affirm what the Church is and what it is meant to do, and thankfully acknowledge that God is faithful even when we are faithless. To all men the Church offers welcome to their Father's home, where they are treated as persons, children of God known to God by name and precious in His sight. In the Church they come into living membership of Christ's body, receiving forgiveness of their sins, partaking in the healing processes of the Spirit, and engaged in the Church's mission to the world. In the Spirit, also, they have the pledge and instalment of their common heritage: of the worship of God and of work in His service, of the communion of saints, of the power of the resurrection, and of the life everlasting.

All this means that the function of the Church is, in the last analysis, to be both the instrument of God's purpose in history and also the first realisation of the life of His Kingdom on earth. It invites all men to share in its life, both as realisation and as instrument. It bids them enter in and possess their inheritance. It also testifies to the nature of the end towards which its hope is set. That end is not an unrelated intervention on the part of God, for which the only possible preparation would be an attempt to escape from the wrath to come; it is the promised climax of what God has done and still continues to do, and the true preparation for it lies in faithful living by these deeds of God.

C. The Unity of the Church

As the instrument and first fruits of God's Kingdom on earth, the Church is in its essential nature one. Where the one Christ is at work, where the apostolic witness to Him is truly set forth in word and sacrament, there is the one Church. We all come from Him, we all go towards Him, and He is among us. This threefold bond is stronger than all discord among Christians, for it is wrought by Christ Himself.

This we must affirm in face of all contradiction. The unity of the Church is so concealed by our many divisions that to affirm it must often appear little better than mockery. But the Church knows of a certainty that at the end of its pilgrimage its unity in Christ will be complete and manifest. Our unity in Christ belongs to the ultimate structure of reality. This is the goal to which all history and all creation move. In pressing forward towards this goal we are one. Let us not forget that when we stand before our Lord at the end we shall stand before our Judge—the Judge of His Church as well as of the world. His judgment will bring about a separation that goes much deeper than all our present divisions and cuts across them all.

Yet even in our present condition He has not left us without tokens of our unity. In our separateness we have attested the operation of the one Christ across all boundaries that divide us. We have heard the voice of the Good Shepherd in the testimony of communions other than our own. We have experienced the power of the Name of Christ in their prayers. We have acknowledged the love of Christ to which they have borne witness in word and deed. In the fellowship of the ecumenical movement we have come together in a way which forbids us, in spite of all stresses, to break away from one another. Thus we have been led to see that the reality of Christ is more comprehensive than the limitations of our confessional traditions, and have confessed in faith our oneness in Christ.

All this we thankfully accept as a token of our Lord's grace to His Church. And yet we are divided. Our true unity remains concealed. There are divisions between the separate communions in which Christians are grouped. There are also divisions within each communion, sometimes no less sharp than those which divide one communion from another. At no point is this scandal of division more grievous in its consequences than in the Church's endeavour to proclaim the one hope of the Kingdom to all nations. All work of evangelisation, however great its history and glorious its results, remains crippled by the divided state of the Church.

This is no mere matter of missionary tactics. Our sense of urgency in the task of overcoming our divisions is something more than a desire to combine in facing hostile forces or unsolved social and political problems. The mission of the Church aims at gathering all men into unity. The disunity of the Church contradicts that purpose.

We are not at one concerning the form which the corporate unity of the Church should take. Our discussions have not yet led us to a common conviction as to a way which we can take all together towards that end. We trust our common Lord to continue to guide us towards that fullness of unity which is His Will for His people. In this situation it is the indispensable condition of receiving further light that each Church should actually take whatever may be clearly indicated as the next step.

To discern what that next step is each Church should face such questions as the following: What are the implications of the discovery which we have made that when we seek to understand together how the whole Church depends for its life on its Lord Jesus Christ we are at once aware of a greater and deeper unity than we have known before? Where Churches have already discovered a large measure of agreement in doctrine, are they justified in remaining separate? In what new ways can we seek to live and to act together in all matters in which no deep differences of conviction are involved? Have we become sufficiently clear-sighted in detecting the purely worldly factors which play their part in our divisions?

D. THE RENEWAL OF THE CHURCH

The Church is God's new creation, united to Christ as the body to the head, filled and quickened by His Spirit, God's holy temple. And yet in this pilgrimage through earthly history there are Christians who are individually and corporately guilty of narrowness of mind, imprisoned in sectarianism, parochialism, or nationalism, and indifferent to the claims of the Church's world-wide mission. Sometimes the Church pitches too low the demands it makes for self-sacrifice and devotion. It often tolerates among its members low standards of faith and knowledge and a worship of Almighty God which is utterly unworthy. Christian believers often reflect the timidities and vacillations and even the despair of worldly men.

The Church knows that it is a society not of the perfect but of those who are in constant need of God's grace and mercy. The life of the Church in the world is a spiritual battle, continuing in Christ's power His warfare against the principalities and powers of evil. Humility and constant self-examination are a necessary part of the climate of the Church's life. An attitude of penitence belongs to the nature of the historical Church; it invites worshippers day by day to make corporate confession of sin. The old Adam needs to die again and again.

Anything that we speak, we can speak only in penitence. Nevertheless we possess a sure and certain hope even for the Church. God has promised and He is faithful. He has promised the presence and power of the Holy Spirit, ever guiding, ever renewing, ever enabling the Church to perform the task to which it is sent. The Church goes on its way ever looking to the heavenly city, knowing that it shares in the life of that city even here and now.

In spite of our unholiness, we know that the Church of God is holy, for it is God's action and not our penitence which sanctifies and renews it. He has sent it, has called it to be His instrument. Though Word and Sacraments may be ministered by unworthy men, they do not fail of their effect. By their means, God acts from moment to moment and from generation to generation, re-creating the Church ever anew by the Spirit who indwells it, renewing its faithfulness, its purity, its self-sacrifice, its courage.

History shows many examples of such renewal, amounting almost to a resurrection of dry bones. And in our time we still find authentic signs of renewal. Amidst persecution and loss of material resources or civil liberty, there are many instances—East and West—in which the community of believers has triumphed and is triumphing by the power of God. These victories lead us to thanksgiving; they lead us also to deeper penitence for ourselves, and to more earnest waiting upon God's quickening Spirit.

E. The Church Triumphant

In Christ, the Church's Lord and Saviour, God has triumphed. In the very defeat of the Cross the Son of God, who made Himself our brother, won the fight. He won it for us. Even in judgment His grace triumphed. He who was crucified for us, for us also rose from the dead. It follows that we His people both share and shall share His victory. But first of all we must let Him win the victory over ourselves. That victory is won when in our sinfulness we are rebuked, consoled, and sanctified by the Holy Spirit. That is the triumph of grace, which gives faith the victory over all the powers of sin and death.

The Church which thus lets itself be conquered by its Lord has part also in His conquest of this world. It is permitted even to help God to win the victory. Where His word is preached and heard, where consciences are first rebuked and then consoled, where the proud are humbled and the despairing lifted up, where the parched ground of dead hearts is changed by the quickening Spirit into a garden yielding fruit to the glory of God, there the Church celebrates the triumph of its Lord; there by faith it triumphs with Him. Where deeds of charity are done, where evil is overcome with good, there the love of God wins the victory over us, in us, and through us. When the Church prays, "Hallowed be thy name; thy Kingdom come; thy will be done," it is taking part, by the grace of God, in God's own triumph.

But here we face a dangerous temptation—the temptation to identify the victory of God with the worldly success of the Church, or to seek a triumph after the manner of the world by worldly means. To do this would be to betray our crucified Lord, to deny Him before the world.

The Church's true privilege and duty is, on the contrary, to humble itself in deep thankfulness because, feeble as it is in itself, exposed to constant attacks from without and always under the shadow of rejection, persecution and shame, it is nevertheless given a part in God's victory of the Cross. In this present age the Church fights its battle of faith, hope, and charity amidst sufferings. Yet in these very sufferings the Church possesses a token of the glory of its crucified Lord. Through thick darkness it marches towards a future that is the Lord's, who as Judge and Saviour will manifest His victory incontrovertibly before the whole world.

The Church's visible structure passes away with this age, but as the chosen people of God it will enter into the glory of the Kingdom of God that is to come. Here at last the true meaning and purpose of its mission will be realised, for all kindreds of mankind will be brought in. Here at last the Church will know fully what it is to be one in Christ.

We must all die, one generation after another. But Christ died—and is risen again. Christ's own people are still members of His living Body. They are with Him. Within the communion of saints they remain united with one another. In the resurrection they will be manifested, each and all, in a new mode of being. They will know God, for they will see Him. In the fellowship of those who are made perfect they will know and love one another. All of them, even those who died immature or undeveloped, the despised, the failures, the defeated, will, in the communion of saints, draw upon the inexhaustible treasury of life which is God's gift to them all in Christ.

Beyond all defeat and persecution, beyond their own sin and guilt, beyond death and hell, the people of Jesus Christ will raise the hymn of triumph, and the new heaven and earth will join the strain. Their worship will have no more need of a temple, for their Lord and Saviour will Himself be a temple for them, as His glory will be their light. The great Supper of the Lamb will be the marriage feast for the Church triumphant, for He will make His triumph theirs. His own will reign with Him. Their highest blessedness will be that God is God; and He will be all in all.

III. CHRIST AND THE WORLD

A. The Christian Hope and the Meaning of History

The centre of world history is the earthly life, the cross and the resurrection of Jesus Christ. In Him God entered history decisively, to judge and to forgive. In Him are revealed the present plight of man, and the end towards which the world is moving. The full character and significance of historical events are known only to God. But in that life and death and resurrection He discloses to men that divine purpose over-arches the whole of the world's history, both the time before Christ and the time that comes after.

God is creator of the world, and all time is within His eternal purpose. Christians reject those philosophies, ancient or modern, that regard history and time as illusory or meaningless. History is being made at every moment by the acts of God and of men; and Christians look to the consummation of God's purpose, in which the full significance of history will be finally disclosed. They know the relative and transitory nature of earthly affairs. Nevertheless they know also that history is within the providence of God. Man's strength and wisdom are small, and he is beset by all manner of irrational powers. But the Christian knows that man and all the powers of this world are under the sovereignty of their Maker whose wisdom and power are infinite.

God not only has created the world and is sustaining it, He moves and acts within it as the ever-living God. There is a divine ordering of history, active and purposeful, however difficult it may be to discern it in particular events. At the same time, the Bible teaches the moral responsibility of man for affirming good or evil. God has established with men a covenant, a living relationship of commandment and promise by which they are called to live as responsible men and women in faithful obedience to His purpose. The commandment is that men should love God and their neighbours. The promise is the gift of abundant life as children of God for those who hear and follow the divine call.

In the actual course of history, men's responses are distorted by sin and the results of sin. Not only are men ignorant, weak, and vulnerable, but by self-seeking and rebellion they break the covenant that gives meaning and direction to their lives. In both individual and corporate action, preferring falsehood instead of truth, exploitation instead of justice, cruelty instead of mercy, they try to set at naught the divine commandment and to achieve an abundant life on their own terms. Not only particular sins but deep-seated and pervasive sinfulness, corrupting the life of mankind and the will of every man, deface God's world. Between God and the enemies of His righteousness, within the life of every person and every group, a continuing struggle goes on as long as there is human life on earth. The struggle is against evil; not against men, but on their behalf, even when they wilfully commit themselves to the enemy. And only God who knows the hearts of men can see exactly where the line of battle lies.

History is full of wreckage that results not only from man's ignorance and weakness, but from man's misuse of the strength and knowledge that God has given him. Upon all such rebellion God's judgment is sure. The wages of sin is death, for individuals and societies. God is not vindictive, but He is inexorably the living God of truth and right. Men and nations violate the demands of His holy Will to their own disaster. But God's patience endures. He is faithful even to unfaithful men. Though they break the covenant, He has maintained it and reaffirmed it—reaffirmed it once for all in Jesus Christ.

Because God is the Lord of history, Christians must reject all doctrines of automatic progress or of fated decline. Man's hope is not in any process or achievement of history. It is in God. There can be no identification of any human act or institution with God and His righteousness. Yet we have been given the assurance that God's grace works in and through and all about us, that He grants us the gift of sharing in His Kingdom even now, and that continually repentant and continually forgiven, we can go forward in hope towards the consummation of all things in Christ. That will be both the judgment and the transformation of history, and also its redemption and fulfilment. The light of that final victory even now shines into our darkness.

B. The Christian Hope and the Hopes of Our Time

Mankind today is uncertain of its future. Most men are confused. Many are anxious. Some are despairing. But it would be a great mistake to suppose that most men are without hope. On the contrary, many hopes of many kinds—some newly born, some revived, some not yet clearly recognised or defined—claim the allegiance of millions. In seeking to declare its hope in Christ, the Church must understand and take account of these other hopes of our time.

In one respect or another, each of these hopes is reaching after truth which the Christian Gospel affirms. Some borrow directly from Christian tradition or deviate from it. All profess to satisfy human longings which Christians have too often neglected, and in that sense the very existence of these other hopes is a judgment upon us. But each of them also in some way distorts the true perspective disclosed to Christian faith, and offers men deceptive grounds for hope, misleading ways to follow, and delusive visions of fulfilment. All these and their followers stand with us under the judgment of God in Jesus Christ, and to each of them we must speak as clearly and fairly as we can the word of Christian hope.

It is plain that we cannot here examine, or even name, all the rival hopes of our time. We have chosen to speak of some that enlist the devotion of many of our fellows, and that seem to us representative though far from all-inclusive. Nationalism, reviving Fascism, devotion to one or another sort of economic and technological order as the way of salvation, nostalgic efforts to recapture the supposed glories of a bygone era, faith in power politics and military force—these and other delusive hopes might have been examined, and must be faced in the spirit of Jesus Christ wherever they appear. Meanwhile, we turn here to speak of four representative hopes of our time.

(i) *Democratic Humanism.* Until very recently, it was widely assumed that the spread of democracy guaranteed a progressively secure, just, and peaceable ordering of life for mankind. Even those movements which today stand in sharpest antagonism to "western democracy" claim for themselves the true democratic faith, and promise to bring in a "People's Democracy." Though chastened by wars and economic crises, confidence in democracy, however conceived, remains for millions the one sure hope for the cure of man's ills. Nor is this confidence confined to those who deny or ignore the Christian faith. Many Christians wrongly identify the democratic hope with the Christian hope for society. For them, democracy is Christianity expressed in social and political structures.

Historically, indeed, the relation of Christian faith to democratic humanism is very close. Modern democracy came to birth and has had its fullest development among peoples steeped in a Christian tradition. In its basic convictions and concerns, democracy is a child, or step-child, of Christian belief and Christian compassion. To Christian teaching it owes, in large part, its recognition of the worth of every person, of the fundamental equality of all men as human beings, of their interdependence, and of their mutual obligation one to another. To the same source it owes its understanding of men's lust for and misuse of power, of the peril of placing unchecked power in the hands of a few, and of the obligation of governments to safeguard each man against injustice, tyranny, and exploitation, and to seek the welfare not of a privileged few, but of all.

But modern democratic humanism has multiple origins. To a variety of sources other than Christian—among them classical humanism, the Renaissance, the Enlightenment, Romanticism, and modern scientific and cultural humanism— it owes other ingredients that vitiate its understanding of man. From these other sources have come faith in the capacity of education or technology to solve all human problems, belief in inevitable progress, and above all, disregard or denial of God's sovereignty over the world, and failure to recognise the imperfect, precarious, and transient character of all human achievements. According to democratic humanism, man is master of his own destiny and can achieve a perfect society. Men should rely wholly on their own powers to realise the good life for themselves and their communities, and their hopes need not reach beyond the improvement of their earthly existence. These beliefs are illusions. In holding them, democratic humanism even when still professedly Christian has become largely a Christian heresy.

The illusions of democratic humanists include also a confusion of ideals and facts. They hold the ideals of equality, freedom, and justice, and assume far too easily that in societies committed to the democratic way of life none of these ideals is denied in fact. But inequality, discrimination, injustice, reliance on naked power, exploitation, and aggression are not absent from democracies; and only man-centred self-righteousness can believe that they are.

Especially because of the historic connections of Christian conviction and democracy, Christians who dwell in democratic societies have the responsibility to bring to bear Christian judgment upon their societies, and to purge them of false assumptions and unjustified hopes. They must affirm men's indebtedness to God for the good earth and their own lives; men's obligation to hold all human possessions and accomplishments as stewards of God, in the service of His purpose for His children; men's dependence upon God for wisdom to do right and forgiveness for wrong-doing. They may share the hope that the institutions of society will be ordered more fully to protect and minister to the needs of all men; but they must know and declare that only in utter reliance upon God and obedience to Him can legitimate earthly hopes be truly discerned and rightly held. And they must insist that all human achievements, like all human persons, must suffer death and final judgment. Men's only sure hope is in the power, justice, and mercy of God in Christ Jesus.

(ii) *Scientific Humanism.* The hope of the scientific humanist is centred in the confidence that man, through the resources of science, technology, and education, can not only mitigate and perhaps remove hunger, poverty, disease, and ignorance, but also create a social order that will satisfy man's deepest needs and resolve his basic conflicts.

The scientific humanist, as we call him, is not necessarily himself a scientist. He is one who sees in science, applied to human affairs, the hope for mankind. He accepts the scientific method as the surest road to truth and most highly values truth of the kind that science gives. He believes that the most clamant needs of men today are needs that science alone can satisfy.

The ground of the scientific humanist's hopes lies in man's past achievement. Man has subdued nature; he has immensely developed his own mental powers; he has created in civilised society a specifically human world in the midst of nature. Civilisation is the sheet-anchor of the scientific humanist's hope. If it disappears, all hope disappears with it. But if it continues to grow, it can provide satisfaction for all legitimate human needs.

The hopes of the scientific humanist sometimes take an extravagant form, but they are more usually characterised by sobriety and hard work. The Christian can welcome a sober humanist as colleague in many common tasks, and thank God for his human compassion and disinterested service. But the scientific humanist by his very centring of all hopes on man must reject the Christian faith as an enemy. Man, he says, ought to carry the destiny of the world, Atlas-like, on his own back, but the Christian keeps man in leading-strings to God. He accuses the Christian, moreover, of thinking too highly of the virtues of suffering to be in earnest about abolishing it. He regards the Christian's doctrine of sin as a morbid influence, of psychopathic origin. Above all, he says that the Christian does not really care about the survival of civilisation, because his hopes are not in this world.

The Christian must accept such criticism as far as it is valid. But he must fearlessly insist that man's hope is in God and not in himself. The hope that man can shoulder the burden of the world is an illusion that leads men through anxiety to despair. Its root is the deadly sin of pride, that will not admit man's dependence upon God, and that may involve him in all the evils of a quest for unbridled power. The Christian's joy in believing that God reigns is, for a consistent scientific humanist, impossible.

Of the Christian's impulsion to relieve and prevent suffering we speak elsewhere. When the scientific humanist sees suffering only as something to be abolished, he does not face the fact that to be human is to suffer, and that Christ has brought joyous hope out of suffering to thousands of people to whom scientific humanism can speak only of stoical endurance.

The Christian doctrine of sin, far from being an antiquated or neurotic theory, describes precisely the situation in which every man stands, the humanist along with all the rest. Out of good intentions evil as well as good arises, to thwart personal endeavors, and to plunge men into tyrannies and wars, civil chaos and social despair. The Christian hope gives strength to men who face this human situation in all its tragic depths. None of man's achievements can be the true ground of hope. But the Christian knows that the sin and evil which frustrate the humanist and blight his hopes are met and mastered by God's abounding grace. With his hope in God, the Christian can labour joyfully for men.

(iii) *Marxism.* Marxism is at once a philosophy of history, a practical programme, and, for many of its adherents, a powerful secular religion alive with hope. Its simplest appeal is to the disinherited multitudes everywhere, who need food, clothes, shelter, and enough security and freedom for decent living. They are the true proletariat, the chosen people of Marxist theory. But Marxism speaks also to more prosperous workers who feel cramped and dehumanized in their work, to warm-hearted friends of the downtrodden, to men and women ambitious to lead or hungry for comradeship, and to highly trained scientists, soldiers, patriots, and statesmen impatient for a new day. To all these men and women in many lands, Marxism offers an exciting word of hope.

First of all, Marxism is a philosophy of history, closely relating theory and action. It finds in conflict both the driving force of progress and the source of evil to be overcome. It teaches that man has no fixed nature, but is continually being made and remade in history, which in turn by social action he helps to make. God and divine sovereignty are denied. History and human existence alike begin when, in his struggle with Nature, man produces the means for his own existence and so differentiates himself from the other animals. Communism (and this is its great strength) addresses itself to the worker, and declares that it is through work that man achieves his humanity and fashions history. The most humble of workers thus has an essential role to play.

But if history is the cradle of humanity, it is also a struggle in which occurs *alienation* of men from one another and of each from himself. For the objects that man produces by his labour, and the parts of Nature that come under his control, are unequally divided between stronger and weaker, and so a class struggle begins. Since economic activities and relations are fundamental in society, the hostility between those who possess and those who are dispossessed poisons all human relationships for both classes. Happiness, justice, and love are no longer possible; and man in the class struggle is no longer truly man. Not individuals merely, but history itself is thus corrupted.

The conflict and the crises it engenders become most acute in capitalist society, and deepen as time goes on. But in that very agony arises a great hope. For the end of the age is at hand: a final cataclysm of revolution, in which the oppressive society will collapse, and the oppressed will be set free. The proletariat, the workers deprived of property, country, and family life, taught and led by a disciplined Communist party and united across national frontiers, can bring the revolution at the opportune moment, and so fulfil a messianic task for all mankind.

The fulfilment of history in the resulting classless society is above all a *reconciliation*. No longer separated by the products of their own work or by private exploitation, men will finally be able to meet one another freely and become real neighbours, as truly social men. The free association of producers will provide for all men the goods they need. Nature itself will cease to be man's enemy. There will be no more social classes, no class struggle, and therefore no coercive government, nor any cause for violence. All the wealth that mankind has amassed through the years will be gathered together, and made available for all.

It goes without saying that the demand for economic and social justice is one that all Christians must affirm, without vindictiveness or partisanship, but without compromise. Moreover, the Church and every Christian must acknowledge their full share of guilt for ineffectual preaching and practice of equity that has helped to open the way for Communist attacks. There is need also to recognize the powerful attraction of the confident Marxist reading of history, and the promise that the end of conflict and alienation is near. The Christian understanding of history and its fulfilment have not often been presented in our time with nearly so much persuasiveness and force.

On the other hand, the means employed by Communist leaders to seize and to hold power in the name of the proletariat, and the explicit teaching that any means required to break the power of class enemies are justified, have repelled many who have been drawn towards Communism by its demand for justice and its promise of peace. In practice, moreover, the Communist doctrine of the dictatorship of the proletariat has led in most cases to totalitarian dictatorship, in which the freedom of man is in fact denied.

But the Christian must press on to point out the illusions by which the Marxist creed itself is vitiated. First, the denial of God and the rejection of His sovereignty over all human history opens the way to the idolising of the party or the economic system. Second, the Marxist belief in the capacity of proletarian man to lead human history to its consummation, to be the Messiah of the new age, is belied by the facts of human nature as we know it. Third, the belief that mere stripping away of economic disabilities can abolish the strife and self-seeking that have marked all human history finds no support in actual Marxist behaviour. The Christian doctrine of man's nature and destiny stands on more realistic ground.

(iv) *National and Religious Renaissance.* In many countries today, especially in Asia and Africa, whole peoples are in the midst of a revolution that is at once social, political, and religious. This vast upheaval has gathered momentum rapidly during the past decade. The Second World War, while it brought untold suffering to many, has opened up a new world to them, and history, once a wearisome repetition of unvarying events, has become for them suddenly alive.

Dwellers in towns and cities, and especially their leaders, had long known the benefits of applied science and political independence. But inhabitants of remote jungles were introduced to some of these benefits for the first time by the armies fighting in their territories. Moreover, the swiftness with which

Western dominion was broken in many countries after the war brought to subject peoples everywhere a new sense of power and national self-consciousness, while those who, as in India, had fought for their independence mainly by non-violent methods found in the outcome a new confidence in their moral and spiritual resources.

At the same time, the religious and cultural patterns of their living show the impacts of the Christian gospel, and of communism and humanism in various forms. In many lands it was through the Christian Church that men first came to see the possibilities of a new and better life. Both Christianity and its rivals have helped to quicken a new awareness of human dignity and of man's responsibility for his fellows. They have helped also to evoke a vigorous counter-assertion of the ancient religions as adequate to meet the problems of our perplexed generation.

The result of all this is a strong and growing nationalism, together with a revival of each people's concern for its own cultural and religious heritage. There is a new confidence among the adherents of Buddhism, Hinduism, and Islam that their several religions hold the answer to the ills of the world. Buddhists today are planning a great world-wide missionary campaign. Neo-Hinduism is never weary of preaching that by virtue of its readiness to recognise truth wherever found, it alone can sum up the best in all traditions. Islam is recovering its missionary zeal, and offering membership in a world-wide brotherhood that transcends race and nationality. African peoples are seeking to revive their indigenous faiths to meet contemporary need.

We rejoice with the peoples of Asia and Africa in the new release of power which they have found, and share their anxiety to use it for the fullest benefit of their own homelands and the good of the whole world. It is good that there should be serious concern here and now for human values—for social justice, for better living conditions, for the preservation of cultural heritages—especially where these things have suffered long neglect. It is good that the cultural awakening in Asia has created a temper of purposeful activity, which seeks to cope with present demands and to shake off the lethargy bred of an age-long tendency to fatalism.

If it be urged, with some justice, that such activity is incompatible with the genius of world-denying religions like Hinduism and Buddhism, it must be remembered that these faiths grant a relative and provisional value to concern for personal worth, social justice, and human community. They regard the events of history with tentative optimism, even though history as such is denied any ultimate validity. This underlying pessimism, in turn, is negated by a transcendent optimism that sees the resolution of all conflicts, fears, and frustrations, and even of all hopes, in ultimate Reality which is beyond all change, activity, and purpose.

Islam, widespread in both Asia and Africa, gives a more positive place to human activity. It is the only one of the great world religions which had its origin within the boundaries of Christendom, and it bears clear traces of this origin, in creed and cult, in characteristic modes of expression, and even in its vehement rejection of the Cross as a blasphemous scandal. Its holy scripture, professing to be God's final revelation, opens with the praise of Allah as Lord of the worlds and King of the Day of Judgment. In the last days a Messiah, the rightly-guided Mahdi, will come in God's time to reform the world according to Muslim ideals. These are set forth in the Sacred Law (Shariat), that professes to be rooted in the revelation given to the Prophet, and that demands scrupulous obedience from the people of God.

But the real force which today is sweeping through the world of Islam is not the expectation of the Day of Judgment and the coming of the Rightly-Guided, but the power of rising nationalism. In this form, at once political, cultural, and religious, Islam is asserting again its confidence that it can heal the ills of mankind. Yet there runs underneath this self-assertion a deep feeling of frustration and bewilderment. The pattern of the ideal Muslim society is believed to be laid down in the unalterable Sacred Law, yet its actual life has to be carried on in the world of today. Modern Islam lives in a state of permanent religious crisis, of tension between the guardians of the old and the various groups of modern, forward-looking Muslims. The peoples of Islam, suspended between violent self-assertion and paralysing frustration, are in deep need of understanding from the side of the Western world.

In this whole situation the Church is called upon to engage far more seriously in its missionary task. This must include a real effort to understand the faith and hope by which so many millions in Asia and Africa are seeking to shape their national and personal lives. We must indeed warn them to remember that wherever absolute claims are made for nations or cultures, disaster follows. But at the same time we cannot stand by unmoved while our brethren of other faiths struggle to achieve social righteousness and the common good of their peoples. The Church needs to be warned against clouding its witness and neglecting its present duty by a disproportionate emphasis on other-worldly hopes. The preaching of the Gospel in Asia and Africa must be related to the immediate tasks in which we are bidden to do the will of God whose Kingdom is at work in the world now.

(v) *The Hope of the Hopeless.* We have spoken of some of the various hopes in which men in our time are seeking refuge. But what of those who, finding no such refuge, are without hope of any kind?

There are those whose experience of life has been so bitter that nothing of value or interest seems left to them. Dogged by disappointment, frustrated in all their dreams, or crushed by injustice and by man's inhumanity to man, it seems to them that they are the victims of a blind fate, or even that things have somehow been arranged by a malicious practical joker set only on their damage and destruction. As they regard the future, they are confronted at best with a bleak and dreary prospect, at worst with a prospect of suffering and misery hardly to be borne. To such embittered souls the whole business of politics and all nostrums for social amelioration appear only as moves in a futile game invented to distract their minds from the profound tragedy of life. When we remember the dreadful sufferings of the vast number of refugees and displaced persons in different parts of the world, we cannot wonder that many of them should fall victim to this kind of hopelessness.

There are others to whom life has not been so unkind but who, having for a time supported their spirits by one or other variety of anthropocentric hope, have now fallen into disillusionment. Their god has failed them, and they are left desolate. It is difficult to exaggerate the extent to which Western man, during the last century and a half, as he lost hold of his traditional Christian faith, has fastened upon some alternative dogma, progressionist or utopian, which enabled him to face the future with confident expectation; and it is difficult also to exaggerate the tenacity with which over a long period these dogmas continued to be held. But in our own time, partly under the pressure of disastrous events, but partly also through a more open-eyed examination of their own presuppositions, a growing number of our contemporaries are abandoning these hopes, even though they have nothing to put in their place. There is here an honesty of thought which can only be respected, but it issues in a situation which should at once evoke our deepest sympathy and cause us the profoundest alarm. However clearly we ourselves may see the illusoriness of such humanistic hopes, we should recognise the responsibility we take upon ourselves when we undertake the negative task of their destruction, lest the last state should be worse than the first.

In certain quarters a still further stage has been reached. There are those among us who, having rigorously purged their minds and their philosophies of every variety of temporising and ill-grounded optimism, of every illusion of progress, of every utopian expectation, of every shoddy or shadowy idealism, and having accordingly faced without blinkers the desperateness of the human situation in a godless world, have found a new courage coming to them from the very clarity and depth of their despair. Such are the atheistic "existentialists" who in some countries are now given so wide a hearing and many of whom write with great ability and with real literary grace. They are atheists, but atheists of a new kind. They no longer flout the issues with which Christian faith is concerned, but take them most seriously. They do not rejoice in the non-existence of God, but regard it as placing us in a situation of the most terrible solemnity. Each of us is completely alone, surrounded only by meaninglessness, so that if his life is to have any meaning or any value, he must create such meaning and value for himself, not forgetting that death swiftly puts an end to all. There is here a certain positive attitude to life, a certain courage, though it can hardly be called a hope, that arises and can arise only out of utter negation, out of the very death of hope. Here we have what is the most honest of all forms of anthropocentrism, and perhaps the only consistent form of it. In its open-eyed realisation of the desperate plight of those who are without God in the world, it repeats what is a central Christian affirmation; while its talk of a courage that can emerge only out of the darkness of the complete renunciation of hope seems to echo, even if only in a perverted form, the Christian teaching that only through the darkness of the Cross, with its cry of dereliction, can hope ever be reborn.

For all who, in any of these ways, are without hope in the world, our only message of hope is that there is One who understands them better than they understand themselves. Jesus Christ has plumbed the depths of human existence as no one else. He passed through the darkest night of the human soul, through utter loneliness and dereliction, before rising victorious over death and hell. In speaking this message to them, we must speak as those who have continued to crucify Him, for we share responsibility for the present hopelessness of so many of our fellow-men for whom Christ died. God give us grace and wisdom to speak the word of hope and to manifest it in acts of love in such a way that they may understand.

We have surveyed, all too briefly, some of the non-Christian hopes of our time on which the eyes of many men are fixed. We discern in their midst the presence of our exalted Lord, who in His earthly ministry moved among outcasts, refugees, political agitators and zealots, sophisticated intellectuals, simple workmen and soldiers, all of them with their thwarted hopes and unfulfilled aspirations. He accepted rejection, suffering, and death at the hands of those He came to save, and on His Cross prayed for them. As the exalted Lord He bids His church, as today it confronts on every side men whose hopes are mocked or starved or fastened upon false gods, to walk the road He trod, for only as it goes the way of the Cross can the Church offer in word and deed a sure and steadfast hope.

C. The Christian Hope and Our Earthly Tasks

We must speak now of the present tasks to which God calls us, and of the hope we have in seeking to carry them out. Here as everywhere Christ is our hope. In Him, the crucified and risen Lord, God delivers us from the power of sin, quickens us into new life, and sets us free to serve Him, without fear, illusion, or idolatry, here and now.

For this world, disfigured and distorted as it is, is still God's world. It is His creation, in which He is at work, and which He sustains in being until the day when the glory of His new creation will fully appear. He is at once the creator and the redeemer. He preserves both those who serve Him and those who refuse Him service. He makes the sun to shine on the evil and the good. He is good to all, and His tender mercies are over all His works. We are forbidden therefore to treat this world as of small account, to turn away from it, to go by on the other side. On the contrary, all who are God's children must find joy in doing their Father's will in the world. God's will has been revealed to us in Christ. In His obedience until death He has manifested that will in action. In Him we have a foretaste of the Kingdom wherein His will is to be consummated. We are to do that will here and now, so far as in us lies. If the only-begotten Son came not to be served, but to serve, those who have been made His brethren are bound to do likewise.

The direction of our service is given in the all-embracing commandment: "Thou shalt love the Lord thy God with all thy heart, and with all thy soul, and with all thy strength, and with all thy mind; and thy neighbour as thyself." What, concretely, does love to God and our neighbour require of us? Most simply it requires us to recognise that in every human being Christ Himself comes to claim our service. God who has called us into the fellowship of His Son, has called us to serve Him in serving men.

Further, His calling lays upon us the obligation to do heartily that share of the world's work which is assigned to us in the place where we now are. Our daily work, indeed, provides the normal context for the many humble and obscure deeds of service which He will own at the last day as deeds done to Himself. We are often tempted to evade the demands of our immediate neighbourhood, giving all our attention to large plans concerning distant goals. But His solemn word about neglecting the daily needs of His humblest brethren we dare not ignore. Moreover, love to God and our neighbour must find regular expression in the faithful doing of that work which occupies the main part of our waking life. The busy scene where thousands of laymen are engaged in their ordinary business is a much-forgotten meeting place between the living Christ, His Church, and the world.

In the third place, our calling lays upon us responsibilities for seeking a better social and political life. Our own day has furnished another terrible demonstration of the suffering that follows the breakdown of stable social order. The misery of vast multitudes of hungry, homeless, and hopeless people is not only a challenge to Christian compassion and brotherly love; it is a reminder to every Christian that he is responsible before God for his due share of political and social action to secure for all men justice, freedom, and peace. For God who in His loving-kindness preserves this world which He has redeemed, sustaining in life even those who rebel against Him, wills that there shall be order, justice, and freedom among men. He has taught us to seek earthly justice, freedom, and peace, and to set our faces against injustice, oppression, and tyranny as evils which He abhors. Obedience to His will requires of us much more than the proclaiming of general ethical principles. It requires us to enter fully into the duties of the common life, understand to the best of our ability the economic, political, and social problems of our time, participate actively in the effort to solve them. We are to seek in all ways the just ordering of society, to promote wise legislation, and to share in responsible planning for the future. And we are to act in no light-hearted or half-hearted spirit, but counting the cost and being ready to pay it.

Obedience to God's will must lead the believer deep into the heart of all the world's sorrow, pain, and conflict. There is no man who does not meet us with Christ's claim for loving service, and no part of human life in which God's will is not to be done. It is God's will that men should have *life*, and have it abundantly. We cannot pray, "Thy will be done," unless we are at the same time willing to go to the help of those who are denied the necessities for human life. The cry of half the world's people for bread enough to sustain life in their bodies must be heard by the Christian as the cry of Christ. He who spoke the parables of Dives and Lazarus and of the Last Judgment will surely not leave us without condemnation if we are content to eat sumptuously while millions are in want. To all who are hungry, without decent clothing or housing, or bearing intolerable burdens in their personal or family lives, we are called to be neighbours. And the fulfilment of that duty will include every kind of responsible action, including political action, that is required to meet their needs. Moreover, while thinking of the physical needs of life, we must not forget the deep longing of men and women the world over for simple human love. Our restless, depersonalised society, with its nervous preoccupation with excitement and movement, does not favour the growth of lasting personal relationships in marriage, friendship, or community. We must show in our lives as Christians the splendour of human love when it is touched by the love of Christ, and do all that is in our power to provide for others the conditions in which human love may flourish.

It is God's will that men should know and love the *truth*. We cannot remain silent while men's minds are being drugged with lies. In our day seekers after truth are often compelled to sacrifice integrity to party orthodoxy, and the means of mass communication have become tools for producing social conformity. We must be ready to speak the truth at whatever cost, and where scepticism and relativism have robbed men of their ultimate convictions, we must lead them to know Him who is Himself the truth, and who requires us to seek and love the truth in every realm of life.

It is God's will that men should be *free*, to know and to serve Him. We cannot remain aloof when man's freedom is threatened. We cannot ourselves enjoy in any kind of self-complacency that inward freedom with which faith endows us, but must step in wherever the freedom of man is denied. We must stand for freedom of belief and conscience and for the right of all to witness openly to the truth of God. We must set ourselves against every political and economic oppression, and against the inhuman terror by which men seek to compel their fellows to submit to arbitrary laws and dictates, and to the service of false gods.

It is God's will that "*justice* roll down like waters and righteousness like a mighty stream." We must be ever alert to seek a greater measure of justice in social and political relationships, and to do battle against every unjust discrimination against class or race, and every denial of human rights, whether political or economic. We do not hold with those who think that they themselves can bring about a perfect social order, if necessary by the employment of terror and the silencing of the individual conscience. But neither do we hold with those who are content to be mere onlookers in the face of the miseries of prisoners, refugees, the dispossessed, the displaced, and the exploited, as if nothing could be done to better their lot.

It is God's will that *peace* should prevail among men. We cannot pray, "Thy will be done," while in the present world situation we do nothing, dare nothing, and sacrifice nothing for the sake of peace. We cannot abandon ourselves to the prospect of a third world war as an ineluctable fate, or regard the present competition in armaments with an easy conscience. Here we are not concerned with rival world views and abstract principles, but with fellow-men, who hunger for peace yet live under the threat of a war that would cast them into utter chaos.

Both the Church in its corporate acts and public words, and every single Christian in his deeds and words are thus required to affirm Christ's Lordship over every part of human life. What that affirmation will involve in the spheres of international politics and race relations, in the development of a responsible society, and in the daily work of Christian laymen, is discussed in other Assembly papers.

Acting in society, the Christian is frequently confronted by the problem of compromise. Group responsibility and group decision are common and necessary features of modern life which often give rise to acute conflicts between corporate loyalty and individual conscience. Further, many situations in real life offer no possibility of doing what is wholly good. A Christian may well find himself compelled by the facts to stand for a lesser against a greater injustice. In extreme situations a Christian may have to take the decision to resign from public responsibilities, or to withhold obedience from civil authority and to challenge its acts at the risk of freedom and even of life. The Church must stand with all its members in prayer, in understanding, in Christian fellowship, and in action. Only if it does so, wisely and patiently, can the Church clearly recognise compromise that is sinful, and rebuke those who fall into it; or support and confirm decisions by its members to withdraw from public office, or to oppose civil authority in the name of Christ.

To such tasks as these God calls us, to act in the power of His spirit. It is God the Holy Spirit who Himself brings forth in us the good works which are His own fruit, and guides our feet in facing the new tasks of every age. Though the Spirit is one, His gifts are many, distributed in rich variety to the members of Christ's body for their various services to one another and to the world. The nature of the tasks to be performed and of the gifts required varies from age to age and from place to place. The Church in the twentieth century is called to duties different from those which God laid upon the Church in the first century. Today our churches face situations and tasks of immense variety, some old and familiar, some new and profoundly perplexing. Yet in the face of all these the Christian may act humbly but confidently, assured that the Holy Spirit will furnish the gifts and power needed for faithful service in the world to those who are willing to ask the Father for His help, to hear His call, and to submit to His will.

In times of trial it is good to remember what God has in fact wrought in and through the Church in the nineteen centuries of its pilgrimage. The very existence of this people of God in the world, growing from age to age as new peoples are drawn into its fellowship, bears witness to God's power and faithfulness. In spite of all man's sin, the light of God shines upon and through His people in the darkness and perplexity of the world's life.

The life of service lived in Christ is therefore a life of unquenchable hope. We know that God's will must at last prevail, that His Kingdom will fully come. That is a certainty which no earthly failure or disaster can take away.

Moreover, we know that what we do here and now for His sake in faith and hope is not in vain. It is not possible for us to know exactly how God will use our work, or what degree of visible success He will grant us in any particular project. The Christian is no more sure of success than his secular neighbour. But he is secure against despair, for he knows that what he commits into God's hands is safe.

At the same time, our actions and expectations will have a certain modesty. We shall not confuse our programmes with God's Kingdom. We cannot know in advance whether we shall achieve a stable and just social order for mankind in any way that we now have in view. The peace and the justice that we seek among men are still not God's perfect peace and God's holy righteousness. Even as we act in the honest intention to do God's will, we must still pray, "God be merciful to me a sinner."

Nevertheless, because God has not abandoned this world, because He rules and overrules its tangled history, and because we have been given a share in the power of His Spirit, we can with confidence hope and expect that what is built upon the foundations which He has laid will stand. We can hope for and expect miracles of help in answer to the prayers we make in our extremity of need. We can hope for and expect the success of concrete plans for the good of our fellow-men. We have no right to set limits to what God may be pleased to do within this present age. Indeed, such hopeful and expectant action for the doing of God's will in the world, in the face of apparently overwhelming odds, is an essential part of our full witness to the present reign of God. All our action will be but humble, grateful, and obedient acknowledgment that God has redeemed the world, and that in it we are called to participate in His ministry of reconciliation. We can therefore live and work as those who know that God reigns, undaunted by all the arrogant pretensions of evil, ready to face situations that seem hopeless and yet to act in them as men whose hope is indestructible.

IV. THE SUM OF THE MATTER

That then is what we have to say, in this present hour, and as delegates of the Christian Churches here represented, in witness to the great truth that Jesus Christ is the hope of the world. It is a human witness to a thing that is itself divine. We are well aware of the poverty and obscurity of our expression of it. Only in part can this defect of our witness be ascribed to the divergencies of thought and understanding which still divide us. Nor can it be ascribed only to the finitude of human knowledge which must condition all our speaking. Rather do we know and confess that all we who venture to address the world, and the Church in the world, are not only fallible men but also sinful men, hard and dull of heart. The mystery of Christian hope deserves altogether more adequate expression than we have been able to give it. We must therefore be ready to place this message of ours under the sign of God's merciful judgment. Among the earthly hopes of which we have spoken we must place also this one —that it may be given to those who come after us, in saying again the selfsame thing, to say it differently, more clearly and more truly. And beyond that we await the eternal light which will at last illumine the darkness that besets even the best thoughts and words of sinful men.

Yet this does not stay us from being profoundly thankful to God for the measure of knowledge which, without any merit of our own, enables and emboldens us to say so much in common and with one voice. Nor does it at all qualify the earnestness with which we enjoin all whom it may concern to consider well what we have here undertaken to say, in good conscience and according to the best we knew, in testi-

48

mony to Jesus Christ as the sole hope, the whole hope, the sure and certain hope of the world. We pray God that He may permit our word—once again quite apart from and contrary to any deserts of our own—to be of service to His own holy and righteous Word through the power of His Holy Spirit.

To whom do we say what we say here? We say it in the first place simply to the WORLD whose hope—whether it be a Christian or a non-Christian, a believing or an unbelieving world—Jesus Christ is. The world in which we and all other Christians live is the world that God has loved from all eternity in Jesus Christ. To this world God has spoken through Him. In Him God has taken upon Himself the world's sin, its guilt, its darkness and its death, that from all these the world might be delivered. In His resurrection God has made manifest to all who believe on Him the world's salvation and its true life. As judge of the world He will appear as God's final revelation to every ear and every eye and as the final goal of all God's ways. To testify to the world concerning the world's hope is the meaning of the Church's existence in every age and every clime, and it is the purpose of all we have said. He that hath ears to hear let him hear! Let him hear not our word as such, but the Word of God which has impelled us to speak—the Word of God which is identical with the Work of Christ which was, and now is, and is still to be. He is not our Lord only but the Lord of all mankind. He is not our future only but the future of all mankind. There exists no man who is not called to find his brother in Him and his Father through Him. There exists no man who is not guilty before Him, beholden and answerable to Him. What is here said is said in solidarity with every man, for every man, and to every man; yet not in our own name, but in the Name of Him who as the world's Saviour is at the same time the Saviour of every man.

But for this very reason what we have said has been addressed also to OURSELVES and to the Christian congregations throughout the whole world whom we here represent. We proclaim no dogma. Even to the Churches we speak as men to men. Yet with brotherly earnestness we speak to them as follows: Through what we have tried to say in this message you and we are confronted by the magnitude of the gift and task which have been entrusted to Christ's Church—by the dignity and responsibility of its mission as bearer of and witness to the only full and certain hope in the midst of a world darkened by so much false hope and also by so much hopelessness. You and we should know that it is not death which is the goal of mankind and its history, but the revelation of the Name, the Kingdom, and the Purpose of the holy and merciful God, that is to say, eternal life. And the meaning and dignity of our Christian existence is just to spread abroad this good news. But, because we look first at our Lord and only then at our own thoughts and words and works, this assignment of ours is at the same time our deep humiliation and a powerful challenge to embrace with far greater faithfulness than heretofore the hope that has been granted to the world and to ourselves. If we Christians, or if our Christian congregations, do not so live in the joy of this hope that others will thereby be brought to share our joy, who else is there who can do this? What are we doing with that which has been entrusted to us?

Here is a question which we desire in this message to engrave upon the conscience of Christ's Church and of ourselves as members of it. Is the Church the authentic witness of its Lord and Head, and so of the whole world's Hope, as it is called to be? Is it the pilgrim people who have here no continuing city but seek one to come, and who reckon not the sufferings of the present time as worthy to be compared to the glory that shall be revealed? Is it the company of watchmen who, because they have seen light in the east, know that the new day has already broken, and are sounding the trumpets to announce it to all their fellows? Is it the fellowship of those who now in this very time are able to recognise the coming King in His hungry, thirsty, naked, sick, captive, and refugee brethren, and are accordingly willing and ready in His Name to give them food and drink and clothing, to visit them and company with them? Is it a confessing rather than a denying Church? It does not lie with us who in this message to our Christian congregations address the whole world, to answer this question for them; but we may and must say to them that this is most certainly the question which is directed to them through our message. And further we must say that they have not understood our message aright unless and until they have understood our question (as we would wish to understand it for ourselves) as an occasion for repentance, for conversion and for faith, and a challenge to a new beginning. And further still, we must say that their and our proper answer to this question can consist only in the prayer that God the Father, the Son and the Holy Ghost may have mercy upon the Church in all lands, making it through His Word to be the Church of hope and thus His Tabernacle among men. And finally, we must say that wherever a Christian congregation answers this question and lives in and through this prayer, the Church of hope is already present and at work—the people of God who, in order that we might proclaim His mighty acts, has called us out of darkness into His marvellous light.